MW00776007

MEANING IN OUR BODIES

AMERICAN ACADEMY
of RELIGION

ACADEMY SERIES

SERIES EDITOR
Aaron W. Hughes, University at Buffalo

A Publication Series of
The American Academy of Religion
and
Oxford University Press

AMERICAN ACADEMY
of RELIGION

MEANING IN OUR BODIES

SENSORY EXPERIENCE AS CONSTRUCTIVE THEOLOGICAL IMAGINATION

HEIKE PECKRUHN

OXFORD
UNIVERSITY PRESS

OXFORD
UNIVERSITY PRESS

Oxford University Press is a department of the University of Oxford. It furthers the University's objective of excellence in research, scholarship, and education by publishing worldwide. Oxford is a registered trade mark of Oxford University Press in the UK and certain other countries.

Published in the United States of America by Oxford University Press
198 Madison Avenue, New York, NY 10016, United States of America.

CIP data is on file at the Library of Congress

ISBN 978-0-19-028092-5

1 3 5 7 9 8 6 4 2
Printed by Sheridan Books, Inc., United States of America

To Brooke.
To my family.

CONTENTS

CONTENTS

ACKNOWLEDGMENTS

A book in the making is a living and growing thing, it is nurtured, pruned, and tended to by many. Over the years, many people have contributed to its becoming. Much gratitude belongs to Deborah Creamer, a mentor and teacher who has generously shared her scholarly excellence, time, enthusiasm, and friendship with me over the years. Her profound theological voice inspires me, her wisdom and trust in me carried the ideas in this book forward from their first appearances to their final form. Edward Antonio and Tink Tinker continuously challenge me to think and articulate clearly, and their scholarly and personal embodiment of theological imagination and rigor are exemplar to me. Jacob Kinnard and Alison Schofield have been tremendous support and provided commentary and encouragement for this project.

There are persons who supported and cheered me on throughout the many stages of writing and editing this book by giving time, feedback, friendship, collegiality, encouragement, and sharing much laughter and righteous anger. Katherine Turpin, Julie Todd, Dave Scott, Ben Sanders III, Eu Kit Lim, Elizabeth Coody, Hannah Ingram, and Emily Kahm grew into the kind of queer family for me that prods and teases, laughs and critiques: In community with them (and Deborah Creamer) I am growing as person and scholar, challenged to answer questions as to why and how what we do matters, so that together we may work toward liberation for all. Yvonne Zimmerman, Letitia Campbell, and Michelle Voss-Roberts earned my gratitude and respect for their generosity, good humor, and extending collegiality to me across geographic and academic distances.

I appreciate having been able to work with Cynthia Read at Oxford University Press who provided support for the book. The anonymous readers offered valuable feedback that improved my work, and I thank them for their generous comments. Drew Anderla, Suzanne Copenhagen, and Rajakumari Ganessin of the editorial and production team have been delightful to work with.

My family—my parents Gernot and Unchalee, my sister Tanja, my ancestors Edith and Kun Yay—continue to show me how to see life through faithfully, to grow wings and tend to the many lands and terrains that sustain me. Their steadfast support, love, and pride across distance and difference are precious gifts. Finally, I am deeply grateful to my loving and supportive spouse, Brooke. She brings wonder and magic to my life. If anything in this book relates to the world we live in today, it is so because she helps me be in it with a heart that attends to the bodies and things that matter, and she prods me to theologize accordingly. Her vital emotional, intellectual, and spiritual support never fail. I could not think of a better partner in this life journey. This book is dedicated to her. *Mit Dir sein ist Zuhausesein.*

PART ONE

BODIES AND THEOLOGIES

I was preparing a presentation on the importance of embodiment to theory and theology at a national academic conference when I received a phone call from my father: "Oma passed away last night." Oma, my paternal grandmother, had been part of the household I grew up in and had been diagnosed with Alzheimer's disease 13 years prior. "Don't come to the funeral," my parents insisted. "We're too busy taking care of things here. Besides, she'd been dying for a long time. You've got other things to do. Go to your conference."

But as family matters often do, bereavement and processing the death of a close relative infused those "other things" (like presenting about embodiment) with emotions and questions. I asked myself, "How could it be that not just my thoughts, but my movements and actions are still centered on a body abroad, now dead? How is it that I move a certain way because of the final passing of a person whom I began mourning almost a decade ago?" Alzheimer's disease had brought on physical, mental, and emotional changes in the loving and doting grandmother who had a significant part in raising me. Changes in personality and physical and mental capabilities required adjustments in our relationship. I had long ago learned to let go of the person I had come to know.

Grandmom spent the last years of her life in a nursing home, requiring
more intensive care than my father, who had been her primary caretaker,
could provide.

  Reflecting on those last years of her at home and in nursing care,
I thought about the peculiarity of our household she had been part of—
my parents, my sister, and I musing out loud about her mental state,
her being "like a vegetable" —and yet so much of our lives, especially
the daily lives and routines of my parents, revolved around this body.
What agency did this body hold? What power did it assert in the physi-
cal space of our home and our experiences together in it, even as we
stopped searching for emotional and mental cues to help us relate? How
did this body with declining cognitive capacities manage and direct the
daily activities of my parents, even when it seemed to us that Oma ceased
to comprehend her environment and even my father appeared to be a
stranger to her?

This book is about bodies, bodily experiences, sense-perception, difference, and theology. It is a reflection grounded in feminist commitments,
a reflection on how theologians interested in understanding and analyzing bodily experiences need to begin by framing them as integral to
the process of our meaning-making, to our socio-cultural expressions,
as integral to how we relate to the world and how we find and invest
value. It joins a long line of feminist theological ventures, asserting the
importance of experience in theorizing, the importance of difference
to experience, and the varieties of embodiments demanding attention
when thinking about difference. However, I set out to do more than
simply elaborate on the merits of specific experiences as resource by
narrating the particularity of the experience and accounting for the
ways in which it is useful to theology. I focus on the significance of
complexly conceiving of bodily experience intertwined with processes
of perception, so that experience is not simply one among many possible starting points, but *the* realm of meaning making. Ultimately, theologies that seek to begin with a critical analysis of the human condition
need to be able to account for the ways in which bodily experience is
the ground for the various dimensions of our lives.

Cartesian/Kantian epistemologies locate the primacy of valida-
tion of knowledge in objective rationality. Feminist theories and
theologies, too, have suffered compartmentalization as a result of
rationalist epistemologies by failing to complexly conceive of the
body-mind-world connection they seek to frame in order to overcome body/mind dualisms. The contribution of this book is framed
by taking another look at the utilizing of experience itself. This is
necessary because theologies that understand themselves as accessing, retrieving, and mining bodily experience as resource themselves
too often end up perpetuating certain Cartesian presuppositions they
aim to overcome, specifically in regards to bodily experience and
perception.

To explore bodily experience as a theological resource, I will take a
closer look at the embodied dimensions of our existence in the world,
rather than approaching bodily experience through the discursive,
through analyses of social constructions (though not neglecting this
dimension). I will utilize "body theology," which I will frame as analytical commitments grounded in and emerging out of understanding
our bodily perceptual orientations in the world. Rather than acting as
theologizing subjects, exploring material reality and turning to access
our bodily experience of it, we need to begin with conceiving of bodily
experience as the fundamental condition of our subjectivity. Thus body
theology needs to approach bodily experience as the realm through
which to understand socio-cultural ideologies traversing and impeding
on our bodies, while also being the realm that constructs and conveys
socio-cultural ideologies through perceptual values and practices evident in our bodily experience. And in a critical theological analysis of
experience, not just in feminist theologies and discourse, but generally
in the Cartesian-based field of theology as well, bodily sensory perception must be our entry point.

3

CHAPTER ONE

EXPERIENCE AND CONSTRUCTIVE THEOLOGY

"Experience is a reality that needs explaining," Mary McClintock Fulkerson charges as she demands that feminist theologians do the work of connecting systems of discourse and social relations to their claims of experienced reality.[1] Though this claim was made over twenty years ago, indeed experience is still a reality that demands explaining, even *after* these critical and complex connections to discourse are made.

The complicated enmeshment of experience and discourse, of embodiment and language, has gained attention with the application of poststructuralist methods and theories of social constructivism. Especially after Judith Butler's *Gender Trouble*, neither feminist theory nor feminist theology has been the same: The implications of language and discourse on embodied experiences are now available to critical investigation.[2] "Experience" has become a resource to be defined and handled carefully. It now needs to be thought of in relation to power structures and linguistic systems, lest we run the risk of oversimplifying and excluding differences to the point of inducing harm for the sake of harnessing experiences of chosen identity groups, for example, "women."

1. Mary McClintock Fulkerson, *Changing the Subject: Women's Discourses and Feminist Theology* (Minneapolis: Fortress Press, 1994), viii.
2. Judith Butler, *Gender Trouble: Feminism and the Subversion of Identity* (New York, NY: Routledge, 1990).

In light of Judith Butler's claim that language and materiality are fully embedded in each other but nevertheless not reducible to each other,[3] methodologies that seek to *access* and *utilize* embodied experience come under question. When appealing to experience as a resource, feminist theologians often rely upon narratives of experience, which makes the need for discourse analysis necessary. But if our bodily experience, the material reality of bodily life, is irreducible to a *thing* we *have*, what are we missing by focusing on discourse, and, what are we presupposing when resourcing bodily experience?[4]

If theologians appeal to embodied experience, we must do the work of attending to the sensory perceptual aspects of embodiment, the bodily capacities and orientation to the world, in order to investigate the complex ways in which our experience is facilitated and shaped in and through our bodily existence in the world. As I began writing this book, questions concerning Oma's experience kept coming up for me: Without much short-term memory and failing long-term memory, how does she experience her life? Does it matter if I am there with her? Does she experience the love and care, the frustration and bitterness extended toward her? Does she still know ____? And how would we know about what she experiences, considering the symptoms of Alzheimer's (affecting brain receptors and neural connections, loss of

3. Judith Butler, *Bodies That Matter: On the Discursive Limits Of "Sex"* (New York, NY: Routledge, 1993), 69.
4. In terms of political analysis of experience, the prevailing mode of accounting for and responding to social events has been what Davide Panagia termed "narratocracy," or "the rule of the narrative." Panagia argues that offering narrative lines is coupling of the visual with the textual, rendering events readable by incising a story line into the field of vision. This commits vision to readerly sight (while at the same time partitioning the body into areas of sensory competency). Panagia investigates the regimes of perception and their political power. He questions political strategies such as those of Judith Butler, who seeks to offer aggressive counterreadings (i.e., changing the story lines), and offers parallel (not replacement) strategies, namely, enacting reconfigurations of the sensible. Davide Panagia, *The Political Life of Sensation* (Durham, NC: Duke University Press, 2009). This project seeks to inquire into the sensible, as to more complexly grasp how it might configure our social life (and inspire imaginations into possible reconfigurations).

neurons)? I had watched my grandmother unresponsive to the smell of burning milk and other sensory stimuli which should have evoked a response. Does she experience ____? Does it make her less alive, less human, if she does not experience ____? How do we begin to understand bodily experience or the criteria for it? If my grandmother does not "have" experiences such as memory, desire, pain, fear, etc., anymore, or at the least, does not have the capacity to express them in ways we consider appropriate and normal, or respond to perceptual stimuli through verbal or physical responses, what does that imply about her bodily existence? Theologically, speaking from a feminist perspective, has she lost her subjectivity, her capacities for meaning-making, for orienting herself in the world? What makes this body an experiencing person? Whose experience is now (more or less) valuable in the sourcing of theology?

My academic interest in theology had put me on a path ready to explore some of these questions, and feminist theology is an important methodological touchstone for its insistence on experience (particularly women's experience) as a resource. Theologians who affirm "women's experience" as a theological resource hold different conceptualizations of "experience" and employ them in a variety of ways.[5] Yet

---

5. "Experience," as we have already discovered thus far (and will discuss throughout this book), continues to be a term accompanied by various presuppositions as well as common sense assertions. This book will explore experience as bodily perceptual orientation. Other scholars, depending on discipline, have defined (or utilized without definition) "experience" in various other ways, ranging from stabilizing universalized frameworks to localized and particular (but no less stabilizing) approaches. Serene Jones, "Women's Experience between a Rock and a Hard Place: Feminist, Womanist, and Mujerista Theologies in North America," *Horizons in Feminist Theology: Identity, Tradition, and Norms* (1997): 34. "Experience" as a term and category has undergone a plethora of philosophical conceptualizations. In general, when I refer to "experience," I aim to refer to the modes of sensing, knowing, understanding, moving in, engaging with, being familiar with, learning, thinking, imagining, and so forth, the world. This incorporates "experience" as practice or skill (as in having experience in typing) but is also much more general in terms of what makes up my grasp and engagement in a situation, "experience" as that which I will explore in chapters 3 and 4 as "bodily perceptual orientation in the world."

7

more often than not, that humans "experience" is presupposed, but the *how* of experiencing is left unexamined, which posits experiencing in an a-contextual way. In other words, feminist theologians may insist on differences in experience, yet the analytical structures framing "experience" itself are considered to be foundational and generalizable, and stable enough to be universally applicable.

Bodily experience is not a dimension of experience separate from, say, socialized or historical experience, but rather it is the one grounding all "other" experiences.[6] It is also a contested space, a space deeply paradoxical, sociopolitical, and intensely personal, as disability scholar Christopher Newell alerts us, because it acknowledges the person experiencing, rather than remaining grounded in the objects experienced and the validated ways of gaining knowledge.[7] Bodily experience is a space that is socially shaped: to analyze the space of bodily experience we can focus on socio-cultural accounts of oppression of people with certain kinds of bodies and specifically the prejudice and injustices bestowed upon them. Yet this personal space is also deeply physical: the realities of flux and deterioration are embodied and undeniable in each of our own existences. This paradoxical nature of bodily experience can create a space for reflections that come from experiences that are deeply personal, unique, and embodied; reflections on the projects of

6. Pamela Young provides a distinction of five categories of experience conceived of in feminist theological reflections: *bodily* experience, *socialized* experience (experience of being made into a "woman" by society with its construction of femininity), *feminist* experience (response to and radical questioning of socialized experience), *historical* experience (recovery of women's history), and *individual* experience. As cited in Elizabeth Stuart, "Experience and Tradition: Just Good Friends," in *Journal of the European Society of Women in Theological Research* 5 (1997): 51. While I do not believe that these categories are necessarily exclusive, they are useful in highlighting what kind of experience an author engages (even if she does not point this out explicitly herself), and this naming of differences is useful to demonstrate the openness and fluidity of the term.

7. Christopher Newell, "On the Importance of Suffering: The Paradoxes of Disability," in *The Paradox of Disability: Responses to Jean Vanier and L'arche Communities from Theology and the Sciences.*, ed. Hans S. Reinders (Grand Rapids, MI: Wm. B. Eerdmans Publishing Co., 2010), 174–175.

culture and theology that are subject-centered, not "subjective" in an individualized sense.

The important question regarding bodily experience is not whether but *how* it will be valued. Is it just one kind of experience, one that brings out particularities of an individual context? If so, then the challenge identified for theology remains that of making room for narratives about bodily experiences, especially those marginalized, and to create space for narratives that speak about undervalued, suppressed experiences, to allow for a voice commonly denied to speak against that which has come to be seen as acceptable. Yet this trajectory still maintains bodily experience as a marginal, subjective, and particular object of inquiry. It maintains that its relevance is always in question and in need of justification in the presence of universalized and generalized critical theorizing and philosophical analyzing. The emphasis of this book is that *all* experience is essentially bodily experience, and theology as a critical inquiry into our being in the world needs to consider experience as a resource by attending to bodily experience and the way it situates us in the world.

REPRESENTATION OF DIFFERENCE IN EXPERIENCE

To explore how to value bodily experiences we must be able to account differences in bodily experiences and their representation. Beyond an acknowledgment of differences, we need to account for how they come to be, and how these differences might "travel" in representations.[8]

My mother, a native of Thailand, still struggles to express herself in German even though she has lived in Germany for over 35 years. Returning home after a post-high school year abroad, I found my mother

---

8. Wonhee Anne Joh discusses the issue of representation in theology after poststructural, postmodern, and postcolonial turns, specifically the questions regarding adequate representation of difference. Wonhee Anne Joh, *Heart of the Cross: A Postcolonial Christology* (Louisville, KY: Westminster John Knox Press, 2006), 5–70.

cooking in an outdoor kitchen, a repurposed garage. Even after some probing, all Mom would tell me then was, "That's just how I like it. It's easier that way." To an observer, the actual food preparation, cooking, and cleaning procedures did not seem "easier." And there was much concern, especially on her daughters' sides, about how we should "explain this" to others who perceive us—about the story or image we desired to convey to those friends and neighbors visiting and seeing and partaking in (or refusing) our newly formed cooking and eating habits. But was there more to this moving of daily home activities to the outside of the house?

Over the now 20 years of outdoor cooking that followed, my mother would sometimes begin to share with me about my grandmother banning her to prepare certain foods at home, particularly foods that would offend my grandmother's sense of smell. I began understanding my mother's actions as resistance and preservation of self and identity. Part of my mother's story, which I have come to learn in bits and pieces over the years, is her suffering under the control and abuse of her mother-in-law (the loving and doting grandmother of my childhood), experiences of which I would not learn until reaching adulthood. Even today, I think I only have heard few and select experiences, and often my mother struggles for words and then says "If you'd understand Thai, I could tell you." If I shared my mother's language, I would have a different (though not necessarily complete) understanding of her practices and rituals at home, which do not always make sense to me, and which do not always have an easily constructed narrative to explain them. Yet there are some things I begin to get a glimpse of, ways in which differences in experience I tend to overlook make themselves known, differences struggling to find their expression through language. One of those glimpses is Mom's insistence on not re-inhabiting certain rooms in the home until renovation and remodeling erased not only visual markers of my late grandmother, but until certain smells associated with Oma had vanished.

In this book, I follow these recounted glimpses of difference and sketch a space for them in/as critical scholarship. Without (creating) a space for the lack of voice, for the inability to communicate to fill common space, we will always fall into speaking about, rather than with, those persons without the ability to access language proper. Newell writes in regard to suffering that "[p]art of the cultural context of suffering is the ubiquitous tendency to worry about its adequate representation rather than actually allowing it to be present."[9] This is a sentiment shared by postcolonial scholars writing on representation, misrepresentation, voice, and agency.[10] My exploration is informed by their work addressing (im)possibilities of adequate representation of cultural difference and the inclinations to represent *for* the other rather than creating conditions that support the (embodied) presence and recognition of difference.

I continue wondering what my mother's communication about her experiences is about. In a sense, we both seem left without access to language when it comes to communicating about our experiences to each other. The narratives she gives me in a language not native and comfortable to her, and the narratives I tend to create for her, are they really adequate? Or are they possibly grossly inadequate to even begin thinking about her experience? Thinking about my mother guides my reflections in two related directions: the already-mentioned presence of cultural difference and epistemic violence inflicted on different

---

9. Newell, "On the Importance of Suffering," 174–175.
10. Gayatri Chakravorty Spivak's often-cited essay "Can the Subaltern Speak?" discusses the dynamics of power and race as epistemic violence inflicted on subaltern consciousness and voice. Spivak argues that the subaltern can speak, but cannot be heard unless the voice is changed. Any attempt to make audible the voice of subalterns is the subjection of the latter to epistemic violence. Granting the subaltern a collective voice by the intellectual expressing solidarity homogenizes the irretrievable heterogeneity of subaltern subjects and, in the same vein, establishes a dependence on Western intellectuals or postcolonial subjects situated in the West to speak *for* the subaltern rather than creating conditions of audibility. Furthermore, in the conceptualization of subaltern historiography, the male remains dominant as subject and thus the female subaltern is doubly effaced. Postcolonial studies, in their attempts to recover subaltern voices and consciousness, are complicit in the re-inscription of colonial and neo-colonial political domination and exploitation. Gayatri Chakravorty Spivak, "Can the Subaltern Speak?," in *Colonial Discourse and Postcolonial Theory*, ed. Patrick Williams and Laura Chrisman (New York, NY: Columbia University Press, 1994), 66–111.

consciousness and voice; and the sought-after manifestation of difference outside of narratives, the difference present in sensory perceptual acts and experiences. What are the glimpses into my mother's experiences that I can gain by paying attention to her perceptual acts, rather than solely relying on narratives? How can I begin to understand my relation to her world of experience, despite the gap between our social and cultural structuring of selves and identity? How do I begin to think about the realms of perception in which difference manifests, and how does it relate to experience?

Reflecting on both my mother and my grandmother, I return to my claim that bodily experiences are grounds of practices, values, meaning-making, and theologies. And in both cases, different as they may be, bodily experience demands attention not as one realm, but as *the* realm from which to understand how our existence in the world makes sense. Bodily experience is the site from which to begin critical theological analyses, and we need to come to this site by inquiring into sensory perception.

CONSTRUCTIVE BODY THEOLOGY

Feminist and postcolonial scholarship on particularities of bodies, bodily experience, and bodily differences (race, class, gender, ability, sex, pain, etc.) insists that bodies make a difference as they situate us in the world, that our embodiment makes a difference in how we perceive and are perceived by our environment, and thus how we actively make meaning, how we do theology in this world. I share this conviction and bring several concerns and questions to their conversations:

- If difference in bodily experience and embodied difference provide the starting point for body theology, what then, is bodily experience, and how does difference come into play? Maintaining that bodily experience is just "something we have" not only maintains the power of (re)definition and (re)narration in the eye of the beholder, but also often leads to universalizing articulations of a generalized "normal" and to pathologizing taxonomies of differences and deviance.

- What might be at stake when references to sense perception and perceptual experiences are made without providing a more thorough investigation of perceptual processes (and thereby implicitly or explicitly referring to commonsense notions of "sensing the world")?
- It seems that most theologies gathered under the label of "body theologies" are better named "body metaphor theologies."[11] How do we move from body metaphor theology to body theology? What would it look like if we would move from exploring metaphors provided in bodily images toward a theology that begins from bodily experience and bodies as the locus and medium of our thinking? What is the difference in these approaches and what difference does it make in the constructing of theologies?

My exploration of bodily experience will be interdisciplinary—traversing philosophy, anthropology, history, and other fields—and employing those disciplines, it will be *constructive body theology*. A few comments are in order to clarify this label.

To some feminist sensibilities, locating theology in/as bodily experience might seem like a self-defeating project. Those committed to the human sciences may wonder whether a discipline like theology, seemingly committed to metaphysical matters, has any regard for the rules and methodologies guiding science (e.g., building theory on scientifically gained evidence). Theologians reading this book may wonder about the use of drawing in scholars who seem to ignore questions regarding underpinning values in their theories. Whichever academic discipline we are trained in, we often come to believe that it is our field that explains the world best. Yet it is only because of the limited scope of scientific methods that we come to produce any knowledge at all. Learning about the limitations of the kind of knowledge that our own field produces can help us appreciate difference and thus be open to dialogue and interdisciplinary (yet still limited) knowledge production. An academic community needs to learn to forego claims of unity and

11. See chapter 2 for evidence of this claim.

wholeness in its disciplinary taxonomies, which tend to impose particular perspectives on the realm of human experience and distort the varieties and differences present around us.[12]

I am convinced that important contributions can be made in anchoring analysis of bodily experience explicitly within the theological, though in an interdisciplinary conversation with other disciplines constructively taking up embodiment. Sociology, anthropology, and phenomenology particularly are the disciplines selected here to speak in a dialogical fashion of the constructive potential offered by theology in the deconstructive age of cultural analysis.

I have two premises in mind. First, as a scholar located in Western culture wherein Christianity has forged so many wider cultural perspectives and habits, I cannot properly understand and work out of my own context without at least referencing Christian theology. I agree with Mieke Bal that one of Western culture's interlocking structures is (Christian) theological in nature, and as such it informs the cultural imaginary, and that relevant theology today must be a cultural discipline.[13] Thus, I understand the study of religion and my theological project as necessarily engaging in cultural analysis while understanding that cultural analysis needs to take into account theological imaginations and frameworks at play in socio-cultural expressions. Further, any investigation into concepts with bodily implications/dimensions today that is located in the Western academy (as this book is) is done within an imaginary that is born and still steeped in religious and Western Christian theological legacies, not the least of these being Cartesian and Kantian infused philosophical frameworks.

The second premise of my working as theologian is based in the conviction that any investigation into the body today must be interdisciplinary.

12. Hans S. Reinders, "Human Vulnerability: A Conversation at L'arche," in *The Paradox of Disability: Responses to Jean Vanier and L'arche Communities from Theology and the Sciences*, ed. Hans S. Reinders (Grand Rapids, MI: Wm. B. Eerdmans Publishing Co., 2010), 5.
13. Mieke Bal, "Postmodern Theology as Cultural Analysis," in *The Blackwell Companion to Postmodern Theology*, ed. Graham Ward (Malden, MA: Blackwell Publishers, 2001), 4–5.

Religion and theology are but one in a cluster of permeable arenas of social life. Knowledge in life is not experienced as compartmentalized, and any discipline today must acknowledge interdisciplinarity if it wants to be relevant in a dynamic present. Much of the feminist theory that has influenced feminist theology has drawn explicitly on what are considered non-religious disciplines (medical sciences, anthropology, philosophy, physics), specifically in order to overcome religious concepts of the body considered oppressive to women. Theology then can neither be a separate discipline, nor be treated as the ignored presence in a cultural theory dialogue, in which other disciplines develop the theory and theology receives/criticizes the pieces it can use to stay relevant as a specialized field.

"Constructive" Theology

As a Christian theologian, I add the descriptor "constructive" to the kind of work I see myself engaging in. First, let me sketch a differentiation. I understand constructive theology to engage in the task of taking up questions and concepts of meaning, world, and humanity for the contemporary context, while attending to the shaping influences of histories of ideas and theological traditions, as well as the particularities of the present location. While sharing certain intersections and overlapping in theories and methods, constructive theology thus is different from, for example, historical, systematic, or biblical theology in that it asserts the possibility of knowledge generation via theological imaginations. Second, I offer a proposition: I understand constructive theology *today* to be most apt to the task I have sketched if it acknowledges and makes use of certain poststructural ideas and methods. This includes attending to the structures of language and the productions of culture, which present a complex context of influences, investments, contesting/conforming discourses, and power dynamics that precede modes of experience, interpretations, and thus theological constructions.[14]

14. I follow here what different theologians have described and exemplified in Serene Jones and Paul Lakeland, eds., *Constructive Theology: A Contemporary Approach to Classical Themes* (Minneapolis, MN: Augsburg Fortress Press, 2005).

Third, and perhaps for some readers most controversially, I propose that constructive theology today must not be, by literal definition, "god-talk." Rather than occupying itself with arguments for the existence of "God" or specific attributes pertinent to a deity, constructive theology traces and utilizes what/who emerges as "God," and may challenge and adjust what/who functions and is posited as "God" as it emerges in the everyday in human experience. If "God" as symbol or living metaphor is not part of the meaning that emerges, a constructive theology, as I propose it here, need not introduce it just for its own sake.

Theology must not be equaled with dogma concerning god/deity/divine, but rather understood as a "method by which to analyze human experience ... [T]heology in particular allow[s] for interrogation of the cultural underpinning found within all human endeavors."[15] Theology is an analytical scheme then, and a constructive theology which investigates bodily experience must be interdisciplinary (because it seeks to engage the vast resource of "human experience" explored in substantial volumes of inquiry in various disciplines) if it wants to attend to the ways in which questions and concepts of meaning, world, and humanity emerge from, come together in, and traverse our human existence and experience as bodies.

"Body Theology": A Brief Detour on Works under This Label

"Body Theology" is most popularly known as the title of James B. Nelson's 1992 publication.[16] Nelson places incarnation at the center

15. Anthony B. Pinn, *The End of God-Talk: An African American Humanist Theology* (New York, NY: Oxford University Press, 2012), 3–4. Pinn grounds his theological inquiries in the experiences of African-American communities in the United States to develop his African-American nontheistic humanist theology, rethinking various dimensions of embodied life. He, too, turns to the resource of embodiment, though choosing photography and architecture.
16. James B. Nelson, *Body Theology* (Louisville, KY: Westminster/John Knox Press, 1992). Though Nelson is credited with coining the term, he is not a contributor to subsequent projects taking it up. Nelson first used the term "body theology" in

of the theological imagination. Claiming sexuality as the grounding reality—the basic dimension of personhood—he seeks to develop a positive account of all aspects of embodiment as source of revelation. Rather than developing norms for the use of the body by means of theological reflection or describing the body in theological terms, he proposes to do theology as "critical reflection on *bodily experience* as a fundamental realm of the experience of God."[17] This turn to bodily experience was significant, yet his resourcing of bodily experience for theology largely framed bodily experiences as metaphors for theological exploration.

"Body Theology" surfaced again in 1998 as the distinct name of a field of study with the publication of *Introducing Body Theology* by Lisa Isherwood and Elizabeth Stuart, in which body theology is categorized as theology that allows "the body and its experiences to be a site of revelation."[18] One might argue that any Christian theology, with its doctrinal claims of divine incarnation in a human body, inherently must be body theology, thus making a separate naming redundant and delineation as a field superfluous. Yet, as Isherwood and Stuart point out, while divine incarnation and redemption wrought through the body of Christ could have laid the foundation of body-positive theologies and practices, the history of theology as it is embedded in various religious, political, and philosophical discourses proves otherwise.[19]

---

an earlier work in reference to embodiment and sexual theology. "Sexual theology is body theology. We experience our concreteness as body-selves occupying space in a concrete world." James B. Nelson, *Embodiment: An Approach to Sexuality and Christian Theology* (Minneapolis, MN: Augsburg Publishing House, 1978), 20. One more book bears this title, published earlier by Arthur Vogel, though it is Nelson's work which gained most attention and is most referenced in a query on "body theology." Arthur A. Vogel, *Body Theology: God's Presence in Man's World* (New York, NY: Harper & Row, 1973). Both Vogel and Nelson ground their understanding of the body in concepts by Merleau-Ponty, a philosopher of the phenomenological movement to whom I will return later in this project.

17. Nelson, *Body Theology*, 43. Emphasis mine.
18. Lisa Isherwood and Elizabeth Stuart, *Introducing Body Theology* (Sheffield, UK: Sheffield Academic Press, 1998), 40.
19. Ibid., 15–17.

Isherwood and Stuart introduce body theology as a field of study that is norm-defying in its being positively body-centered, albeit still an emerging way of doing theology.[20] With their volume situated in a series called "Introductions in Feminist Theology," it is not surprising that the framework within which the authors present, evaluate, and critique body theologies is that of taking the female body (in its particularity) as normative,[21] and emphasizing bodily experience as central in order to "create theology through the body and not about the body."[22]

As introduction, this volume presents a range of theologies which "do" body theology, for example, feminist, womanist, and disability theologies; lesbian, gay, and queer theologies; and ecofeminist theologies each receive mention in this volume, and the future direction of body theology is projected to develop the concerns of gender, sexuality, and ecojustice further. The authors point to the phenomenological and suggest future attention to the sensual dimension of bodily experience, as well as the need for new constructions in theological anthropology as aim and constructive contribution of body theology.

Importantly, the methodological approach put forward in this introductory volume suggests to place "what we feel and experience in our everyday lives at the heart of how we begin to understand God"; it suggests that experience is contextual and situated, and fundamental assumptions underpinning experiences must be named; that "interpretation is as embodied as the experience itself"; and that "we are related to the things we experience."[23] I resonate with these suggestions, yet much of the introductory exploration points toward theologies that nevertheless frame "the body" as a site of investigation (asking how a specific body comes to be in a specific context), a site of revelation (what does a specific body "mean" in a specific context), as locus of speech (what is said through a specific body), questions that may

20. Ibid.
21. Ibid., 9.
22. Ibid., 22.
23. Ibid., 39–40.

maintain "the body" as an object of and through which we learn. This kind of approach upholds a dualism of body/mind in implicit ways by treating "the body" as some*thing* to *do with* theologically. And though "body theology" is framed as "theology through the body and not about the body,"[24] the theological examples and theologians featured more often than not present bodily experience (or narratives thereof, as for example in biblical stories) as symbol or metaphor to construct liberative theological visions.

When "Body Theology" again appears in a title ten years later, it is in the series "Controversies in Contextual Theology," in which editors Marcella Althaus-Reid and Lisa Isherwood seek the continuation of dealing with the "harsher realities of the body and the way in which it manifests and reacts in the world and most importantly to the world."[25] Here, too, it is women's and/or sexual bodies that provide the ground for critical inquiries, from matricide and the Marquis de Sade to mutilation of bodies to trans- and intersex bodies to women's bodies and dieting/fitness crazes in Western contemporary culture. The editors call this a highlighting of "some of the important current themes in the discussion of a body theology pertinent for the twenty-first century," hoping for new development of dialogue on "some of the hard issues of women's bodies, the theological, political and social implications of which we are just starting to unravel."[26]

That both books, given the feminist theological commitments of the editors, are prefaced with grounding inquiries into the body, specifically in female bodies, is not necessarily surprising or troubling to me. What I want to note in comparing these two volumes, though, are certain significant disappearances or omissions. Mentioned in *Introducing*, ecofeminist concerns disappear in *Controversies*. *Introducing* gives some attention to disability studies and disability theology (fields that significantly challenge and enrich inquiries into embodiment that take up

24. Ibid., 22.
25. Marcella M. Althaus-Reid and Lisa Isherwood, eds., *Controversies in Body Theology* (London: SCM Press, 2008), 3.
26. Ibid., 5–6.

ability and normalcy), presenting a few pages on Nancy Eiesland's *The Disabled God* within a chapter discussing the construction of bodies that need redemption or might signify the divine. *Controversies* does not include disability among the themes mentioned; disability appears only in a brief reference in a chapter on the intersections of Christian diet programs with capitalist, racist, and misogynist ideologies.[27] And *Introducing* highlights reflection on embodied (sensual) experiences, specifically laughter, as very promising in being able to avoid the pitfalls of biological essentialism in body theology. Such embodied experiences "of the flesh" are taken up in *Controversies* by a chapter inquiring into cosmetic surgery and cultural representation of women and a chapter on cutting (self-mutilation) of women as embodied deconstruction of pain and Christian communities.[28] But the explicit references to disability theology and phenomenological approaches in *Introducing* have vanished in *Controversies*.

The disappearances of certain embodiment differences between the publications is disconcerting to me, because these works are most commonly cited in queries on the term "body theology" and thus set the

---

27. Lisa Isherwood, "Will You Slim for Him or Bake Cakes for the Queen of Heaven?," in *Controversies in Body Theology*, ed. Marcella M. Althaus-Reid and Lisa Isherwood, *Controversies in Contextual Theology* (London, UK: SCM Press, 2008), 174–206. To understand why certain diet programs could be supported by Christian religious framing, Isherwood explains biblical and historic connections of sin with physical disability over against holiness equated with perfection, health, and beauty. "Women with disabilities have carried an extra burden since they are viewed as doubly transgressive" (191). This makes disability only one of the additional markers of a woman's body; the experience of disability being subsumed under the experience of being a woman, and thus, in this chapter, the experience of surveillance and oppression from religiously framed consumerism and aestheticism is experienced as woman first, as disabled person second.
28. Inga Bryden, "'Cut'n'slash': Remodelling the 'Freakish' Female Form," in *Controversies in Body Theology*, ed. Marcella M. Althaus-Reid and Lisa Isherwood, *Controversies in Contextual Theology* (London, UK: SCM Press, 2008), 29–47. Elizabeth Baxter, "Cutting Edge: Witnessing Rites of Passage in a Therapeutic Community," in *Controversies in Body Theology*, ed. Marcella M. Althaus-Reid and Lisa Isherwood, *Controversies in Contextual Theology* (London, UK: SCM Press, 2008), 48–69.

parameters of how body theology as a term and field is framed. Body theology then appears as an outgrowth, subgroup, niche work, or synonym of feminist and sexual liberation theologies: the framework is given by feminist/sexual theology (though grounded in a variety of feminist theories), and the main concerns of "body theology" today (still) focus on the effects of social constructions of (gendered female, lesbian, queer, or transgender) bodies.[29] Therefore, "body theology" as presented in these works might be more aptly named "body metaphor theology," as bodily experiences are resourced most often in a symbolic or metaphorical way.[30]

While the critical analysis done in the works discussed so far is certainly important, especially as it concerns real live bodies and suffering experienced, analytical dialogues must be pressed further. Body

29. In *Doing Contextual Theology*, Angie Pears reinforces this connection, though she groups body theologies in line with sexual theologies and queer theologies under the larger rubric of liberation theologies. In surveying body theologies (and referring mainly to the authors I mentioned earlier: Nelson, Isherwood, Stuart, and Althaus-Reid), she names as identifying characteristics the body as fundamental resource for theology, a rejection of spiritual/material hierarchical dualisms, and a positive reading of the body. But she also reinforces the impression of body theologies as those inquiring into human sexuality and sexual bodies as *the* point of reference for embodiment—a delineation I find neither useful nor desirable. For example, disability theologies are referenced in one passing sentence under body theologies and receive no further mention in the book. See Angie Pears, *Doing Contextual Theology* (New York, NY: Routledge, 2010), 117–123.

30. By no means do I intend to dismiss theologies that seek to provide liberative metaphors, as I am convinced that it does matter how we speak about the sacred/divine we experience or wish to see in the world. The critique of Sallie McFague, for example, challenges traditional theological language as exclusive. Because she understands language to qualify human reality, and metaphors as irreducibly structuring our knowing, she seeks to affect the religious imagination through models and metaphors that will bring about positive relations in the world. Thus she conceptualizes the human body as dependent, liable to contingencies, and vulnerable, and then employs it as a metaphor to posit the world as body of God in order to encourage a focus which prohibits the spiritualization of pain or the focus on existential anxieties, but rather affirms all life as imbued with intrinsic value. Sallie McFague, *Models of God: Theology for an Ecological, Nuclear Age* (Philadelphia: Fortress Press, 1987), 72–74. Sallie McFague, *The Body of God: An*

theology must not be understood as a niche interest/project or analogy for feminist theological work. Doing so submits to strategies of containment employed to delimit the critical challenges and contributions presented by theologies attending to embodiment to the larger field of theology and the humanities. Emphasizing contextuality and embodied particularity may point out the pretense of disembodiment in universalizing intellectual projects. Yet it also undercuts the critique brought from particularized and contextualized marginal positions by placing the burden of proof for wider relevance on those theologies described as contextual, situated, or emerging from so-called particular (read: non-White, non-heteronormative, non-Eurocentric) locations. To label body theology as a niche theology is to compartmentalize and dismiss the insights offered through body theology analysis for and by the larger normative/operative intellectual structures that legitimate knowledge and theological projects.

OUTLINING "CONSTRUCTIVE BODY THEOLOGY"

This book proposes a robust and complex notion of "body theology" and demonstrates what kinds of analyses this re-envisioned approach can do. My underlying commitments and presuppositions are that theological reflection is always done as embodied selves yet bodies have not been taken seriously in the doing of theology.[31] Having grown out of liberation concerns related to gender and sexuality, and highlighting the political and the experiential, body theologies take as starting point a conscious focus on embodied experience, using it as a critical source for reflection on and construction of theology. These theologies

Ecological Theology (Minneapolis: Fortress Press, 1993), 18, 168,171–173. For a critique on how her body metaphor still depends on a concept based on whole, well-functioning "normal" bodies, see Deborah Beth Creamer, *Disability and Christian Theology: Embodied Limits and Constructive Possibilities* (New York, NY: Oxford University Press, 2009), 66–69.

31. "Theologies have always been embodied because all theologies have been explored and lived by people with bodies." Creamer, *Disability and Christian Theology,* 57.

acknowledge the role of particularities of embodiment and make credible arguments about the role of bodily particulars such as gender, race, sexual orientation, and so forth in establishing a difference in one's position and experience of the world.[32]

"Body theology" in this book begins with these acknowledgments and commitments. Bodily experiences are significant, even fundamental, starting points for and concerns of theological reflection and construction. More than simply affirming bodily experience, body theology as inquiry with particular critical commitments begins with attention to complex differences and inherent ambiguities of particular embodied experiences, and demands that these bodily sites of experience are recognized as significant, if not crucial, to our understanding of the human condition of all. It is neither an unequivocal celebration of the particular body (which might produce romantizations similar to those found in some early feminist theologies celebrating the feminine), nor is it marginal with little value to the dominating mainstream discourse. Depending on context, a body theology might find a home in feminist theology, womanist theology, mujerista theology, disability theology, queer theology, contextual theology, or postcolonial theology, but it is more broadly cast to be adequately contained by any of these labels. I want to establish body theology as analytical commitments in conversation with different theologies which hold concerns and commitments in regard to engaging and exploring varied embodiments and their effect on our orientation in and interpretation of the world.[33]

In conversation with and indebted to the theologians who have shaped my own theological interests, skills, commitments, analyses, and desires, I offer "body theology" as a set of commitments that seeks to claim the concern for specific and particular bodies as relevant to all. The "body" in "body theology" then is not an adjective, but rather a verb (as much as that is grammatically possible) indicating an

32. Ibid., 56–57.
33. Ibid., 58.

em-body-ing of theology, a concern with lived, embodied experiences as source and grounding for the doing of theology, common to various theologians otherwise differently grouped. It is then not a theology *of* the body, which starts with theology and seeks to inform and direct bodily issues;[34] rather, it is a theological stance beginning with bodily experience and seeking to speak back to or engage in a dialogue with theologies, social theories, cultural analysis, and so forth. It is those embodied/body theologies I want to engage with, and ultimately, suggest critical commitments for.

I will argue that body theology does not need to be "god-talk," though it certainly can be. Rather, body theology is a critical inquiry into and within human experiences, beginning with and taking seriously bodily experiences. If we consider history of religions scholar Charles Long's definition of religion as orientation in/to the world, as "how one comes to terms with the ultimate significance of one's place in the world," and assert that orientation is more than just structures of thought but "experience, expression, motivations, intentions, behaviors, styles, and rhythms,"[35] then our bodily experiences are orientation in the world. Our means of situating ourselves in the world is in our being embodied selves: in and through our bodies we come to perceive the world and are perceived by it; our bodily experiences give rise to thought. This implies that our orientation to the world takes place in a vulnerable space, susceptible because of its deep, flexible physicality and because of its exposure to social forces.

Body theology begins by seeking a more complex understanding of how and why human existence manifests as bodily inhabitation of time and space. Any theological enterprise, god-talk or not, explicitly attending to embodiment or not, is always, as Gordon Kaufman noted, a constructive project following experience, because all theologizing and analyzing is based on and follows experience and articulates that

34. As, for example, John Paul II, *Man and Woman He Created Them: A Theology of the Body*, trans., Michael Waldstein (Boston, MA: Pauline Books & Media, 2006).
35. Charles H. Long, *Significations: Signs, Symbols and Images in the Interpretation of Religion* (Aurora, CO: The Davies Group Publishers, 1995), 7.

experience and its meaning through a particular lens.[36] Thus "body theology" in this project is the doing of theology within a body framework. As such, it begins by seeking to appreciate bodily experience and sketching an understanding of it in regard to our embodied existence. Body theology as analysis of human experience places bodily experience and expressions of the embodied subject in time and space at the center of meaning-making, and frames bodily experience by attending to sensory perception, the interplay of bodily experience and the complex productions of culture, and inherent power dynamics within which both are found.

I consider this move as critical to grounding any theological enterprise in bodily experience. While remaining committed to feminist theory and analysis, I reposition the theoretical lens with which we approach bodily experience at an intersection with other disciplines. If particularities of embodment make a difference, as feminists claim, then I need to know not *what* the body is, but *how we are bodies*. As I mentioned earlier, my reflections on personal experiences provided me with a hunch that there is something to sensory perception that might help to explore bodily experience. I turn to phenomenological concepts, particularly Maurice Merleau-Ponty's exploration of bodily experience as perception, to follow the cues of the living (and dying) bodies of my grandmother and my mother. The senses and perceptual experience are the juncture at which my various questions and pursuits are usefully explored. As exploration into perception and bodily experience, the potential scope and breadth of this project is vast, and so inevitably, this books weaves together selective and eclectic strands of philosophical, historical, anthropological, and ethnographic perspectives to frame a theological reflection.

Attention to sensory dimensions of embodment is a fundamental component of bodily experience and thus can lend complexity and strength to other approaches, such as religio-cultural analysis or

---

36. Gordon D. Kaufman, *An Essay on Theological Method* (Missoula, MT: Scholars Press, 1975). Gordon D. Kaufman, *The Theological Imagination: Constructing the Concept of God* (Philadelphia, PA: Westminster Press, 1981), 21–24.

theo-ethnographic studies. What I offer is an integrated view of the role of perception in bodily experience; and bodily perceptual experience both as a relationship to a world and as in itself a kind of structuring of world and defining of meaning.

While the very act of critical analysis on bodily perceptual experience demands certain abstractions and presuppositions (such as presuming that distinct perceptual capacities can be identified and discussed analytically), I show that (and how) the dimensions of bodily perceptual experience are intimately connected to our emotional, intellectual, and other personal experiences; in fact, that bodily perceptual experiences *are always implicated in, embedded in, and subtending of* our existence, and there is no experiencing that is not bodily perceptual. Moreover, any given context and culture provides perceptual matrices through which bodily experiences are made intelligible, and in turn, individual and culturally informed bodily experiences shape our sensory perceptions. By developing a better understanding of what bodily sensory perception is, I encourage new theological investigations into bodily experiences and processes beyond potential essentializations of bodily perceptual functions.

I turn to feminist theology because of the explicit commitment to embodiment and the difference bodily experience makes that is found in this field. In chapter 2 I review and critique theoretical perspectives on perception explicitly or implicitly drawn on in feminist theologies. I offer representative indications of phenomenological conceptions found in feminist theologies, which feed into understanding bodily experience. I discuss how these conceptions factor into theologies that have sought to construct theological claims by returning to bodily experience in one way or another. I critique the challenges inherent in embedded concept of perception, and how they may undermine the theological project they are supposed to support, most significantly by resorting/succumbing to Cartesian dualisms sought to be overcome.

In the second part of this book I make a case that our existence in the world is always fundamentally and significantly a bodily perceptual orientation. In other words, we are always feeling, tasting, touching, hearing, thinking, imagining beings; and these perceptual acts are how we exist in the world and how the world makes sense to us. It also orients us toward the world in specific ways. At stake in not carefully conceptualizing our sensory perception is that, although we might point out differences in embodiment or bodily experiences, conceptual shortcuts regarding perception might lead us to "flatten" bodily experiences into examples of our situation, rather than understanding them as integral to our situation in the world. I make my case by exploring phenomenological concepts such as bodily intentionality and habit, and I do so in separate chapters by pivoting through the concepts of gender, race, and normalcy. In each chapter I add historical and cultural comparisons in order to deepen our understanding of our existence in the world as fundamentally bodily sensing. The differences and incarnate possibilities regarding bodily perceptual orientation, regarding the being, feeling, thinking, touching, speaking, and so on in the world, are not only potentialities to imagine, but also already did/do exist. Encountering these differences will bring our own orientations to gender, race, and normalcy in the world more complexly and viscerally to our attention.

In the third part, I take us back to body theology, now as commitments that ground our analysis and investigations in bodily experience, and frame our approach to experience via bodily perceptual orientation. I return to theological projects that attend to body/bodily experience, particularly the works of Carter Heyward and Marcella Althaus-Reid, to demonstrate the difference a re-envisioned body theology as analytical commitments can make. Returning to my personal questions raised in this introduction, I frame answers by approaching my own familial bodily experiences through "body theology." I conclude this project by looking out into further fields of study or issues of interest which might benefit from body theology queries.

CHAPTER TWO

SITUATING FEMINIST THEOLOGIES PHENOMENOLOGICALLY

Both feminist theory and theology have significantly shaped and influenced the concerns I bring to my research. To demonstrate the importance of carefully attending to sensory perception in order to complexly understand bodily experience, I review the spectrum within which perception is conventionally framed in feminist theologies, implicitly or explicitly. This will help us better understand the stakes involved regarding under-articulating or ignoring to frame a concept of perception and its place in bodily experience, and it will support my search for a complex and integrated view of the role of perception in bodily experience.

I will begin by situating my interest and concern regarding bodily experience and perception within a conversation of feminist theory and theology. After a broad sketch of the feminist dimension informing my theological work with highlighting approaches to bodily experience and perception, I will switch angles and provide an outline of the spectrum within which perception has been conceived in traditional phenomenologies. The feminist theologies which I deeply appreciate and yet begin to critique employ phenomenological concepts along this spectrum in efforts to bolster theological claims, implicitly or explicitly. I will show how this resorting to perception in an effort to overcome body/mind dualism and revalidate bodily sense experience as epistemological resource may nevertheless implicate and undermine the theological aim precisely because of the way perception is conceived.

To conclude this chapter, I will provide a conception of bodily experience and perception that avoids the problems highlighted; a conception I will explore in depth in the following chapter to propose as the theoretical frame for exploration of bodily experience as theological resource.

SITUATING BODILY EXPERIENCE
AND PERCEPTION IN FEMINIST THEOLOGY

After René Descartes' epistemological base of *cogito ergo sum* ("I think, therefore I am"), the body and those associated with it (i.e., women, racial others) have largely been dismissed from Western intellectual traditions. Descartes had worked out that, as human beings who are primarily thinking beings (rational and detached from the sensual world), we can only be certain of objects (the worlds outside of our minds) if they conform to the representations we hold of them in our minds. We can even be sure of our own existence only as and within "I think, I am." The body/mind split of the Enlightenment was not a new development, but the emphasis shifted from the body as a mundane (though suspect) factor to being considered an obstacle to rational thought.[1]

---

1. Certainly, Descartes and Enlightenment as philosophical movement neither mark the founding of body/mind dualisms nor are they the greatest progenitors. These dualisms have roots in Hellenistic philosophy and can be found in the New Testament; one can see them in Augustine, as well as Paul, and repeated in the Middle Ages in Aquinas as well as other thinkers. The philosophical roots of judging the physical senses as distorting perception of objective truth, or even incapable of perceiving such, and of only the discerning mind being capable of accessing true essences are found in Plato and Socrates. But it is Cartesian philosophy that first provides a systematic philosophical account, building on Hellenistic traditions. Descartes articulates the mind/body dualism in *De Homine*, conceiving of body and mind as separate entities, the former affecting the latter through sensations, but the mind affecting the actions of the inferior body. A philosophical critique of mind/body dualism might begin with a genealogy and context of dualism. In this book, I choose to remain within the feminist theological critiques of Cartesian dualism, for one, because the blame is often (though not necessarily justly) laid at the feet of Descartes and by engaging Descartes and his feminist critics, showing how these criticisms fall short of their own task. But more importantly, my

The post-Cartesian body was a fixed biological object, some "thing" to be transcended to free the person into full subjectivity by pursuit of rational activity.[2] Because women were considered too steeped in their bodies, their rationality and intellectual ability were questionable because of their supposed sensuous nature. Early feminist theory challenged this and focused on the body/mind, female/male binary split in order to elevate the feminine from its position of the other, the less than fully human.[3]

The feminist theory emerging in the 1960s out of and in tandem with the feminist movement of that time set the intellectual course for a developing Euro-American feminist theology.[4] Feminist theories and

utilization of phenomenology as intellectual movement warrants a close look at Cartesian legacies more than Hellenistic or medieval articulations, because phenomenology itself is a philosophical trajectory made possible because of Cartesian formulations (see more in what follows).

2. Descartes' concern was to establish reason as the foundation for a universal science. He sought to establish systematic doubt as the method to establish a firm foundation for comprehensive scientific philosophy and knowledge. This foundation was the intuitively perceived existence of the finite self. This self subjected the realm of physical facts, events, and experiences to scrutiny and investigation. Sense experience can be deceiving, and thus any experience needs to be subjected to doubt. While Descartes left a lasting legacy, this is not to say that Cartesian trajectories have been left without critique. For a sample of early and later rejections of Cartesian dualism, see Stuart F. Spicker, ed. *The Philosophy of the Body: Rejections of Cartesian Dualism* (Chicago, IL: Quadrangle Books, 1970).

3. These strategies are not confined to early feminist theories and theologies, but their trajectories continue today, as for example found in the feminist philosophy of Luce Irigaray or feminist theologies turning to bodily experiences/faculties traditionally associated with women to value their epistemological and theological meanings. See Luce Irigaray, *An Ethics of Sexual Difference* (Ithaca, NY: Cornell University Press, 1993). Paula M. Cooey, "The Word Became Flesh: Woman's Body, Language, and Value," in *Embodied Love: Sensuality and Relationship as Feminist Values*, ed. Paula M. Cooey, Sharon A. Farmer, and Mary Ellen Ross (San Francisco, CA: Harper & Row, 1987), 17–33. See also Carter Isabel Heyward, *Touching Our Strength: The Erotics as Power and the Love of God* (San Francisco: Harper & Row, 1989).

4. Neither feminist theory nor feminist theology begins at that time. One of the ways feminist thought has been traced is by referring to what has been coined "first

theologies took up new philosophical and theological frameworks to promote the affirmation of women's full humanity. They began affirming women's experiences as valid, even indispensable, resources for theorizing and theologizing and saw women's praxis as liberating activity central to political and cultural (and for theologians and some theorists, spiritual) life.[5] The move to explicitly value experience is not necessarily a new methodological move, as the appeal to experience in the study of religion and theology has roots in (masculinist) Enlightenment thinking. The methodological revolution was *women's* experience as the primary resource. Placing women at the center of theoretical and theological reflection reframed epistemology as it had been defined. Valid knowledge and the means of its production were no longer solely limited to that which passed as scientifically objective, namely the uncritically male and masculinist Enlightenment thinking.[6]

Seeking to challenge sexism in religious traditions, early feminist theologians pursued a variety of strategies, and commonly a spectrum between two broadly sketched ends is used to frame the approaches taken (though many might be better described as falling somewhere in between): There are those feminist theologians who sought to detect and remove androcentric symbols and practices, using women's experiences as a starting point for dialoguing with and within their respective

wave feminism," a period of women's activism during the 19th and early 20th century which saw a focus on suffrage and the production of Stanton and Anthony's *Women's Bible*. The emergence of feminist theology as a discipline does not occur until the 1960s, which is why I begin my discussion with this time. However, one could also argue that when/wherever women have been/are oppressed one could find instances of what is now called feminism, though not gathering under the name of this modern concept.

5. Linda Hogan, *From Women's Experience to Feminist Theology* (Sheffield, UK: Sheffield Academic Press, 1995), 16.

6. For discussion of the epistemological shifts, see Alessandra Tanesini, *An Introduction to Feminist Epistemologies* (Malden, MA: Blackwell Publishers Inc., 1999). Linda Alcoff and Elizabeth Potter, eds., *Feminist Epistemologies* (New York, NY: Routledge, 1992). Or for more explicit connections to theology, see Lucy Tatman, *Knowledge That Matters: A Feminist Theological Paradigm and Epistemology* (Cleveland: Pilgrim Press, 2001).

religious traditions. They came to be known as "reformists" (key figures among them are Elisabeth Schüssler Fiorenza and Rosemary Radford Ruether). Others, known as post-Christian or radical feminist theologians, determined Christian traditions to be too deeply steeped in androcentrism and sexism, so they sought to theologize outside of Christian texts and traditions, hoisting new symbolism, metaphors, rituals, and so forth, or re-appropriating ancient, pre-Christian religious symbolism (e.g., Carol P. Christ and Mary Daly).

Regardless whether one most identifies with the reformist or the radical end of the spectrum, the smallest common agreement among feminist theologians is that bodily difference (and/or discourse thereof) has social consequences; different bodies leads to different (bodily) experiences, and different experiences are valid sources of evidence. Roughly, feminist theological uptake of "body issues" ranges from following a masculinist standard (rejecting the body in pursuit of intellectual equality), to reclaiming and revalorizing the body and cultural associations with it (nature, nurture, cycles) as the very essence of the female, to the most recent poststructuralist concern with instability, cultural inscriptions on bodies, bodily experiences, and embodied potentialities.[7] Feminist theologians today are routinely challenged to not only address the gendered dimensions of life, but also be able to attend to intersections of race, class, abilities, nationality, and other dimensions leading to marginalization of bodies. Experience remains a significant factor in theorizing from a variety of standpoints and toward various ends.

While most contemporary feminist theologians might agree that the instability and flexibility of the concept of "woman" is desirable and useful for feminist theology, not all might agree that the same is true for the concept of "experience."[8] With the category "women's

7. Margrit Shildrick and Janet Price, "Openings on the Body: A Critical Introduction," in *Feminist Theory and the Body: A Reader*, ed. Janet Price and Margrit Shildrick (New York, NY: Routledge, 1999), 3.
8. Remember, for example, the famous Sojourner Truth speech *Ain't I a Woman* decrying the racism and exclusion of black women from the category "woman" in the mostly white women's movement of the time. Mary Daly is another popular

experience" under scrutiny (very much from the beginnings of feminist articulations), how a feminist theologian decides to employ this category depends on the epistemological framework and methodology chosen, a choice which then marks the emerging theological perspective.[9] Appeals to experience are most commonly distinguished between essentialist and constructivist frameworks. On either side of this divide (with feminist theologians now often acknowledging that a strict binary division is neither possible nor theoretically desirable), experience is highlighted as *embodied* experience. Theologians who operate within the essentialist framework anchor their work in gender fundamentals

---

example of attracting criticism for essentializing "woman" as white; most known is Audre Lorde's charge against Daly as either excluding black women's experience or essentializing non-white women as victims.

9. For example, making corresponding connections between a certain feminist vision and divine reality, revealed through accessing and expressing a certain "experience," runs the risk of conceptualizing said "experiences" as unmediated, untainted material to be accessed. Assigning ontological normativity to select "experience" is evident when patriarchal religion and myths are critiqued and followed up with "recoveries" of more authentic matriarchal origins or feminine spiritualities. A recovering construction has the potential to become ideology itself when it becomes more reflective of a cultural critique of a modern crisis that, for example, seeks to reconstruct the female goddess symbol in the image of what is considered to be lacking in the current context. This reads contemporary concerns into a historical situation in order to use this constructed history to legitimize a project and the validity of such a method. Moreover, simply accepting appropriations of accounts of, for example, medieval women's spirituality often does not account for differences. These accounts often characterize women's spirituality as bodily-affective, which upholds and reifies traditional stereotypes of the feminine. Yet historically, women's spirituality emphasizing embodied devotion and mysticism was no oppressed activity but was even supported by contemporary religious authorities. It was the women who advocated for other kinds of spirituality (esp. one's emphasizing intellectual activities and interpretation outside clergy supervision) who were persecuted as heretics and had their writings destroyed. See Monika Jakobs, "Auf Der Suche Nach Dem Verlorenen Paradies? Zur Hermeneutik Von Ursprüngen in Der Feministischen Theologie," *Journal of the European Society of Women in Theological Research* 5 (1997): 128–132. Anke Passenier, "Der Lustgarten Des Leibes Und Die Freiheit Der Seele: Wege Der Mittelalterlichen Frauenspiritualität," *Journal of the European Society of Women in Theological Research* 5 (1997): 196–197.

and differences and seek to craft and/or employ universalizing frames of reference to structure their account of human experience. Theologians on the constructivist side follow postmodern trajectories and investigate the social roots of experiences of gendered personhood.

To sketch the wide field of feminist theologies today, let me point to feminist theologians who prominently contributed in the emergence and shaping of feminist theology as a discipline, like Mary Daly, Rosemary Radford Ruether, and Elisabeth Schüssler Fiorenza. The first two began with the observation that women and female bodies have historically been degraded by means of theo-philosophical and scientific discourses of the time. Therefore, updating philosophical and scientific evidence on the body provides the arguments with which to make a case for equality of the sexes (I will return to Daly and Ruether again later).

Elisabeth Schüssler Fiorenza focuses on methods of interpreting Christian scriptures, and in *But She Said* and other works also presumes women's experience as determinant of the validity of theological traditions.[10] When referring to experience, she explicitly seeks to utilize "feminist experience" or "feminist analysis of women's (socialized) experience" as resource and perspective on reality against which theological interpretations need to be tested.[11] However, when Schüssler Fiorenza posits "feminist" experience as the source of liberating theologizing,[12] she frames the creation of a feminist critical consciousness as originating "breakthrough" or "disclosure" experiences of suspicion

10. Elisabeth Schüssler Fiorenza, *But She Said: Feminist Practices of Biblical Interpretation* (Boston: Becon Press, 1992). Elisabeth Schüssler Fiorenza, *Jesus: Miriam's Child, Sophia's Prophet. Critical Issues in Feminist Theology* (New York, NY: Continuum Publishing Company, 1994). Elisabeth Schüssler Fiorenza, *Sharing Her Word: Feminist Biblical Interpretation in Context* (Boston: Beacon Press, 1998).

11. Schüssler Fiorenza, *But She Said*, 21, 34.

12. This comes close to the a priori access to truth found in Mary Daly, who would have only "women-identified women" at the center of all "true" interpretations, in Schüssler Fiorenza, it appears that only persons within the *ecclesia of wo/men*, and engaging in the processes she describes, are able to appropriate "experience" correctly, that is, in a liberating fashion.

about the supposed naturalness of patriarchy.[13] While she does not
explicitly appeal to the utilization of perception, she reveals an implicit
leaning on poststructuralist tools (see following) in her drawing on
Foucault's articulation of docile bodies and the disciplining of bodies to
illustrate women's oppression through cultural forces.[14] Experiences of
pain, suffering, oppression, violence are mediated through the surface
of the body, and while important, gain traction only in and through
discourse, through a critical feminist consciousness, which enables
"correct" perception.

Theologians who plow the field of theological resources of embodied experience with poststructuralist tools (e.g., Sallie McFague and
Marcella Althaus-Reid) may be eclectic in their methodologies and
draw on linguistic, cultural, social, and political theories, yet all are
influenced by and employing themes of subjectivity, language, and
social construction of identity. These theologians seek to affirm the
instabilities as well as the generalities articulated in "experience"
by particularizing social location. Poststructuralist methodologies
allow theologians to focus on language, symbolism, and myths and
the power inherent in linguistic systems to shape social structures
and therefore experience. This kind of focus often supports theological aims of subverting dominant and oppressive symbolism. New
understandings and models of the body allow for new metaphors
and re-symbolization in theology to express and address embodied

13. I chose to discuss Ruether and Schüssler Fiorenza here at length, because
much of what is popularly understood to be "feminist theology" has followed
these two scholars or at least used their trajectories and/or taken cues from their
methodologies. One reason might be Schüssler Fiorenza's employment of Marxian
language and method as well as her liberationist language appropriated form liberation theology, which is useful in theologies seeking to do a material analysis.
Radford Ruther's methodology might find its popularity and resonance in many
(feminist) audiences, western and non-western, as she charts an accessible middle
way between the liberal and romantic types of feminist thinking (women are equal
and equally capable as men; women are aligned with attributes that need to be
validated).

14. Schüssler Fiorenza, *Sharing Her Word: Feminist Biblical Interpretation in
Context*, 143–145.

experience. For example, Sallie McFague understands language to qualify human reality, and metaphors as irreducibly structuring our knowing. She therefore seeks to affect the religious imagination through models and metaphors that will bring about positive relations in the world.[15] Her epistemological claim connects the quest for truth and meaning to embodied locations, as she defines experience in its basic sense as the act of living.[16]

Yet McFague acknowledges that one has no access to a *raw* experience of reality, and, utilizing theories on metaphors (particularly Ricoeur's hermeneutical phenomenology), argues that all experiences are expressed in metaphorical constructions. Moreover, she asserts that human access to reality is partial and always mediated through linguistic metaphors. At the same time, metaphors are productive of reality, meaning that metaphors can produce and offer new/different experiences, and her works attempt to find metaphors to express radical relationality between all that lives.[17] While experience begins with bodily sensations, the latter serve in constructive processes of associations,

15. For example, in *Models of God* and *The Body of God* she uses scientific theories and other texts concerning North American experiences of the ecological crisis as touchstones to investigate cultural models and paradigms that construct experiences and with it Christian identity and practice. Salley McFague, *Models of God: Theology for an Ecological, Nuclear Age* (Philadelphia: Fortress Press, 1987). Salley McFague, *The Body of God: An Ecological Theology* (Minneapolis, MN: Fortress Press, 1993). For example, she uses the Big Bang theory as a cultural text and "common creation story," which informs contemporary experience and through it theorizes unity and diversity and applies this to a theology of nature. See McFague, *Models of God*, 45–46. McFague situates her project in an epistemological discussion between idealism and positivism, in which she is critical of both, though more so of the latter than the former. She is skeptical of unitary tendencies in some idealist immaterial epistemological claims (direct correlation between metaphor and reality) and resists tendencies to deny reality outside of language, but frames human existence as hermeneutical in nature. Sallie McFague, *Metaphorical Theology: Models of God in Religious Language* (Philadelphia: Fortress Press, 1982), 39.
16. McFague, *The Body of God*, 47.
17. McFague, *Models of God*, 26, 51.

connections and interpretations within signifying systems.[18] While metaphors are central to knowledge and language, McFague acknowledges "sensuous, affectional, and active lives at the most primordial level," providing the base for metaphors and symbolic systems.[19]

Mujerista, womanist and postcolonial theologians (like Ada María Isasi-Díaz, Delores Williams, Kwok Pui-Lan), often share concerns and methodological features with poststructuralist theorists regarding embodied experience. They often seek to make explicit the connections between particular and historicized social locations and embodied differences to make use of historically marginalized experiences as a central resource in doing theology. Often using socio-cultural and ethnographic accounts or localized "thick descriptions," they make an effort to point to the abjected, embodied experiences that provide the grounds for emancipatory and liberating theological formulations.[20] This strategy borrows (or at least echoes) the concerns and methodologies of more explicitly poststructuralist theologians, albeit from different locations.

Delores Williams describes triple inscriptions of racialization, masculinization, and sexualization on black women's bodies (using historical experience to analyze contemporary socialized experience of black women). In *Sisters in the Wilderness,* she draws on novels which describe and ground the experiences of African American women,

---

18. McFague, *Metaphorical Theology*, 32–35. Perception is a "seeing-as," it is not simply reception of sense data, but involves recognition of what is seen. This recognition is part of an interpretation process, and McFague argues that perceiving is always interpreting; it always takes place in our contact and response to reality and our environment. Analogies and metaphor guide us in our interpretative acts and are also created by us to re-interpret and continuously respond and engage our contexts and rereading historical experience. McFague, *Metaphorical Theology*, 34–38.

19. McFague, *Metaphorical Theology*, 37.

20. "Thick description" is a methodological concept offered by anthropologist Clifford Geertz. He proposes to provide dense descriptions of small, real-time lived experiences (rather than aiming for broad, all-encompassing descriptions devoid of detail). Clifford Geertz, *The Interpretation of Cultures* (New York, NY: Basic Books, 1973).

making experiences of race and class intersect with gender to articulate women's experience.[21] Williams, in a womanist methodological vein, retrieves embodied experience (e.g., motherhood, surrogacy, ethnicity, wilderness experience) hermeneutically and for the purposes of developing reading strategies of biblical texts and other literary sources supporting full moral agency of black women. Important in this constructive theological work is critical reflection on experience (embodied and narrated), especially as it concerns the body doubly marked by race and sex; this often takes the shape of analyzing stereotypes and cultural images of black women and the construction of race.[22] Her conception of perception is less explicit, yet what leaks through is an understanding of perception as sensitivity to lived experience, particularly regarding oppressive structures. While embodied knowledge can be found expressed in bodily movement (singing, dancing, gestures), highlighted is often the making intelligible of embodied experience through critical intellectual attention.

Kwok positions the "Asian woman" as a multiple, fluid identity, grounded in communal (rather than individual) experience and in particular historical contexts and struggles, and signifying a political position rather than an essential definition.[23] Discussions of experience, particularly Asian women's experience as theological resource, most often center on experiences and feelings of fragmentation, displacement, alienation, and oppression under colonialism and its aftermaths. Kwok points out that to talk about Asian women's experience generally, "experience" needs to be understood as a social construct. Asian feminist theologians resource this experience often via utilizing narratives (since story telling has been the chief means of transmitting

21. Delores S. Williams, *Sisters in the Wilderness: The Challenge of Womanist God-Talk* (Maryknoll: Orbis Books, 1993).

22. See also, for example, the work of ethicist Emily M. Townes, *Womanist Ethics and the Cultural Production of Evil* (New York, NY: Palgrave MacMillan, 2006).

23. Kwok Pui-Lan, *Discovering the Bible in the Non-Biblical World*, ed. Norman K. Gottwald and Richard A. Horsley, The Bible and Liberation Series (Maryknoll, NY: Orbis Books, 1995), 26. Kwok Pui-Lan, *Postcolonial Imagination and Feminist Theology* (Louisville, KY: Westminster John Knox, 2005), 36.

wisdom between generations of women) and social analysis.[24] Similarly to Williams, perception in regard to experience becomes a tool utilized for critical analysis, particularly hermeneutical approaches to narratives of experience.

These are just few examples of what can be found in today's feminist theological field, in which "embodied experience" as a category is accepted as dynamic and conceptually unstable. The challenge for feminist theory and theology in using "women's experience" is that of acknowledging and accounting for and theorizing with difference.[25] The plurality and the diversity of the lives, choices, and values of women are all bound to class, race, culture, physical make-up, and other factors. Theologians utilizing "experience" today need to attend to how human experiences are bound up in bodies and the particularities through which we encounter the world.

The body matters; and the most basic feminist consensus is that any theoretical investigation needs to begin with this acknowledgement.[26] It is also important to realize how dangerous the vulnerable body appears to us: The body vulnerable to disease, decay and death terrorizes the human imagination, and modern medicine embodies a war on this body in the form of therapy or ennobling duties of care in the name of love. The dominant social approaches to the vulnerability of the body reveal that within the larger project of modernity, human bodily experiences of finiteness and mortality are abject to a culture which normalizes idealized images of able-bodiedness. Bodies that defy the norm appear as dangerous "other," and in a world which worships reason and intellect, the vulnerable and disturbed mind incites terror.[27]

This concern is highlighted in the feminist theological landscape by feminist disability theologians (like Nancy Eiesland and Sharon

---

24. Kwok Pui-Lan, *Introducing Asian Feminist Theology* (Sheffield, UK: Sheffield Academic Press Ltd, 2000), 38–41.
25. See Mary McClintock Fulkerson, *Changing the Subject: Women's Discourses and Feminist Theology* (Minneapolis: Fortress Press, 1994), 13–18.
26. Shildrick and Price, "Openings on the Body," 1–3.
27. Newell, "On the Importance of Suffering."

Betcher) who frame the body as the locus for theological reflection, yet explicitly seek to deconstruct persistent notions of "normal" embodiment. Paying deliberate attention to the physical body and its representations, these theologians resource lived experiences of persons with disabilities to utilize this multifaceted body knowledge for doing theology, for grounding symbols, metaphors, and models of God.[28] These theologians highlight the ambiguities of nonconventional bodies and their potential as resource for reconceiving notions of wholeness, mutuality, survival, and care. Lived experiences of persons with disabilities are tapped for the alternative knowledge regarding the disabled body and the specific social and existential bodily experiences of it to "think with" it about difference.[29]

If "the body," as it is presented to me, is always an inconsistent production, then there is never an unmediated access to a pure corporeal state or to pure bodily experiences. Even the so-considered neutral, biological body itself is an effect of language, a product of the representation of scientific "objectivities" that materialize the body within normative charts, in stages, to be manipulated or (more or less) intelligible diagnoses. That even the medical body is far from fixed or factual can be observed in how changes in cultural understandings are reflected in scientific language and descriptions of bodies.[30] The methodological issue here is that when we name our bodily experiences, we are always

---

28. Nancy L. Eiesland, *The Disabled God: Toward a Liberatory Theology of Disability* (Nashville, TN: Abingdon Press, 1994).

29. Sharon V. Betcher, *Spirit and the Politics of Disablement* (Minneapolis: Fortress Press, 2007).

30. See, for example, Lynda Birke, "Bodies and Biology," in *Feminist Theory and the Body: A Reader*, ed. Janet Price and Margrit Shildrick (New York, NY: Routledge, 1999), 42–49. She describes changes in conceptualizations of the immune system as a defense system of a closed body system to a flexible response system of a permeable body. See also Emily Martin, "The Egg and the Sperm: How Science Has Constructed a Romance Based on Stereotypical Male-Female Roles," in *Feminist Theory and the Body: A Reader*, ed. Janet Price and Margrit Shildrick (New York, NY: Routledge, 1999), 179–189.

involved in a dialogue that is already framed by the discourse(s) we find ourselves in, and we materialize our bodies at the moment we represent it with the references we choose.

While feminist theorists and theologians have become skilled in reading bodies as signifiers of culture and detecting inscriptions on bodily surfaces, there are still remnants of conceiving of the interior body as biologically fixed and either "passive," inaccessible, or universal.[31] This stance rests on biology being conceptualized as fixed and reductionistic, rather than within parameters of indeterminacy and transformation.[32] This kind of binary leaves liberal humanist parameters of health/disease, whole/broken, and so forth, in place and unproblematized; for example, corporeal distress (pain, physical suffering) is an experience of vulnerability that

31. Interestingly, while bodily surfaces, such as skin, have received much attention in regard to social values inscribed on the skin, the skin as sense organ is also more complex and undifferentiated than the other sensory faculties. Skin therefore is a sense organ *and* a social-bodily canvas; it enables perception as well as the site of where tactility is "seen"; this links tactility and sight closely together. Sander L. Gilman, "Touch, Sexuality and Disease," in *Medicine and the Five Senses*, ed. W. F. Bynum and Roy Porter (Cambridge, MA: Cambridge University Press, 1993), 198–224. With this linking, it appears that the visual investigations "into" skin have eclipsed explorations of skin in regard to its complex tactility and related sensory dimensions. Mark Smith notes that tactility was deeply implicated in modernity (e.g., in a kind of skin consciousness regarding race, gender, class, comfort, capitalism; the look, haptics, protocols of touch), and rather than touch losing importance, it was that ideas about it changed. He also cautions against too closely linking touch and sight, and even collapsing the two so that inquiries into the visual aspects of skin/touch stand in for exploring tactility more complexly. Mark M. Smith, *Sensing the Past: Seeing, Hearing, Smelling, Tasting, and Touching in History* (Berkeley, CA: University of California Press, 2007), 95. For a volume of essays discussing touch/tactility, see Constance Classen, ed. *The Book of Touch* (Oxfod, NY: Berg, 2005). Also note a compilation of essays into the history of touch, particularly the role of tactility in early modernity and its relation to epistemological organization and definitions of subjectivity. Elizabeth D. Harvey, ed. *Sensible Flesh: On Touch in Early Modern Culture* (Philadelphia, PA: University of Pennsylvania Press, 2003).

32. Birke, "Bodies and Biology," 44–48.

happens to a subject in a body previously or otherwise "whole"/
"healthy."[33]

Bodily experiences of pain and suffering are then bodily signs to be
interpreted, to be used as indicators in an analysis. Control over one's
body and being human is kept in close theoretical connection (and threatens the loss of humanity or subjectivity for those who cannot control
their bodies).[34] This approach also forecloses potential theoretical and
theological thinking *in* and *through* (not just *about*) our "real" bodily
experiences. It prevents theologizing from bodily experiences *as* bodies
in pain, *as* "bodies out of control," from *within* the very bodies that
actively inform our perception and experience of ourselves in the world.

CONCEIVING PERCEPTION

Feminist theologies may name (women's) bodily experiences and
thereby make it a conceptual category, holding up specific bodies and/
or experiences to "truth," be it via ontological epistemological access
to it, or be it as indicator or text offering truth about social and cultural forces. Sometimes experience is used to demonstrate the power
of cultural inscriptions on embodiment, sometimes experience is the
site of identity. Sometimes embodied reality is investigated for the wear
and tear of the effects of sin/oppression, sometimes it is held up to
demonstrate the body as a site of contestation over who gets to control
whose body.

What I will diagnose as inattention to perception is what leads to
conceptual problems when bodily experience is used as an access point
for theology. Rather than talking *through* the body or bodily experiences, feminist theologians more often than not end up talking *about*

33. For intriguing and exciting theologies that take up this issue, see Creamer,
Disability and Christian Theology. Also Betcher, *Spirit and the Politics of
Disablement*.
34. Margrit Shildrick and Janet Price, "Vital Signs: Texts, Bodies and Biomedicine,"
in *Vital Signs: Feminist Reconfigurations of the Bio/Logical Body*, ed. Margrit
Shildrick and Janet Price (Edinburgh: Edinburgh University Press, 1998), 5.

the body. This may be traced partially to the ways in which theological scholarship in the Anglophone academy has been framed and validated, it is also connected to the ways in which our language limits us in our theological expressions (after all, there is no existing English word that describes what we might want to see as body-mind unit). But it is also partially due to the ways in which the body/mind dualism leaks back into our theologies, and I am making the case that it can leak back because we have not paid attention to carefully articulate our conception of bodily experiences and perception.

The theologians surveyed earlier employ different methods in accessing and conceptualizing the body, experience, and perception. When it comes specifically to sensory perception though, what emerges is a spectrum between two perspectives on perception: an empiricist view on perception, and an intellectualist view. In other words, the descriptions or implied conceptualizations of perceptual experience fall on a spectrum between considering perception a mechanical bodily function (the senses as bodily channels for truth "out there") or as a function of the mind (the senses as providing the data, which the mind then perceives, judges, and interprets).

To be able to more fully engage with the phenomenological aspects of a feminist theology, I will now turn to sketch the spectrum within which traditional philosophical works have framed perception, frameworks that make their way into theological projects. I will show how even those phenomenologies (philosophies of perception) which seem to be on opposite ends of the spectrum still share common underlying presumptions and are complicit in continuing the pervasive dualism of body/mind. Theologies that point to sensory perception as a way to overcome body/mind dualisms, but implicitly or explicitly embrace phenomenological concepts upholding them, end up undermining themselves and maintaining this separation of body and mind by not giving careful attention to the understanding of perceptual processes.

The scholars solicited as exemplars for what is at stake in theological projects do not necessarily fall clearly on one end or the other of the phenomenological spectrum, often because their phenomenological concepts are not explicitly articulated or do not receive the sophisticated attention other philosophical issues receive (such as discourse). I am drawing on the works of some key thinkers in feminist theological discourse that have influenced feminist theology as a field as well as my own theological formation. Overall and most generally, common to these theologians is the concern with theological imagery. This selective survey, neither exhaustive nor fully representative, is not to showcase the only or "worst" perpetrators. Rather, given their influence on my own feminist theological journey, they exemplify the theologies which refer to bodily experience in one manner or another, and they have been conversation partners in my initial quest to explore bodily experience for constructive theological projects. Next, I offer a phenomenological spectrum with inserted theological connections to highlight the importance of being attentive to our theological conception of bodily experiences and perception.

Concepts of Perception: Relevance in and to Theological Projects

Sensory perceptions have often been conceived of as either mechanistic or intellectual functions, positions that are still commonly held today. These theoretical stances should come as no surprise and neither should the confusion surrounding perception. We hold commonsensical notions of perceptual capacities, and tend to "know" what they are—we define vision as "seeing with my eyes," or olfaction as "smelling with my nose." Yet we continue to inquire into the complexities of different perceptual capacities in a variety of ways, though not necessarily in an interrelated manner.

Take vision, for example: It is not intuitively evident what vision is and how it functions. Philosophers since antiquity have developed theories on vision and have come up with diverse concepts of processes regarding visual perception.[35] Questions regarding visual perception are engaged in a diversity of fields: there are *empirical* questions

35. For an exploration of the many conceptions of vision, see Nicholas J. Wade, *A Natural History of Vision* (Cambridge, MA: MIT Press, 1998). Wade describes

inquiring into the physical mechanics (e.g., examinations of lenses, the retina, projections), scholars investigate *psychological* aspects (e.g., questions regarding the inversion and reversion of projected images, brain processes that appear to transcribe data into "right side up single vision"), and we also find *philosophical* questions regarding the nature of perception (nature of knowledge, images, language, etc.). When different approaches are aligned with varied disciplines—some inquiring into the bodily mechanics, some inquiring into the workings of the mind—body/mind dualism might be upheld, though this is not to be read as a scholarly determination or conspiracy to perpetuate this Cartesian split. Rather, it points to the depth of the perpetual mystery surrounding perception itself.

The pervasive mystery (or shall we say: conceptual uncertainty) regarding the processes of perception is also traceable in traditional phenomenological theories. Conventionally, the spectrum along which perception has been conceived falls between the empiricist/objectivist and the intellectualist/idealist ends. Very roughly sketched, empiricism considers perception a mechanical bodily function, a reception of sense data that carries meaning through sensory bodily channels; intellectualism considers perception a function of the mind that receives perceptual data through sensory channels which the mind then perceives, judges, and interprets. Empiricism and intellectualism hold similar views of the world as object of perception, the world as self-contained "nature." But the two positions disagree about the role of consciousness in the process of perception.

I will discuss these positions in more depth and embed critiques provided by Maurice Merleau-Ponty, the phenomenologist who provides the phenomenological perspectives for my exploration of bodily experience in this project.[36] Woven into the exploration of this spectrum of

Plato and Euclid, for example, who defined optics mathematically and conceived of vision as reception of geometrical projections. Descartes traced vision to the movement of light through air. Hobbes conceived of color as an apparition through motion working in the brain.

36. Maurice Merleau-Ponty is the phenomenologist of choice for this project for two reasons. While other scholars have critically expanded and appropriated his

phenomenological positions are the connections to theological projects. I will not provide full reviews of the scholarly corpus of the theologians selected, but will focus on the phenomenological aspects in their work to provide useful illustrations, and theological questions and connections. This will demonstrate how different theologians explicitly or implicitly take up positions along this spectrum, and we will discover what is at stake in holding the respective conception of perception.

EMPIRICISM DESCRIBED AND CRITICALLY ANALYZED

In empiricist thought, the world is distinct and separate from the perceiving person, but we can come to know about this world through perceptual processes. Sensation is a bodily capacity, perception an activity of the mind, and the mind obeys the laws observed in nature.

thought further, Merleau-Ponty remains useful as this book seeks to discuss and analyze phenomenological presumptions present in feminist theologies, as well as point to ways beyond the drawbacks and problematic consequences inherent in different positions. Merleau-Ponty provides just this kind of discussion with his own contemporary conversation partners, a discussion complex enough to make it valuable for transfer to my own interests. Further, he maintains the focus of discussion regarding embodiment on perception, a focus that I would like to maintain as well. However, Merleau-Ponty's work is not without criticism. For example, Shannon Sullivan critiques Merleau-Ponty for obscuring differences in his account of intersubjectivity by grounding embodiment in pre-personal functions. She also challenges his embodied subject for its inherent maleness, challenges also made by Elizabeth Grosz and Judith Butler. See Shannon Sullivan, "Domination and Dialogue in Merleau-Ponty's *Phenomenology of Perception*." *Hypatia: Journal of Women in Culture and Society* 20, no. 4 (1997). Grosz, Elizabeth. *Volatile Bodies: Toward a Corporeal Feminism* (Bloomington and Indianapolis: Indiana University Press, 1994). Judith Butler, "Sexual Ideology and Phenomenological Description: A Feminist Critique of Merleau-Ponty's Phenomenology of Perception," in *Thinking Muse: Feminism and Modern French Philosophy*, ed. Jeffner Allen and Iris Marion Young (Bloomington, IN: Indiana University Press, 1989), 85–100. Others have challenged Merleau-Ponty's phenomenological assertions for its erasure of difference regarding race. Jeremy Weate, for example, employs Frantz Fanon's critique of phenomenology to contest Merleau-Ponty's notion of bodily freedom with Fanon's geneology of unfreedom of the black body. See Jeremy Weate, "Fanon, Merleau-Ponty and the Difference of Phenomenology," in *Race*, ed. Robert Bernasconi (Malden, MA: Blackwell, 2001), 169–183.

In short, empiricism involves a view of perception as the reception of simple, basic sensory units (e.g., a certain intensity of light as simple retinal stimuli) that are independent of one another in quality and quantity. Bodily perceptual faculties (eyes, nose, ears, etc.) are independent channels and "recorders" for these independently received sensory units (the units recorded via my eyes are not the same as those recorded through tactile channels). To achieve the perceptual outcome of, say, seeing and touching a body, is to combine the received perceptual units and based on previous experiences, having learned that these perceptual units belong together so that we can account for them as distinct perceptual whole, such as "body" or "apple."[37]

An early empiricist conception of perception is found, for example, in Aristotle, in which the mind receives the form of the object: Seeing an apple is to receive in the mind via the eye the form of the apple, though not the juicy fruity substance. The mind itself is a tabula rasa into which experiences of the world enter through the senses. This is a skeptical kind of empiricism: While we might not know the things themselves, we know how they appear to us in our mind, and only what appears to us, our mental pictures of the world, are the objects of knowledge. Thomas Aquinas critically builds on this Aristotelian view, though he finds fault in the concept that the mind knows only its own ideas. Aquinas asserts that what we perceive is not a form or an idea, but we perceive external objects through our ideas, through our mental pictures. The mind perceives through images provided through the senses; images are the means by which we perceive objects in the world experientially.

Philosophers like John Locke carry on this school of empiricism and argue that the only knowledge achievable is knowledge based on experience, a posteriori. Our ideas about the world are derived from experiences, from sensation and reflection on it. An object has primary qualities (the structure which makes it an apple) and secondary qualities (varieties of color, size, texture, but varieties which still adhere to

---

37. David R. Cerborne, "Perception," in *Merleau-Ponty: Key Concepts*, ed. Rosalyn Diprose and Jack Reynolds (Stocksfield, UK: Acumen, 2008), 122–123.

the primary qualities). What is received in the mind through perceptual processes is an idea or picture of the outside world. Significant to the processes of perception are sense data transfers made possible through bodily capacities, the bodily derived and transmitted sense data then causes ideas in the mind of the perceiver.[38]

David Hume is more skeptical about the perception of the world as ideas in the mind. Although we perceive the world through our senses, which deliver images to our mind, the perceptual senses are conveyers or channels which cannot necessarily be trusted. It is convention that leads us to suppose that our sensory perceptions deliver accurate representation of the external world. Yet because we can also experience hallucinations or dreams, the senses appear to be unreliable and deceptive. Only experience can prove and justify what we know about the world, though experience cannot help us (dis)prove the doubt we might have about the very perceptions we have in experience.[39]

Considering the empiricist camp, Merleau-Ponty criticizes its views of perception for separating sensation from perception. Presupposed in empiricist views is "sensation" as building blocks on which perception rests. Sensation is presented as readily available to analysis. This kind of distinction breaks down perceptual processes into cause and effect mechanisms, separating though linking sense data and bodily sensory capacities via sensation. One way for empiricists to conceive of sensations has been to invoke sensation as impression sensed by the subject: Color, for example, is not a property inherent to the object, but an impact made on the eye; my visual faculties are affected in a particular

38. Locke also differentiated between complex ideas (ideas which can be broken down in component ideas such as the idea of an apple, which can be separated out into ideas of round, red, sweet, juicy, etc.) and simple ideas (ideas which cannot be further broken down, e.g., the idea of "red"). All ideas are caused by the material world, mediated/transmitted by our perceptual faculties. John Locke, *An Essay Concerning Human Understanding* (New York, NY: Oxford University Press, 1975).
39. David Hume and L. A. Selby-Bigge, *Enquiries Concerning Human Understanding and Concerning the Principles of Morals*, 3rd ed. (New York, NY: Oxford University Press, 1975), 149–162.

way by the object causing a sensory impression.[40] In other words, the ripe apple I am about to eat is not inherently red; rather, my eyes pick up light waves, and I make a judgment that the sensory units of shape, size, and color come to me from an apple.

Merleau-Ponty notes that conceiving of sensation as distinct from perception differentiates between lived experiences and sensation: Experience is filled with meaning to me, whereas pure sensation—understood as undifferentiated impact such as light waves hitting my retina, sound waves entering my ear—has no meaning in itself. Empiricists consider meaning as found in the impression formed within me, created in my mind through conscious processes of evaluation and judgment. For example, to experience color, I receive sensations on my retina, certain wave lengths of light reaching my eye, and I perceive this sensation in my mind and through convention or evaluation perceive the color red. This view of sensation, Merleau-Ponty points out, has several significant implications to my experiencing in the world: There is a strong delineation between me and the object I perceive; there are objectifying processes undertaken by me; there are implied strong delineations in the causal relationship conceived of between sensation (the reception of data, the experience of a sensorial impact by me) and perception (the forming of meaning).[41]

When theologians appeal to sensory perception as equivalent to knowing (as akin to receiving ideas about the world) they may uphold the inherent mind/body dualism of this empiricist phenomenological perspective. When perception is reception of knowledge and apprehension of reality, feminist theologians may charge women with recovering their ontological ability to perceive/receive knowledge through their senses.

40. See note 38. Locke, for example, has conceived of primary and secondary qualities of objects. Only primary qualities (such as solidity, number, shape) exist in the object itself and are certain; secondary qualities, color being conceived as such (also taste, smell, sound), are not possessed by the object, but are affected in the subject and do not provide measurable truths about an object.
41. Maurice Merleau-Ponty, *Phenomenology of Perception*, trans. Colin French (New York, NY: Routledge, 1962), 7–8.

Carter Heyward and Elisabeth Moltmann-Wendel, for example, through their positive association of embodied sensory perception with nature and the sacred, imbue sensory capacities of the body with the ability to access unmediated, untainted information or truth about a situation.[42] Both theologians seek to overcome body/mind dualisms by conceptualizing body and mind as a unit: Heyward uses the term "bodyself" to articulate a subject or self not separated from the body and defines the "soul" not as an essence or separate spiritual component of the bodyself, but as the "relational spark" connecting all creatures.[43] Moltmann-Wendel articulates body and soul as a unit, a field of energy, the seat of feelings, the sphere of thought and relationship,[44] and asserts the importance of the senses to conceptualizations of the body, as the senses extend the body.[45] Meanings are not natural or biological occurrences, but the ensemble of potentialities which are given value in a particular society.[46] But it is the senses which are charged with the reception of meanings, from socially assigned meanings to divine revelations, and the bodily capacity for sensation affirms the epistemological authority of bodily functions which reveal the world to us and make it intelligible for us.[47]

These strong empiricist conceptions, however, are fraught with theoretical problems. Understanding sensation as such, framing meaning-making processes as social or intellectual processes only, renders bodily sensation itself devoid of meaning and separate from the structures of perception. It implies that my bodily taking in the smell of a person's skin, feeling it, seeing the color of it and touching it, is simply the intake of independent sensations, whereas *perceiving a lover* or *perceiving an*

42. Heyward, *Touching Our Strength*. Elisabeth Moltmann-Wendel, *I Am My Body: A Theology of Embodiment* (New York, NY: Continuum, 1995).
43. Heyward, *Touching Our Strength*, 18, 89, 93.
44. Moltmann-Wendel, *I Am My Body*, viii, 42, 46.
45. Ibid., 90.
46. Heyward, *I Am My Body*, 163, n3.
47. Ibid., 93–94. Heyward uses the example of encountering difference to show the connection between sensory intelligence and bodily boundaries. To Heyward, bodily boundaries in the encounter with the bodily-different other need to be fluid and permeable, while sensory apprehension in a strange environment

abuser is an intellectual or social process (their differentiation unclear) of putting sense data together. Yet empiricist conceptions can only explain the deduction that indeed all these sensations taken in with my bodily sensory tools add up to *a person in close proximity*. The emergence of meaning needed to judge this person to be a lover or a perpetrator of violence, or possible connected revelations of the divine, remains unaccounted for.

This kind of positing bodily sensations as building blocks in a theory of perception is also problematic in other ways. It constructs sensation as something that allegedly explains perception while at the same time sensation supposedly has nothing to do with perception as activity of the mind.[48] It presents the sense data of the person (visually received image of a specifically shaped body of a certain type, size, and color, I am receiving tactile data and a scent, etc.) as something that effects and leads to my perception of a person; therefore sensation explains how it is that I come to perceive anything. Yet it makes a distinction between sensation and perception as if the two could exist independently of each other, as if I could ever sense something without necessarily perceiving it.

In addition to highlighting the theoretical error of separating sensation from perception in empiricism, Merleau-Ponty also points out that the lived experience of perception is that of always perceiving meaningful wholes: I experience sensations within a figure-background structure. Without the latter, we would have no sensation

registers difference as dangerous and evokes thick, self-containing boundaries. Heyward, 110–113. Moltmann-Wendel affirms experience when she also assigns epistemological value to female bodily functions such as giving birth. Yet Moltmann-Wendel overlooks the socially constructed link between sex and social preferences when she lists social differences related to gendered bodies (e.g., linking gendered differences in preference for sports or other types of play to essential male/female differences). This misses the link between female body experiences and social restrictions on female bodies. Moltmann-Wendel, *I Am My Body*, 86, 100.

48. Monika M. Langer, *Merleau-Ponty's Phenomenology of Perception: A Guide and Commentary* (London, UK: The Macmillan Press LTD, 1989), 4.

of *something*.[49] I always perceive a person first, and already within a given context, before I can then abstract and tease apart the different components (color, smell, size, texture) of this perception. The concept of undifferentiated sensation without meaning in itself, however, cannot explain how I would come to perceive something meaningful, like a friend at a party or a stranger on the street.[50]

Theologians conceiving of the senses as bodily receptors of knowledge concerning a person's world fail to account for how perceived meanings then are formed or changed (how new or additional sense data can invoke different meanings in the mind). We actually do experience a person in an immediate perception with associated meaning, and the same person can be perceived with various meanings in different contexts. Theologians appealing to the senses as channels for perception run the risk of maintaining that ultimate "truth" about a

---

49. Merleau-Ponty is strongly influenced by Gestalt psychology on this point. More specifically, he learned about Gestalt psychology from Aaron Gurwitsch, who combined a reading of Husserl's phenomenology with the Berlin Gestalt School (Max Wertheimer, Wolfgang Köhler). Gestalt theory rejects mechanistic assumptions and argues that sense experience has a holistic and dynamic character, perceiving intelligible forms and shapes (Gestalt). Experience rests on meaningful, coherent configurations, which often fail to correspond to sensory stimuli in a direct way (i.e., sensations do not show constancy in their relation to stimuli). Merleau-Ponty recognizes the enormous philosophical implications of this Gestalt claim, not just for thinking perception as an aspect of psychological functions, but for thinking perception as essential to our being in the world. Taylor Carman, *Merleau-Ponty*, ed. Brian Leiter, Routledge Philosophers (New York, NY: Routledge, 2008), 20–21.
50. Merleau-Ponty, *Phenomenology of Perception*, 4–5. For example: Where empiricism conceptualizes perception as passive reception of sensory data (e.g., the data of light, color, shapes are received by the eye, odor is received by the nose), sensory faculties become independent organic receptors. The perception of an object is the result of combining and accounting for the received data ("I see and smell a flower"). Merleau-Ponty charges that this position is untenable: Perceptual experience is that of sensing *things*, and we sense them in *context*, that is, perception is not awareness of sensory data ("I see light and colors and feel a smooth hard surface") but of sense data in context (I see red as the red of an apple, I feel softness as the softness of a blanket) and of objects ("I see and feel a table"). Empiricism also problematically presupposes but leaves unaccounted for an interpreting consciousness, as we will discuss at a later point.

perception is connected to egocentric reflective judgments of a cogito, a separate mind in a body, a concept which is exactly what the feminist theologians mentioned seek to refute, yet reinstate.[51]

Not all empiricist philosophers posit this differentiation though. Some of those who recognize the flaw in conceiving of pure impressions or sensations move to situate sensory qualities in the object. Sensations received by the subject, such as color, taste, and smell, are then theorized as inherent properties of the object. Yet Merleau-Ponty rightly diagnoses this approach as equally flawed in replacing one extreme version of object-subject dualism with another. Sensory perception and meaning have simply been reworked from a radically subjective process to a radically objective and determinate property. Objects are posited as existing in a world that is in-itself: Everything has clearly defined boundaries, inherent properties and meanings. The subject's perceptual experience is now conceptualized as analogous coherence between sense impression and the properties of an object that is isolable, self-contained, and determinate.[52]

As in the aforementioned approaches, this empiricist view upholds a strong subject-object differentiation, presupposes strong and singular specific object-perception connections, favoring analogous connections. This discounts sensory ambiguity as a deficiency in the subject (e.g.,

---

51. Consider also Mayra Rivera's comment regarding sensuality and materiality in theology: "The senses do not belong or give access to a 'natural' realm and they are constantly changing in relation to things, including the technologies that we invent to approach the world. Nonetheless, when it avoids the illusion of having escaped the realm of discursive influence, an appeal to the senses may call attention to the non-human [...]."Approaching material things as relations, rather than as objects encountered by fully constituted human bodies, suggests a promising way to theorize the materiality of bodies as well as of things. [...] The crucial affirmation of materiality and the body in theology must resist the tendency either to reify or idealize them, instead theorizing materiality in its dynamic, complex relationality and incompleteness." Mayra Rivera Rivera, "Corporeal Visions and Apparations: The Narrative Strategies of an Indecent Theologian," in *Dancing Theology in Fetish Boots: Essays in Honour of Marcella Althaus-Reid*, ed. Lisa Isherwood and Mark D. Jordan (London, UK: SCM Press, 2010), 92–94.
52. Merleau-Ponty, *Phenomenology of Perception*, 9.

inattention, sensory deficits). Indeterminacy is a perceptive blunder by the subject, not a possibility of the perceived object.[53] Theologians relying on these kinds of conceptions do not account for how more complex meanings can be perceived through the utilization of bodily channels simply transmitting sense data.

Mary Daly, for example, asserts that a feminist consciousness awakens deprived and dormant senses to allow women to perceive the dimensions and effects of patriarchal oppression. The newly sharpened senses allow women to perceive "gynaesthetically" (i.e., to perceive and recognize patterns of oppression), and this newly honed perceptive ability also aids in the implementation of liberative action.[54] In Daly, women's sensory ability is framed ontologically as well as epistemologically: women are biologically different. This has ontological dimensions, and it makes perception ontologically sexed. In an empiricist vein, the senses then become bodily functions operating like channels: they may be congested or cleared, but they are passive receptors of knowledge. Daly conceptually separates sensing from perceiving, thinking, imagining, acting, and speaking; even as she attempts to hold them together, she connects sensation to perception and knowledge in a mechanistic way. The senses function as receptive organs whose capacities are biologically-ontologically determined and, once "re-awakened," aid in the use of other capacities such as perceiving, thinking and speaking.[55]

53. The point-by-point correspondence between stimulus and elementary perception is the "constancy hypothesis" of empiricists. The objective world is given, and emits stimuli received by the sense organs, this connection is a constant. This, however, fails to account for discrepancies such as optical illusions (e.g., of size or color). Ibid., 7.

54. Mary Daly, *Gyn/Ecology: The Metaethics of Radical Feminism* (Boston: Beacon Press, 1978), 341, 401–405.

55. Considering speech as an action and expansion of the self/mind/body, a linguistic revolution is Daly's (theological) solution, and she seeks to strategically invent and reappropriate words and grammar to speak and write "woman" in order to create a female mystic symbolism that will allow a "re-membering" of the creative integrity in women. This shares similarities with the philosophical

While Daly's larger theological project involves highlighting and struggling against persistent mind/body/spirit separations imposed on and maintained through patriarchy and androcentric language, her framing of perception with empiricist conceptions undermines her project significantly. Daly attempts to frame body/mind/soul not as separate entities, but rather as different aspects of the same self. Daly describes women as being deeply connected to the world and as capable of tapping into the interconnection of the world through women's range of subtle and complex sensory powers, accessing what she calls "deep memory."[56] When addressing the patriarchal split and control of

project of Luce Irigaray. Critics of Daly's project point to her exclusive dismissal of differences and her universalizing of women's oppression, the patronizing, racializing undertones when Daly essentializes non-White women as victims. In my reading, it is not the victimization of non-White women where I locate the strongest indictment of her racial stereotyping. Daly mirrors the patriarchal gaze when she draws the biology-oppression-symbolism connections in her discussion of women's global oppression: The Indian wife stands in for gender oppression in marriage, the Chinese woman symbolizes oppression of sexuality and erotics, the African woman illustrates bodily sexual violations, while the European and American women become illustrations for the oppression of female wisdom, spirituality and autonomy of mind. Daly keeps bodily associations and hierarchies common to Enlightenment taxonomies intact. Mary Daly, *Pure Lust: Elemental Feminist Philosophy* (Boston: Beacon Press, 1984), 175. Daly, *Gyn/Ecology*, 24.

56. Daly, *Pure Lust*, 80, 91, 353. The soul as the animating principle is wholly present in each part of the body as the intellectual principle that is united to the body as the body forms. This also grounds her claim of ontological differences based in biological differences. Insisting on women's biological ontological difference, Daly valorizes female bodily functions like menstruation, pregnancy, childbirth as biological and symbolic—they are ontologically different experiences which need to be perceived and expressed grounded in feminist consciousness. Daly, *Gyn/Ecology*, 83. Daly, *Pure Lust*, 344–345. This conceptualization also explains Daly's preference for bodily integrity and her valorizing and normatizing of bodily wholeness and sex/gender conformity. Daly, *Gyn/Ecology*, 57, 238. Transgenderism and transsexuality might be judged to be bodily mutilations caused by or effecting a mind/body/soul split, which might explain Daly's expressed contempt for male-to-female transsexuals (claiming that most transsexuals are men, trying to take creative capacity away from women). Also not faring well are gay men, lesbians who are not sufficiently "woman-identified," and more or less everybody who is not a

mind/body/spirit and the "pollution inflicted through patriarchal myth and language on all levels,"[57] Daly diagnoses the effects of this oppressive split in the pervasive sensory deprivation of women, a deprivation that destroys women's capacity to feel and perceive and know deeply and therefore act authentically.[58] The world in which women live is not ambiguous; rather, inattention or sensory deficits/deprivation results in flawed perceptions and inauthentic knowledge.

Daly's appeal to the senses resorts to a strong dualism in which the biological capacity to sense the world is causally connected to the epistemological capacity to perceive truth *about* the world. Daly's conception of sensory capacities and perceptual abilities makes linear connections among biology, symbolism, power, and language, but rather than overcoming dualisms, she reinforces them by positing the senses in a bio-mechanical manner as channels to perceive truth, which then gets expressed in language according to this perception in the mind. Granting women "naturally" special or particularly keen perceptual capacities maintains dualistic biological essentialism and universalizing of "woman." It remains unclear how exactly it is that female perceptual capacities are different or better than male perceptual capacities, especially if the uniqueness of female bodies is located in bodily functions such as pregnancy, menstruation, or lactation, bodily organs not immediately connected to, say, the capacities of sight or hearing. Resorting to a connection between perception and consciousness to support a sexed/gendered perceptual difference is equally unsound, because it upholds a consciousness/senses dualism, and makes consciousness the cause and the receptor or perceptual insights.

Merleau-Ponty assesses that dissecting perception into sensations, qualities, stimuli, response, etc., upholds an objectification of the world with a rigorous subject-object divide and presupposes an objective world in-itself accessible through mechanical perceptual processes.

---

radical/Lesbian feminist is considered a traitor to the feminist cause, conforming to an androcentric worldview.

57. Daly, *Gyn/Ecology*, 9.
58. Daly, *Pure Lust*, 63, 342.

The various theoretical takes of empiricism conceptualize perception by theorizing how an object affects perceptual experience. "Sensation" is often the empiricist notion of choice to explain perception: It seems commonsensical that objects are sensorially perceived and bodily senses are the physiological tools available to the subject. But no matter where empiricists locate the process of sensation, perception is reduced to a causal process of an object bringing about a sensory impact; felt sensation is conceived as the experience of impact on sensory organs. The perceiving subject has at her disposal a physical system which receives stimuli to which she responds in ways determinable by empirical observation.[59]

But in any possible empiricist stance (sensory impressions formed by the subject upon stimulation, or sensory qualities inherent to the object and analogously received by the subject with her sensory capacities), causal theories of perception still fail to explain exactly *how* an object can cause a perceptual experience. When empiricists attempt to answer the question of how a sum of independent sensations can lead to the perception of an object (e.g., how does a figure stand out from a background), the go-to explanation is to invoke sensation along with mental functions like association and memory.[60] That is, particular

59. In one possible empiricist conception, sensation is a differentiated building block: it is implicitly independent of perceptual processes and by implication cannot serve in an explanatory function. In another empiricist conception, sensation is understood as an unambiguous correlative process between object qualities and perceptual experience, but the ambiguous nature of perception (with perceived information and meaning depending on context) is unaccounted for and produces mischaracterizations of our actual perceptual experience. Merleau-Ponty points to ambiguities in perceptual experience and the dependencies on context by using examples like Müller-Lyer's optical illusion (two lines which are equal in length, but appear as various in lengths). Merleau-Ponty, *Phenomenology of Perception*, 6.
60. Another notion invoked to explain perceived object unity, but also discrepancies between perceived object and immediate sensory effect (as in an optical illusion), is *attention*. I will return to this notion in more detail shortly in my discussion of Merleau-Ponty's take on intellectualism. But in terms of empiricist theorizing, attention is invoked to explain why, if all sensations are equally present and available to the perceiver, some qualities are perceived and others are not. Attention equals perceptive focus in this framework. Yet again, as we will see later

distributions of sensations are thought to invoke similar distributions experienced in the past and with it invoke the references we learned to associate with them. This, however, simply defers the problem of how sensations invoke perception of a unified object standing out against a background: the past event to which the association refers still poses the same question, and our search for the original invocation of meaning is caught up in an infinite regress.[61]

This is a theoretical bind Rosemary Radford Ruether encounters when appealing to perception. Like other feminist theologians, she understands that dualisms of any kind distort reality and, as such, cause and perpetuate structural and individual sin. Her method of choice is to employ dialectical thinking, construct syntheses between posited dualisms, and recover positive aspects of what traditionally has been devalued: mind/body, man/woman, white/black, human/nature, orthodoxy/heresy, transcendent/immanent, and so on.[62]

Ruether paints a complex picture of human embodiment and existence in a matrix of energy-matter. Energy and matter are not separate; energy is organized in patterns and relationships and is the basis for what is experienced as visible things. Human consciousness and intelligence are a most intense and complex form of inwardness of material energy itself.[63] The individual self, which is an individuated ego/organism, ceases in death (the cessation of consciousness as interiority of that life process which holds an organism together), and dissolves back into cosmic matrix of matter/energy which is the basis for new

with memory and association, what exactly triggers attention/inattention is unaccounted for. Empiricism, by explaining perceptive processes as external, mechanical relations only (in an attempt to leave out acts of consciousness), puts the notion of attention into infinite regress: what triggers attention must be triggered by something else, but no original trigger can be given. Ibid., 26–27.

61. Ibid., 13, 19–21.

62. See Rosemary Radford Ruether, *Sexism and God-Talk: Toward a Feminist Theology* (Boston: Beacon Press, 1983).

63. Ibid., 86–87. Ruether draws on Teilhard de Chardin's theory of evolution for a philosophical-scientific concept of the body.

life.[64] This cosmic matrix is what enables "revelatory experience," the breakthrough experiences beyond ordinary fragmented consciousness which provide the grounds for theologizing.[65] Because oppressions are social and cultural products, they can be overcome through resocialization, which revelatory experiences make possible.

In Ruether, the subject (the energy-matter-ego-organism) has experiences, and these experiences appear to be organized by the mind (complex form of material energy). Revelatory experiences, brought about by a honed utilization of bodily and intellectual senses, are equaled with consciousness of evil (the perception of evil).[66] Ruether uses brain research to argue that women already have a biological and cultural advantage for psychic wholeness due to their advanced integration of rational and relational modes of thought.[67] And because of women's socialization toward rational and relational modes, women have a "perceptive edge" in terms of psychic integration and revelatory experience.

Because she is describing consciousness-raising processes as intellectual processes (though we remember that she understands intellect/mind as a form of complex matter), Ruether is employing an empiricist

64. Ibid., 257. Ruether's conceptualization of the body as energy/matter fits with her concept of "experience." If the energy released from the organism in death returns to the cosmic energy cycle, then the breakthrough revelatory experiences are a tapping into this cosmic matrix.
65. These feminist (because brought about through consciousness-raising) experiences provide interpretive symbols illuminating the means of the whole of life. Starting with the experiencing individual, they become socially meaningful only when translated into communal consciousness and becoming collectively appropriated by a formative group. Ibid., 13.
66. Ibid., 159–164. Ruether calls this "conversion." To Ruether, this ability to perceive evil and name sin is not an individual conversion, but one that requires (feminist) networks of communication and support. Ibid., 184–185.
67. Ibid., 113. She specifically investigates research into the relation between the two brain halves. However, Ruether neglects that scientific research into the brain itself might already be culturally ordered, research in which cultural gender divisions are read into "objective" biological observations. For an example of how culture shapes scientific facts, and casts scientific observations in gendered terms, see Martin, "The Egg and the Sperm." See also Part Two of this book.

separation between intellectual perception and biological sensing. Her concept of experience also rests on a presupposition of perception being different from experience, with (accurate, revelatory) perception functioning as the result of a heightened consciousness applied to experience. Once a woman is open to a feminist consciousness, she is able to perceive her individual, bodily experiences from a feminist perspective, and now needs to move from deepened senses of anger and alienation to a sense of a redeemed, liberated self.[68] Perception functions as the unexplored tool or channel of consciousness, and serves the mind to interpret experience.

The cosmic matrix (which enables revelatory experiences of truth by collecting the energies of previous lives and their experiences) about the world still defers the problem of how sensory experiences invoke perceived meaning; the origin of truth ends up being projected into a matrix which has no beginning. Positing perception as correlative process of sense experience and qualities of the world renders "truth" and "meaning" in the world as static and fixed. This implies that perceptual differences now have a hierarchical aspect in regard to truth. In other words, it ties knowledge to the external world, and posits hierarchies of perceptual consciousness in regard to perceivers. For example, if I do not perceive and associate certain embedded structures (say, sexism) as connected to my experience in a certain way, I either fail to sufficiently tune my senses or my feminist consciousness to the overarching "truth" in the world. This stance undermines any attempts of conceptualizing contextual and historical differences or shifts and interrelations of meaning. Effectively, this universalizes certain interpretative methodologies by adding fixed perceptive associations as a biological and theological capacity for theological work.

Summing up Empiricist Conceptions and Connected Theological Dilemmas

Empiricist notions of perception are caught up in a dilemma. By invoking memory and association, they presuppose that which they seek to

68. Ruether, *Sexism and God-Talk*, 184–189.

explain (the actual process of association), and defer to a consciousness for which they cannot account via empiricist methods. Furthermore, they undermine the positing of sensations as building blocks. If a specific sum of sensory data invokes an association or a memory, it cannot be neutral. It must possess more than just factual qualities and inherently hold a guide for its own interpretation. Resorting to memory and association then only highlights the circular theoretical explanations of empiricism and the shortcomings of sensation as main explanatory principle.[69] The latter is especially evident when expanding the equation of sensation with experience to more complex perceptions, such as spatial and temporary relations: If all experience is dissectible and analyzable in terms of quantities of differentiated sensation, then knowledge cannot be more than an anticipation of impressions.[70] The process of association and recognition of unity (seeing a thing as a thing) remains unexplained and relegated to a consciousness equally unexplained (though crucial in the operation of identification of configurations).[71]

Empiricism, Merleau-Ponty thus asserts, is descriptively wrong in the claim that perception is simply an awareness of sensations: describing experience via sense impressions fails to explain sensation itself. Also, it is incoherent when it attempts to capture the content of experience in terms of sensation while at the same time putting forward experience as brought about by sensory stimuli.[72] In other words, the empiricist position is not accurate in the claim that perception equals attending to the

---

69. Merleau-Ponty, *Phenomenology of Perception*, 22.

70. This is a position Hume is content to rely on. While the external world is "out there," perceptions are only evidence from which we can infer existence of exterior objects and knowledge about them, but we cannot perceive things as they "really" are.

71. Merleau-Ponty, *Phenomenology of Perception*, 17.

72. Ibid., 3, 13–17. Empiricist phenomenology in the eyes of Merleau-Ponty reverses the order of explanation by taking the consequence of perceptual significance (e.g., taking a red sign in a landscape signifying a specific meaning to me) for the ground. "In doing so we relieve perception of its essential function, which is to lay the foundation of, or inaugurate knowledge, and we see it through its results." Ibid., 17.

senses. Nor is it logically consistent to define experience as consisting of *and* caused by sensation. Such a position bestows sensation with the dual, but discordant purpose of describing *and* explaining experience.

Attempting to hold on to sensation as a concept and fix loopholes in their own theorizing, empiricists can no longer maintain purely empiricist methodologies. Theorizing perception via empiricist avenues in the end fails to adequately account for structures of perception, structures which allow us to perceive whole objects and qualities. It also conflates felt sensation and associated meaning, presenting a linear or consistent relation between sensation, perception, and knowledge. Empiricists externalize these structures and imbue them in the elementary sensation perceived by a stimulus via the constancy hypothesis. But because this cannot explain perceptive confusions or varieties in association, it leaves processes or dynamics of perception unaccounted for in the end.[73]

Turning back on their concerns with dualist notions of body/mind, even theologians like Daly, Heyward, Moltmann-Wendel or Ruether, who passionately argue against a separation of body-mind rendering female bodies passive and biological-mechanical, have rendered it passive yet again by appealing to sensory capacities which turn bodily sensation into purely receptive channels and/or by implying perception to be the intellectual grasp of bodily sensorially received data. Being unclear about how bodily experiences are connected to or brought about by sense data and perception curiously separates the body from the mind. It relegates the body to the role of mere vessel for sensations with perceptual capacities which can be honed and utilized by a consciousness.

Epistemologically, rendering sensory perception a biological capacity (however spiritually or intellectually honed) in empiricist conceptions (even those which may allow for socio-cultural influences) makes it difficult to account for any knowledge gained through perceptual

73. Taylor Carman, "Between Empiricism and Intellectualism," in *Merleau Ponty: Key Concepts*, ed. Rosalyn Diprose and Jack Reynolds (Stocksfield, UK: Acumen, 2008), 46.

ability, especially different knowledge acquired from a different stand-point (be it the female body, the racialized body, or the poor body). In other words, it makes it difficult to explain how embodied experience can be the sensing of, for example, oppression, without resorting back to conceiving of knowledge as associating and anticipating certain patterns of experience and identifying them as "oppression." Either this association must have a specific origin which was clearly identified as oppression and is easily transferable to other experiences (thus universalizing and simplifying either oppression or experience), or this association is made by a consciousness (but how is still not explained).

When appeals to the senses are made in feminist theologies, they may be connected to liberative epistemological strategies of tuning into the "real world," or of tapping into traces of a "world untainted by sexism/oppression" (as in Ruether). Yet this upholds divides of natural vs. cultural, and often associates this "natural" world with an ideal world free of oppressive structures. This nature/culture divide, deliberately placed or not, frames sensory perception as a biological, but somehow "culturally sensitized," tool which is supposed to be able to bridge the dualism it was conceived within in the first place. For example, the perceiving woman has at her disposal either a physical system which she simply needs to hone or "fine-tune" in order to receive knowledge about the world (e.g., in Daly or Moltmann-Wendel), or the perceiving woman has innate bodily and mental capacities to perceive her environment which she needs to reawaken in order to make perceptive and interpretive associations (as in Ruether).[74]

---

74. Serene Jones cautions against establishing universal principles or themes under which "women's experience" become subsumed, such as posing "relationality" as intrinsic to female human existence. As Jones comments, relationality can serve as the structure to appropriate or fit in that which is marginal, and she also wonders if valorizing traditional stereotype of women being more relational can really be liberating. Also problematic is the thinking of relationality as essentialized female experience, based on care and nurture in the essentially female (biological) capacity to reproduce and mother children. Valorization of bodily experiences described as uniquely female, such as menstruation, seems useful in countering social constructions of menstruation as symbol for female excess, lack of control and messiness. Serene Jones, "Women's Experience between a Rock and a Hard Place: Feminist,

It does not matter if the empiricist conceptions of perception found in theologies are expressed explicitly or implicitly, or if they show more or less theoretical sophistication. Any resourcing of bodily experience which utilizes a plea to the senses as "better" access to "truth" or "meaning" maintains caught in dualisms of many kinds and on many levels and ends up perpetuating them in significant ways (though it may be unintended). In empiricist conceptions sensory capacities remain fixed in a biologically determined body, and this obviously undermines any attempts to move beyond body/mind dualisms.

INTELLECTUALISM DESCRIBED AND CRITICALLY ANALYZED

Intellectualism (also called idealism or cognitivism, depending on discipline and context) is the most pervasive theoretical thread in the phenomenological movement. Traceable (though not exclusively originating) in the diverse manifestations of Cartesian and Kantian rationalisms, intellectualism conceives of our essential relation to the world—of the content of our attitudes about the world—as thought.

Descartes conceived of the mind as that which apprehends ideas, rationally formed. Body and mind are two distinct entities; bodies

Womanist, and Mujerista Theologies in North America," in *Horizons in Feminist Theology: Identity, Tradition, and Norms*, ed. Rebecca S. Chopp and Sheila Greeve Davaney, 137–153 (Minneapolis: Fortress Press, 1997), 139. Also Serene Jones, *Feminist Theory and Christian Theology: Cartographies of Grace*, ed. Kathryn Tanner and Paul Lakeland, Guides to Theological Inquiry (Minneapolis: Fortress Press, 2000), 47. I echo this concern. Relationality, if used in an undifferentiated way, can easily neglect to take a postcolonial analysis into account, in which relationality is complicated by relations to colonial power and within imperialist structures: Relationality is not necessarily inherently innocent, thus a women's experience of relationships can be marked by oppression as well as complicity, be it in deference to cultural customs or survival struggles. This potentially falls back on regarding the reproductive body as something essentially female, regardless of intention or ability of individual women to exercise that capacity. Theologies that valorize women as life-givers valorize biological capacities and connect affirmation of women to their considered biological (reproduction) and social (relationality) capacities. This kind of deduction raises questions about the humanity of those women who cannot or want not bear children, or who fail to show nurturing and caring traits.

are made of physical properties, the mind takes up properties such as thinking, seeing, feeling, and sensing. Edmund Husserl, the considered founder of the phenomenological movement, alludes to Descartes as the "patriarch of phenomenology," describing his own phenomenological approach as a new Cartesianism.[75] Cartesian conceptions undergird our habit to think of the body as an object, and of perception as an action of the subject. From this perspective, bodily experiences and perception as mental activity are at best causally connected, and this makes it difficult to conceive how physiological, spatially grounded facts can be commensurable to psychic facts not located in time and space.[76]

Immanuel Kant, more known for his epistemology, nevertheless leaves a legacy on phenomenological thinking. He distinguishes between the way objects are "in themselves" (called "noumena," which one cannot directly experience), and the way objects are interpreted in one's perception and understanding ("phenomena").[77] Kant drew a contrast between receptivity and spontaneity, a distinction which comes close to basic intellectualist aspects of perception, the sensory and motor dimensions.[78] For analytical purposes, I could make a distinction between two aspects of perception that underlie the traditional objective-subjective, physical-mental divide: a) the relative passivity of sense experience, and b) the relative activity of bodily skills.

A Cartesian cogito of some kind is common to both empiricist and intellectualist approaches: a mind that synthesizes and "manages"

75. Edmund Husserl, *Cartesian Meditations: An Introduction to Phenomenology,* trans. Dorion Cairns (The Hague: Martinus Nijhoff, 1964), 3–5.
76. Merleau-Ponty, *Phenomenology of Perception,* 77. Or posing this as a question: How can there be a connection between something that exists somewhere in space (is spatial-physiological), and something that exists nowhere (is psychic), and what would this connection be?
77. Immanuel Kant, *Critique of Pure Reason,* trans., Marcus Weigelt (New York, NY: Penguin Group, 2008), 251–260.
78. Dennis Schulting, *Kant's Deduction and Apperception: Explaining the Categories* (New York, NY: Palgrave Macmillan, 2012), 139.

sensory information. Yet intellectualist theories conceive of perception fundamentally as cognitive and subjective activity. The "I" actively transcends itself and grasps the world. The world exists as such, though only for the conscious mind which "knows" it. As a form of idealism, intellectualism is a response to the considered flaws of empiricism, especially the positing of the consciousness as just another thing in the world subject to natural laws (such as causation). Intellectualism conceives of consciousness as wholly different from the world. Taken to its logical conclusion, intellectualism then has to argue in support of a consciousness constituting the world, a consciousness that *is* the "I" transcending into the world. There is a world in itself "out there" existing independently of the conscious "I," but we cannot know about this world "as it is," only as it is constituted in my consciousness.

Intellectualism, though it seeks to overcome the mechanical sensory model of empiricism, renders perceptual experience just as static and shares much with the empirical views it seeks to overcome, for example, the conceptions that raw data is passively received through sensory faculties and knowledge conforms to independently existing objects. Intellectualism understands perception as the exercise of thought and judgment involved in experience, executed by an evaluating subject. Phenomenologically, this describes sense experience as distinct from, but analogous to, thinking. Consequentially, rendering experiencing akin to thinking absorbs sense experience into thought and cognitive structures without accounting for the ways in which thinking and bodily perceptual experiences differ.[79]

More specifically, intellectualists attempt to address the concept of attention, used by empiricists to theorize how it becomes possible that in the reception of sensory data an object stands out against a background for the perceiver.[80] Where empiricists fall short because of their theoretical inability to resort to consciousness (though they imply it), intellectualists propose that it is the constituting activities

79. Merleau-Ponty, *Phenomenology of Perception*, 28.
80. See note 49 of this chapter on Gestalt psychology and figure/background perception.

of consciousness which create the structures of perception.[81] Whether or not this structure is perceptible to the subject has no consequence in intellectualist theories. Consciousness, by its very existence and activity, produces structures which aid the subject in perception.[82] Intellectualists do not need "attention" in order to explain perception, but use it to help illuminate perceptual structures.

However, if consciousness in its activity produces structure, it must have these very same structures itself. In other words, if consciousness provides the structures of perception, then in the moment of perception we already possess perceptual structures. This makes certain actual perceptual experiences theoretically untenable: I could not possibly be perceptually deceived (as in optical or other sensory illusions), and contingency and learning remain unaccounted for theoretically. Conceiving of a consciousness possessing and producing structures of perception implies that perception is always complete, determinate and definite. Yet our lived experience shows that we continue to explore and learn about that which we perceive.

Intellectualist perspectives are unable to meaningfully employ concepts such as attention. Indeed, "to attend" is to progressively formulate that which initially occurs as indeterminate and ambiguous to us. Therefore, the experience of attention shows that at the beginning of perception, there is neither sensory chaos nor unambiguously perceivable qualities; at the end of perception, there is no complete transparency and coherence.[83] Attention itself is creative, and this creativity is motivated exactly by this initial indeterminate horizon of perception.[84] Intellectualism thus needs a different concept to link sensory data impinging on the subject to the perceived sense image of unified objects.

---

81. Merleau-Ponty, *Phenomenology of Perception*, 27–28. For example, my consciousness, by virtue of being active, produces structures of time and space; therefore, I perceive my world temporarily and spatially.

82. Without this structure-inducing consciousness, there is either perceptual chaos, or a Kantian noumenon (the thing in itself). Ibid., 29.

83. Ibid., 30.

84. Merleau-Ponty discusses psychological studies with patients who cannot locate a specific point on their body, yet who are not completely ignorant of it either. Their

The problems inherent in intellectualist conceptions may make their way into theological projects which emphasize consciousness-raising. For example, Ada María Isasi-Díaz's theological project is that of detecting, describing, and valuing Hispanic women's moral agency and subjectivity.[85] Among those themes, she uses, for example, the experiences of particular community struggles and that of *mestizaje* (signifying the racial and cultural mixed-ness of U.S. Hispanics), mined for processes of meaning-making.[86] Her method is strong on being sensitive to culturally specific historical, socialized, and feminist experiences, and she constructs insightful theological formulations.[87]

---

vague locating of a body part overturns empiricist and intellectualist concepts of attention. The same is evident when considering infants learning to distinguish color. Child development studies show that children first conceive of color/colorless, then warm/cold hues; they then begin to distinguish colors. Merleau-Ponty claims that it is not that they saw colors all along but failed to pay attention; rather, the structure of their perception changed. Ibid., 30–31. Langer, *Merleau-Ponty's Phenomenology of Perception*, 12.

85. Ada María Isasi-Díaz, *Mujerista Theology: A Theology for the Twenty-First Century*(New York, NY: Orbis Books, 1996). Ada María Isasi-Díaz, *En La Lucha = in the Struggle: Elaborating a Mujerista Theology*, 10th anniversary ed. (Minneapolis: Fortress Press, 2004). Hispanic women's experiences as theological source are called *lo cotidiano* in Isasi-Díaz: The struggles and processes of Hispanic women's lives, the "stuff" of Hispanic women's reality makes up shared (not common) experiences.

86. Isasi-Díaz, *Mujerista Theology: A Theology for the Twenty-First Century*, 66. When Isasi-Díaz elicits processes of meaning-making she focuses on acts of interpreting and understanding one's actions and statements. Isasi-Díaz's balancing act between thick descriptions and normative generalities is mirrored in other feminist theologies from non-Western locations, as found in the essays compiled by King, Fabella and Oduyoye, and Brock, Jung, Kwok and Seung. See Ursula King, *Feminist Theology from the Third World: A Reader* (Maryknoll, NY: Orbis Books, 1994). Virginia Fabella and Mercy Amba Oduyeye, eds., *With Passion and Compassion: Third World Women Doing Theology* (Maryknoll, NY: Orbis Books, 1988). Rita Nakashima Brock, Jung Ha Kim, Kwok Pui-Lan, and Seung Ai Yang, *Off the Menu: Asian and Asian North American Women's Religion and Theology* (Louisville, KY: Westminster John Knox Press, 2007).

87. For theological projects with similar aims of constructing theology from particular locations, see, for example, Joh's engagement of the Korean concept *jeong* in Wonhee Anne Joh, "Violence and Asian American Experience: From Abjection to

Perception is significant to Isasi-Díaz where consciousness and conscientization are concerned. Sensory perception to Isasi-Díaz is the most basic level of sensitivity in consciousness, a level shared with animal life.[88] But understanding (she refers to Bernard Lonergan's use of Hegel's term *Aufhebung* or sublation)[89] is used to describe complementation and interpretation of what is sensed. Unique to humans is the incorporation of sense perception with other, higher, levels of judging and choosing.

Because conscientization as critical reflection on action leading to awareness is connected to higher levels of consciousness Isasi-Díaz describes, sensory perception in her work is the raw material, but nevertheless needs to be absorbed into a consciousness which "pays attention" in order to be put to use for processes of liberation. Knowledge about the world still conforms to a world that exists independently and offers meaning to the person sensing and reflecting on her sensory bodily experiences in her environment. Conscientization is the exercise of thought and judgment; the evaluative perception employed by a person who holds perceptual structures in her mind which aid in her perception of her world.

Theologians leaning in intellectualist directions in terms of phenomenological conceptions are bound to the ways in which they (implicitly or explicitly) propose a judging and evaluating mind processing perceptual data gained in bodily experiences. Judgment in intellectualist conceptions assumes the coordinating function within consciousness, whilst also taking on the explanatory burden for phenomena such as optical illusions (or even the discrepancies between what is projected

---

Jeong," in *Off the Menu: Asian and Asian North American Women's Religion and Theology*, ed. Rita Nakashima Brock, Jung Ha Kim, Kwok Pui-Lan, and Seung Ai Yang (Louisville, KY: Westminster John Knox Press, 2007), 145–162. See also Joh's christological construction based on *jeong* in Joh, *Heart of the Cross: A Postcolonial Christology* (Louisville, KY: Westminster John Knox Press, 2006).

88. Isasi-Díaz, *Mujerista Theology: A Theology for the Twenty-First Century*, 154.
89. Bernard Lonergan was a Catholic priest and theologian. Part of his philosophical work includes explorations of empirical methods to investigate exterior sensation as well as internal processes of consciousness.

on a retina and the perceived object).[90] Within this theoretical assembly, perception is rendered an intellectual construction. Sensory data is received, but to perceive is to interpret, elaborate, or use that data to conclude and determine. The experience of perception is now the intellectual activity of judging: Every time we see, hear, taste, smell, or touch, we actually judge that we see *this*, hear *that*, smell *this*, or touch *that*.

Merleau-Ponty argues that this intellectualist version is not how we experience perception in real life. Purely physically, we do "see" (receive an imprint of an image on our retina) upside down, but we do not experience upside-down images which we then judge or interpret right-side up. And we do experience differences between sensing and judging, as evident in attempts to make sense of sensory illusions or to explain hallucinations.[91]

Contrary to intellectualism's conception, perception is not thought. The latter is based on and presupposes perception. There is an irreducible phenomenal difference between perception and thought: we perceive before we think, and we learn how to think about what we see, rather than attaching preexisting thought to a sensed world encountered

90. "Judgment is often introduced as *what sensation lacks to make perception possible*." (Emphasis in original) Merleau-Ponty, *Phenomenology of Perception*, 32–33. Merleau-Ponty sketches intellectualism's take with Descartes' example of seeing hats and coats below our window, but using judgment, we declare that we see men.

91. Regarding hallucination, Merleau-Ponty explains that intellectualism makes sharp distinctions between true and false perceptions. But it is incoherent to say that, if I experience a hallucination, I simply *think* I am seeing something which I do not really see, because by definition, I *do* see it. Because if saying that I see something = I think that I see something, then the intellectualist stance implies that I think I see what I don't think I see. If I argue that I simply execute bad judgment (perhaps by holding false premises), the problem of explaining the process of my hallucinating is merely deferred. The process of distinguishing between adequate and inadequate impressions still requires explaining. And such an explanation would require conceiving of an elementary sensible holding immanent signification, a concept already ruled out by intellectualism's theoretical stance. Ibid., 39–44. Langer, *Merleau-Ponty's Phenomenology of Perception*, 14.

by the act of thinking.[92] At the same time, thinking itself is structurally much more like perceiving than rationalistic concepts account for: both are intentional,[93] both share some underlying structural features (e.g., perspectival orientation), because both are anchored in the body.[94] But judgment is secondary, not integral, to perception. The intellectualist trajectories of phenomenology (beginning with Cartesian rationalism and moving through Kantian a priori categories of judgment enabling perception) posit an autonomous and disembodied consciousness. In the Cartesian model, the mind holds "ideas" (or "representations" in Kant) and therefore is able to imagine and perceive. These ideas are objects of consciousness: the subject is aware of ideas and has attitudes about ideas. This fails to acknowledge that all subjects (including their mind and its functions) are inherently embodied and situated.

Even theologians who explicitly and adamantly seek to do theology from embodied perspectives and grounded in bodily experiences may be tripped up by intellectualist notions making their way into their projects. Marcella Althaus-Reid, for example, grounds her theological engagements in the lived, embodied experiences of women in Latin America, who face multiple layers of oppression.[95] Althaus-Reid

---

92. Maurice Merleau-Ponty, *The Visible and the Invisible*, trans., Alphonso Lingis (Evanston, IL: Northwestern University Press, 1968), 11. Carman, *Merleau-Ponty*, 12.

93. "Intentionality" as a technical term in phenomenology is *not* understood as a synonym for "on purpose." Rather, as the feature of our mental life, it describes our perceptions, thoughts, emotions, beliefs, etc., as being "of" or "about" something. I will explore this concept in depth in the next chapter.

94. Merleau-Ponty, *The Visible and the Invisible*, 33.

95. Using socio-cultural analysis and ethnographic tales, Althaus-Reid argues that economic, political, sexual, and religious structures all work together to form systems and orders of decency which determine the lived reality of women. Althaus-Reid names this kind of liberation theology "Indecent Theology" and argues that this is the case because it exposes and deconstructs the relationship between the sexual and the theological, a relationship defining the order of decency which underpins other oppressive orders. Decency/indecency operate to define what stands as "normal" in terms of the economical, sexual, racial, and theological, and this decent and normal masks the multiple oppressions and interrelated structures

investigates lived realities of bodily experiences, comparing them with religious narratives and symbols, looking for possibilities of identification and liberation in sexual metaphors employed for the theological imaginary.[96] Constructively, she then proposes a perverting and "indecenting" of theology by constructing positions from sexual marginal epistemologies: telling sexual stories and doing theology of sexual stories, bringing them into dialogue with economics and politics and the oppression occurring through them.

Because Althaus-Reid connects perception to recognition of meaning *and* reception of sense data, perception can be conscious or not, but conscious perception is linked to particular standpoints and social location, revealing particular (hidden) truths.[97] While she does not articulate it specifically, at times she implies perception to be bodily function which can be put to use in accessing experience and providing information useful to processes of interpretation and meaning-making. Other times, she implies perception to be something that is also socially influenced, particularly when it comes to recognition and reception. What is perceived/recognized is already shaped by the social and cultural imaginary, for example, certain physical appearances of a person are already shaped as perception of a criminal.[98] In her theological project, Althaus-Reid invokes employing a phenomenological method which understands perception as the capacity for objective observation and for "truthful" description of sensory information of a lived experience/phenomenon.[99]

of oppression at work. Marcella M. Althaus-Reid, *Indecent Theology: Theological Perversions in Sex, Gender and Politics* (New York, NY: Routledge, 2000), 2, 17, 22–26.

96. For example, she finds subversions in theologically engaging the poor raced transvestite who seeks to survive marginalization and oppression by prostituting in a nightclub. She resists essentializing of "the poor" as well as their desires, and complicates religion, citizenship and notions of justice through her theological readings of sexual practices and embodiments. See Ibid., 32–33, 85–86, 112–114, 136–137.

97. Ibid., 38,55.

98. Ibid., 105.

99. Ibid., 80.

When Althaus-Reid specifically seeks to tap into (sexually and economically) marginalized bodies and experiences as theological resources, her phenomenological stance binds her to utilizing bodily experiences as metaphor (albeit lived).[100] She indicates that perception is more than physical sensing, more than accessing objective data to receive knowledge. Perception and affect are linked to each other and to one's social location; neither is free from social and cultural inscriptions. Althaus-Reid links perception and recognition, the latter being shaped by the cultural imaginary, though she also sometimes likens perception to a bodily mechanism which accesses experience and aids in meaning-making. We can also detect how this inadvertent employment of intellectualist conceptions upholds the body/mind dualism and its cause and effect mechanisms. The mind receives data of the external world, and in a separate internal zone the world is represented. An isolated body causally affects the mind, though the purely mechanical relations of a physical universe are upheld: an external physical world shapes the organization of the interior mental world, and this relation can be reduced to physical laws of causation.[101]

Summing up Intellectualist Conceptions and Connected Theological Dilemmas

Theologians drawing on intellectualist notions allow for the person to play a role in the process of perception and in formulating meaning as it appears for her. But this subject stands outside the world of experience and imposes meaning on the world. Even when theologians insist that

100. Althaus-Reid both has been lauded for her radical, subversive, and liberatory theological images and metaphors derived from bodily experience. But she also has been challenged for their limitations, particularly for the failure to spell out what a "Queer God" or a "Bi/Christ" *really* means, in other words, what the actual substantial difference in using these bodily groundings *is*. Thomas Bohache, *Christology from the Margins* (London, UK: SCM Press, 2008), 223.
101. Dorothea Olkowski, "Introduction," in *Merleau-Ponty, Interiority and Exteriority, Psychic Life and the World*, ed. Dorothea Olkowski and James Morley (Albany, NY: State University of New York Press, 1999), 1–2.

to be embodied in the world implies a situatedness in time and space, implying a particular perspective which is only possible when one is *in* the world, the embodied subject is still caught in transcendental frames, as mind disconnected from body and world when perception remains an intellectual function.[102] When sensory perception is mostly thought of in terms of awareness but remains a lower or subordinate function of consciousness (as in Isasi-Díaz), bodily experiences become subordinated to or absorbed in cognitive structures.

Where perception is understood as bodily mechanism *and* socially influenced process (as in Althaus-Reid), we have observed that the theologies constructed by resourcing bodily experience mine the latter for metaphorical and symbolic purposes. Aiming to reshape the cultural imaginary, perception is a link and interrelated with embodiment and social location and shaped by social inscription/cultural imaginary. Yet inadvertently, a nature/culture dualism is upheld if the focus of theologies becomes the reshaping of theological and cultural imagery: If perception is a biological mechanism which is also socially influenced, it remains unarticulated how sensory perception is also a factor in the shaping of the social and the cultural, and it becomes a "natural" ability over against "cultural" powers. Consequentially, these theologies are about bodies and of bodily metaphors, rather than theologies grounded in bodily *experience*.

102. Merleau-Ponty maintains that the intellectualist position holds that the world has no role in determining meaning, which resolves to idealism and implies a detached subject. ("For to acknowledge a naturalism and the envelopment of consciousness in the universe of *blosse Sachen* as an occurrence, is precisely to posit the theoretical world to which they belong as primary, which is an extreme form of idealism" Merleau-Ponty quoted in Christopher Watkin, *Phenomenology or Deconstruction? The Question of Ontology in Maurice Merleau-Ponty, Paul Ricoeur and Jean-Luc Nancy* (Edinburgh, UK: Edinburgh University Press, 2009), 37.). A constituting subjectivity implies and demands that the world is affirmed/assumed to be bare of meaning. Against this extreme idealism, Merleau-Ponty proposes that the self and the world are inextricable in the constitution of sense, an un-analyzable Gestalt in which meaning emerges in the interaction of self and world, while remaining reducible to neither. Watkin, *Phenomenology or Deconstruction?*, 19.

Perception as intellectual capacity bearing on bodily sensory information conceives of things and structures in the world as constituted by my perception, and thus dependent on and even confined to my constitutive consciousness. Although I am real and I exist, any oppression perceived, and structural violence sensed, would be "less real" without me and my grasp on it. Experience is a resource for theology, but never more than raw material on which to critically reflect. Experiences from a specific embodiment and particular location can give rise to theology via conscientization (intellectual processes) *only*. To paraphrase Gayatri Spivak, the subaltern may experience, but cannot do theology.[103] This maintains certain hierarchies, not just of body and mind, but also of intellectual processes.

Any theological focus on identity and subjectivity (often considered multiple, fragmented, or intersectional in feminist and postcolonial thought) still upholds an explanatory gap regarding perception. Articulating cultural forces on subject formation and bodily experience and thereby forming cause-effect mechanisms still maintains nature/culture, body/mind dualisms, and places processes of perception alternately in either category. In other words, simply using either category or both to explain experience (or identity, subjectivity) does little to overcome any dualism itself.[104] Curiously, the subject itself, or

---

103. See chapter 1, note 10. Spivak famously wrote that the subaltern can speak, but cannot be heard without significant changes to consciousness ultimately demanding the subaltern not be subaltern. I believe the same is true for theologies. Though I do believe that critical reflection is important and is a significant step in liberative projects, I also believe it is not the most important in terms of understanding what it means to experience and perceive the world.

104. For example: Explaining subject formation alternately as social forces inscribing meaning on bodily markers and thereby shaping experience (e.g., heteronormativity inscribing sexual practices and thereby experiences which in turn produce heterosexual subjects and "others"), and also describing subject formation as resistant bodily practices taking up and reshaping existing cultural imagery (e.g., queer practices taking up recognizable positions while at the same time resisting and reshaping stereotypes). This strikes a balance between two perspectives which are not necessarily opposed to each other. However, the mind/body dualism is muddled, rather than overcome, in this method.

subjectivity, falls into an "explanatory gap" in some versions of this kind of approach, for example, when the brain is rendered an organ which carries out thinking, remembering, imagining, acting, and so forth in a system based on physical mechanics. The mind is either reduced to the brain or becomes an unaccounted-for third party in this cause-effect model, a mind that nevertheless somehow has experiences as a subject.[105]

When the perceived world is rendered as separate from myself, things and others exist and relate to each other independently of me. As detached perceiver, I can sense the world from nowhere and everywhere and am simultaneously connected to the world only as another alienated object, and my perception of the world is irrelevant to its existence. The world and its goings-on are real, but I as perceiver am not necessary, do not have to be a person involved in it. Even when interrelation of me-other and me-world is thought of as constitutive of my identity, as long as conceptions of perception remain caught in a subject-object divide, then "deep down" my subjectivity remains prior to interrelations with other subjects and objects (the independent "I" comes before any relation/perception of the world). Unwittingly, perception in empiricist *and* intellectualist conception can (re)shape the subject of feminist theologians into the dis-embodied universalized male, either by suggesting access to (universal) truth through sensory channels or by employing phenomenological notions which disconnect the perception of the world from one's bodily location.

SITUATING THE THEOLOGICAL SENSE REGARDING PERCEPTION

Lacking at present in feminist theology are methodological tools to address how exactly the body is not just the passive material molded by

---

105. Scott L. Marratto, *The Intercorporeal Self: Merleau-Ponty on Subjectivity*, ed. David Pettigrew and Francois Raffoul, Contemporary French Thought (Albany, NY: State University of New York, 2012), 13.

language and social inscriptions. How *do* we experience in our bodies, how *does* the body move into the imagination, into concepts, into perceptions of the world? In other words, what exactly can theorists and theologians alike learn about the "inner life" of the body and embodied experience, and what influences are at work in how we come to feel it, perceive in it, talk about it, and look at the world from and through it? And how can a theologian conceptualize (from) a particular bodily experience (be it disabled, raced, gendered), without universalizing an able ideal, a white norm, or a naturalized gendered concept, and also avoiding exclusive, segregated theological conversations? And as a caution to myself, working within the Western academy, how should I entertain this project without simply presenting dominant discourses with yet another tool to appropriate or exploit other/othered bodies to "improve" Western discourses?

Surveying the spectrum of phenomenological approaches I have presented the two ends of the spectrum within which perception has been conceived (empiricist and intellectualist). At the ends of this spectrum, one can conceive of perception as a mechanical bodily function (the senses as bodily channels for truth "out there") or as a function of the mind (the senses as providing the data which the mind then perceives, judges, and interprets). Neither position might seem palpable to a feminist theologian concerned with body/mind dualisms, yet when perception is unattended to, one may fall anywhere in between. My goal in presenting the ends of the spectrum has been to highlight the shortcomings of the phenomenological positions via their extremes, and to allow us note where these conceptions of perception leak into theological projects.

Pursuing the questions which initiated this project, and turning to feminist theologians who employ bodily experience and sensory perception in their work, I seem bound to remain within the same spectrum they find themselves in. In other words, I appear caught between a methodological rock and a hard place: seek to hone my sensory perception to receive truth about my experiences in/with my family, or install my perception and interpretation as a superior mind. Let me illustrate more clearly the dilemma I find myself in.

I could attempt to ground my theological reflection on my grand-mother's experience, for example, by employing sensory perception as access to experience. But for lack of communication (verbal or gestural) I am left with "objective" data of what her experience might or could be like, based on detached scientific observation and collected sensorial evidence on persons with Alzheimer's disease. My attempts at accessing and utilizing her experience, what she might perceive sensorially, remain speculative, though they gain a certain clout of authority backed by scientific inquiries into the universal. Or I can shift my attention to *my* experience, my first-person perceptual account and descriptions of grandmother. This would correct the speculative utilization of what Grandmom's experience might be (should be) like, but shift the focus on experience toward my personal perspective, to meaning and truth as only I experience it. Grandmom's experience and its meaning are either universal and exist independently of my witnessing them, or I am bound to my perspective and can attest to experience and meaning only as I perceive them myself. Neither approach addresses complexly how it might be that bodily sense experience (mine or hers) informs my theological reflections, and, as this statement also reveals, maintains inadvertently a body/mind dualism in which the body experiences and the mind reflects.

Relating to my mother, I can pretend to perceive her meaning-making in the world as if I am not part of her situation and not enmeshed with her in her experiences of suffering and resistance. Theologically, I am then observing her bodily movements through my perceptual capacities as if my sensory perception is capable of grasping all meanings emerging *for her*. Or I can acknowledge that I am left with my own subjective grasp of her experience; I cannot perceive of *her* experience, but only draw on *my* experience of her, my perception and description of her experiences. Yet honing and employing my sensory abilities to perceive of my mom's experience like an outsider is imprudent not only (though significantly) because *I* am involved. Positing my perceptual capacities as adequate for theological reflection and interpretation on her experiences like an insider is imprudent because *she* is involved. And I still have not accounted for the ways in which bodily experiences and perception are implicated with each other so that I am not a mind evaluating my bodily perceptions.

Within this spectrum of empiricist-intellectualist approaches to perception, the nature and processes of perception are insufficiently explained. Perception cannot be adequately conceived as either a causal link in a mechanic, bodily process or as an event or state in the mind or brain. When theologians employ embodiment to voice dissatisfaction with pervasive mind/body dualism, perception cannot remain conceptualized within a dualistic frame. What has emerged so far in this chapter is that some phenomenological conceptions posit bodily experiences as offering up "truth" accessed through perceptual processes. Theologies naming (women's) bodily experiences, and thereby making it a conceptual category, then may imply that these bodily experiences may be accessed via ontological epistemological sensory capacities, or they may serve as indicators or text offering truth about social and cultural forces evaluated and interpreted through intellectual capacities.

In the phenomenological spectrum presented, sensori-perceptual processes are established as common universal. Theologies falling within this spectrum—either by hailing sensory perception as the go-to avenue for women (or all persons) to access truth/knowledge, by likening perception uncritically to apprehension (albeit from different standpoints), or equaling it to recognition of reality—fall prey to the problems inherent in this spectrum. This does little to deconstruct binaries of experience (e.g., male/female) or metaphysical dualisms (material/transcendent), but again constructs idealized bodies and bodily functions, and particularly neglects implications of those bodies doubly inscribed with difference (racialized women, women with menstrual complications, intersexed persons, transgender persons, impaired bodies, dying bodies, etc.).[106]

---

106. See Jones, "Women's Experience between a Rock and a Hard Place," 139. Also Jones, *Feminist Theory and Christian Theology*, 47. See also Paula Cooey's discussion of constructions of motherhood and "bad" women, in Paula M. Cooey, "Bad Women: The Limits of Theory and Theology," in *Horizons in Feminist Theology: Identity, Tradition, and Norms*, ed. Rebecca S. Chopp and Sheila Greeve

Turning back on their own concerns, even theologians who explicitly seek to overcome body/mind dualisms render the biological body mechanical and passive, either by appealing to the senses and therefore making the body no more than a vessel for reception, by appealing to bodily function while at the same time applying normatizing ontological ascriptions, or by focusing on the intellectual perceptual capacities to evaluate social forces impinging on bodily experiences. These approaches, however, tend to establish evidence of different bodies and bodily experience as evidence for the fact of difference (I see different bodies, therefore our bodies are different). This kind of shortcut might prevent us from undergoing a more complex exploration of *how* difference is perceived and established and how bodily experience and perception may play part in it. An appeal to the senses does not grant access to unmediated truth or untainted experiences, revelations of meaning or the divine; bodies, and their sensory capacity themselves, are always differently constituted. To "be in touch with one's feelings" is always simultaneously less and more than just that, as we will discuss in depth in the following chapter.

MOVING BEYOND THE EMPIRICISM-INTELLECTUALISM SPECTRUM

We have seen in the preceding describing and evaluating of the different positions that empiricism posits a perceptual process which in effect renders the subject ignorant (because consciousness is denied a role in the process, though invoked for other functions). In contrast, intellectualism conceives of a subject completely cognizant of what is perceived. But despite some of our actual sense experiences being ambiguous or vague,

Davaney (Minneapolis: Fortress Press, 1997), 137–153. On the problem of gendered implications in reproductive health and childrearing for moral agency and full personhood of women, see Helen Marshall, "Our Bodies, Our Selves: Why We Should Add Old Fashioned Empirical Phenomenology to the New Theories of the Body," in *Feminist Theory and the Body: A Reader*, ed. Janet Price and Margrit Shildrick (New York, NY: Routledge, 1999), 64–75.

both positions theorize perception as determinate and corresponding to a (self-evident) objective world: Empiricists understand this world to exist in itself, imposing on the perceiver, and construct an absolute objectivity via this theory of perception. Intellectualists conceive of the world as the immanent end of knowledge, posing a concept of consciousness which sustains the objective world constructed by empiricists.[107]

Merleau-Ponty charges that the inadvertent denial of the embodied nature of perceptual experience is common to both empiricists and intellectualists. The former treats the body as a mechanism; the latter treats the body only as an afterthought or contingency to consciousness.[108] Both positions take for granted that there is an objective world "out there," a world described by science. Human beings are but one of the objects in this world, and "experience" is the result of inter-object cause-and-effect relations. This approach is mistaken in its starting point: It is from embodied experience that any scientific theories are derived, that is, we interact with the world before we develop our theories about it. This prereflective dimension cannot be explained away by mechanisms or after-thoughts.[109]

We do not experience (in) the world as a thinker musing about an object of thought. Thus we ought not conceive a perceiving subject solely as consciousness which executes cognitive functions like interpretation of data, or which orders the matter and meaning of objects according to ideal laws inherent to the object.[110] Hence, if perception is not what empiricists or intellectualists propose, what is it? For Merleau-Ponty, this question can only be answered by maintaining the focus on embodiment. He turns to the inherent embodiedness of perception to frame the subject as able to access to the world *only* through the body and *only* as already situated in the world. Merleau-Ponty

107. Merleau-Ponty, *Phenomenology of Perception*, 29, 35–39.
108. Ibid., 24, 39.
109. I will discuss "prereflective dimension" more explicitly in the next chapter.
110. Maurice Merleau-Ponty, *The Primacy of Perception and Other Essays on Phenomenological Psychology, the Philosophy of Art, History and Politics* (Evanston, IL: Northwestern University Press, 1964), 12.

considers the paradox or mystery of perception to be that (a) the world is disclosed to as at all, that we are aware of things outside of ourselves, and (b) that we are living beings encountering the world via bodily perspectives, bodies which we *have* and *are* (I only *have* a body *as* a body).[111] Perception is bodily; it is as bodies that we perceive. We are not subjects positioned over against objects, but bodily agents in and of the world.[112] More concisely, perception is an integral aspect of our bodily existence.

Merleau-Ponty's famed thesis is the primary of perception, though he does not bestow perception with exclusivity of evidence.[113] Rather, perception in Merleau-Ponty is that which constituted the grounds for all knowledge, and as such its study has to precede all other layers of investigation. Merleau-Ponty's originality lies in his attempt to develop a non-Cartesian understanding of perception: he seeks to find a new, innovative unity between the empiricism of traditional sciences and the philosophical intellectualism he considered too narrowly centered in the Cartesian tradition.[114]

Maintaining distinctions between interior and exterior, mental and physical, subjective and objective, is misleading when using them to

---

111. Merleau-Ponty, *The Visible and the Invisible*, 8. Merleau-Ponty, *Phenomenology of Perception*, 144.

112. Merleau-Ponty, *Phenomenology of Perception*, 41–44. Carman, *Merleau-Ponty*, 26.

113. If the philosophical and scientific purpose of phenomenology is to describe and clarify the meanings of concepts found in our language and culture by getting back to the source, the phenomenon originating the meaning, then perception must be primary, because it is perception which reveals the phenomena which in turn are the source for abstract ideas. Merleau-Ponty, *Phenomenology of Perception*, xxi, 241–242.

114. Herein lies Merleau-Ponty's challenge to his predecessor Husserl and his contemporary Sartre, who both desired to overcome the Cartesian and Kantian object-subject dualisms, yet whose points of departure in phenomenology were still a version of the Cartesian cogito. To Merleau-Ponty, there is no pre-given objective world which is put together by attention or judgment of a subject. Herbert Spiegelberg, *The Phenomenological Movement: A Historical Introduction*, 3rd ed., 6 vols., vol. 5 (Boston, MA: Martinus Nijhhoff Publishers, 1982), 542.

frame sensory perception. Merleau-Ponty conceives of these percep-tual aspects as interrelated and inseparable.[115] His understanding of the various aspects of perception is always both: always passive and active, situational and practical, conditioned and free.[116] He insists that our own bodily experience shows us this, because we do not experience an "I" in a body that is simply a living organism func-tioning in a mechanistic manner.[117] Merleau-Ponty refers to pain to support this point: I feel pain not as caused by my body, but as inhab-iting my body. In other words, pain is not something that is distinct from my body, a sensation inflicted on me by a pain-wielding body as agent, but I experience the sensation of pain in me, in my body-self.[118] I *have* pain and I *am paining*. Pain can be scientifically measured and it is something that I feel and describe subjectively and cannot relate objectively.[119]

Furthermore, Merleau-Ponty posits that perception is always in the middle of two traditional categories, it is in fact the *ground*: the dualist categories employed depend on and presuppose perception as the middle ground of experience. That is, I can have subjective sensa-tions and experience sensory qualities, but only because I can some-times generate them by abstracting away from my original openness to the world and zoom in on isolated features of things and on bits of experience. I then suppose (rightly or wrongly) that my sensations must correspond to those isolated features. This can go the other

---

115. Merleau-Ponty, *Phenomenology of Perception*, 130.
116. Carman, *Merleau-Ponty*, 79.
117. Though we might ridicule the rigidity of Cartesian body/mind split and the overly mechanical understanding of the body he held, the ontological assumptions are still widely held in scientific common sense.
118. Merleau-Ponty, *Phenomenology of Perception*, 90–93.
119. On the incommunicable personal bodily and emotional aspects of pain, see Elaine Scarry, *The Body in Pain: The Making and Unmaking of the World* (New York, NY: Oxford University Press, 1985). On her argument related to language, see chapter 5, note 3. On pain and other sensations felt emotionally and physically, and an analysis of the political role of emotions at intersections of race, gender, and sexuality, see Sara Ahmed, *The Cultural Politics of Emotion* (New York, NY: Routledge, 2004).

direction as well, taking my zeroed-in sense experiences and abstracting them away from myself toward a world I posit as independent of perspective.[120]

The human subject exists as embodied perceiver: I am a body perceiving; my bodily experience is always perceptual; my perceptual experience is always bodily. This is the presupposition unattended to in traditional concepts of perception which understand perception as either causal (empiricist) or conceptual (intellectualist). For Merleau-Ponty, to insist on perception as essentially bodily affirms that perception cannot be theorized or understood when abstracted from its concrete corporeal condition and/or when separated into bodily and mental functions. We have a prereflective understanding of our own experiences, that is, we do not think of our experiences as linked to our bodies in a causal or conceptual way, but we understand our experiences to coincide in relation with our bodies: our thinking, feeling, judging, remembering, etc., is always coinciding with our seeing, feeling, touching, smelling, hearing, etc.

Thinking of bodily experience as experiences of us as living bodies shows that there are significant untapped ways to think about how more complex experiences (such as oppression or structural violence) are embodied and experienced *in* and *through* ourselves, not just inflicted *on* us. I might be able to draw on studies correlating social location with bodily markers and specific physical/medical conditions, but these studies alone cannot help me access bodily experience in a way that helps me understand *how* exactly a bodily condition or social location might orient me in the world via my bodily experiences. To do theology complexly grounded in experience, I need to begin by seeking to understand my existence in the world as constituted by my embodiment and by my perception of and in the world. Thus far,

---

120. Carman, *Merleau-Ponty*, 78. Again we can see how the projects of aforementioned theologians might be undermined by their own presuppositions regarding perception if perception is not placed as the ground, as that which gives rise to bodily experience and intellectual processes alike.

I have sketched that to exist in this world is to be embodied and to perceive a world:

> There is no me without my existing as bodily perceptual orientation in a world.[121]

What does this mean? To exist in this world is always to already be *as* body, and as body I always already am touching, feeling, hearing, smelling, and seeing the world. As perceiving body, I am always already directed toward the world, as I turn my head to see another person, turn my body to listen to a song, focus my bodily attention to the touch and feel of another person: I am always existing by being bodily perceptually oriented in the world.

We are our bodies, and we experience the world as we are in the world through our bodies, as body-subjects. This leaves no room for an ontological separation of the subject "I" and the body of the subject. Furthermore, I and the world are enmeshed with each other, and what pervades this interrelation is perception. Perceiving always implies a situatedness in time and space; it implies a particular perspective which is only possible when I am *in* the world. And it is because I am *in* and *of* the world, that I perceive the world inevitably as structured, meaningful, and whole.

In the next part of this book, I will continue to explore the question of how to conceive of experience by supporting the assertion that my existence in the world is always fundamentally a bodily perceptual orientation in the world. I will investigate what this assertion entails and provide arguments to support this assertion, but also show how understanding experience as bodily perceptual orientation is useful when seeking to understand specific conditions of human existence. This will provide me not only with a more complex (and I believe more useful to my project) conception of perception, but it will allow me to understand how bodily experience and perception might be interrelated. This in turn will present a robust framework with which to resource bodily experiences for theological purposes.

121. Ibid., 30.

PART TWO

BODILY

PERCEPTUAL

ORIENTATIONS

I have asserted heretofore that my being in the world is always fundamentally a bodily experiencing in the world, and this bodily experiencing is a perceptual experiencing. I am in the world as a bodily being. And my encountering the world, my shaping by the world, my learning about the world and myself is always already based in and mediated by my seeing, touching, feeling, intuiting, evaluating, remembering, and so forth, in and through my being a perceiving body. This is *bodily perceptual orientation,* my condition for existence and interacting in and with the world.[1]

---

1. In this part and throughout the rest of this project, I will continue to use combined terms such as "bodily perception" or "bodily perceptual orientation." Unless otherwise clearly noted, this is not to indicate that there might be other kinds of perception or perceptual orientations. Rather, it is to remind myself and the reader that perception and perceptual orientations are always inherently bodily, and I seek to hold in close linguistic connection that which has often been conceptually separated and maintained through philosophical body/mind dualisms.

In Part One we sketched out the scope of this project, and discovered that uncritical theological appeals to sensory perception that may lead to an impasse in the quest for identifying meaning. As body theologians, we seek to affirm bodily experience as inherent to our existence in the world, and theologize to overcome hierarchies and taxonomies that emerge out of body/mind dualisms. Yet when we uncritically employ perception for epistemological purposes, we access experiences as something we *have*, as content to recall, access, apprehend, and mine for meaningful content to be turned into text and metaphor to be read. Thus we undermine the overall aim of our theological reflections and reinstate a dualistic body/mind split and a consciousness-subject that can turn toward experiences accessed via sensory perception.

Experience is important and connected to meaning, but where to go from here, and how? I find myself in a curious methodological bind: I can turn to those bodily experiences and functions which are considered "common" and derive ways to analyze meaning-making in the world. For example, I could invoke widespread bodily experiences (death or pain) or common gendered experiences (such as pregnancy or menstruation). But tapping select specific bodily experiences for meanings and truths leads me down empiricist methodological avenues which tempt me to essentialize or universalize bodily functions and/or fix associated inherent meanings disconnected from context. I could try to prevent this by taking a first-person approach to embodied experiences and employ personal narratives and subjective descriptions of experience. Yet here, any analysis of meaning and truth may remain a subjective intellectual enterprise.

Theologians utilizing the senses sway between equally disembodying positions: Either fixed meanings are "out there" which are received through perceptual channels, or subjective meaning is created through intellectual interpretation of perceived raw data. This impasse is partially due to the lack of attention and clarity in how bodily sensory perception functions in our experiences, and also to our linguistic limitations. The English language, for example, makes it difficult to express our existence as unified body and mind. I am linguistically led to express the feelings I *have*, talk about the *something*

I feel, express concerns about the body I *have*, or that pain I feel *in my* foot.[2] It requires some work to explore how I exist as body experiencing, how my reflecting on experiences is in itself an experience, how I am a body perceiving, and how my attempts to understand perception are bound to my perceiving. Because our linguistic limits can too easily constrict our theories and methods and turn on our efforts to overcome body/mind dualisms, it is crucial to work out our conception of bodily experience and sensory perception when grounding theology in experience.

Even when explicitly challenged, body/mind and subject/world dichotomies are still permeating the link between perception and bodily experience in theological projects. If theological language and power dynamics within and between discursive structures were the sole concern of a theological project, then this lack of theoretical attention to sense perception could be defensible. But I am convinced that theologians who want to take seriously the charge to overcome harmful body/mind dualisms must consider and move beyond these dualisms found in concepts of perception, lest we undermine our own projects. Drawing on my own initial questions again: Focusing on language and power dynamics in linguistic structures shifts attending to Grandmother's experience toward a discursive framing of her situation and experience. But it remains unclear how a change in discourse about Alzheimer's disease and aging might actually influence *her* experience, or how it might influence the meaning created for/by her, especially as her cognitive abilities decline. Is she just a body without a mind? Can she perceive and with what? Am I the mind observing her body as object? Similarly, I can understand my mother's experience to a certain extent by focusing on her self-understanding as shaped by concepts (of whose choosing?) of "foreigner," "daughter-in-law," or "immigrant." But what do *I* know about her experiences and meaning-making beyond what she tells me in broken German? How would I understand how her

2. Some feminist theorists and theologians then construct terms to signal something beyond the body/mind dualism partially enforced through language, such as body-self, body-subject, corporeal self, incarnate subject, just to name a few.

bodily perceptual experience is involved? Am I the educated perceiver-judge interpreting meaning for her sensory experience and acts?

Challenging body/mind dualisms by making women subjects and elevating bodies from a pure object status is not enough if we still continue to conceive of perception in ways that uphold body/mind separations. Therefore, body theology cannot just claim and/or describe a sense experience and assert a role for it in the constitution of theologically valuable experience. Body theology must theoretically attend to perception to grapple with the complex nature of body-world-culture relationships and what constitutes a "real" embodied experience at a given moment in a given context in time and space. Only thus can body theology be grounded in experience and answer questions regarding what experience *is* and what it tells us about the human conditions we seek to inquire into.

My task now is to show how we can understand bodily experience and sensory perception in interrelated ways. I claimed that perception is a bodily experience inherent and significant to our being in the world: to be in this world is to be in a body, to feel, touch, smell, see in a body; to experience the world and be experienced by the world in a bodily way also positions us toward others and the world in specific ways. Having asserted *that* bodily perceptual orientation is how I am in the world in the previous chapter, I now turn to exploring this claim: What is bodily perceptual orientation? What does it do? How does it take place? I will show that it is important to theorize beyond appreciative nods toward an interrelation of body-mind-world. It is crucial to think through this interrelation in its complexity.

This part of the book is a development of a framework for a robust body theology. I will begin by detailing the fundamental theoretical affirmation regarding bodily perceptual orientation as condition of being: Experience *is* bodily perceptual orientation. To experience in the world is to experience through and with our senses, the world we experience is always shaped by our perceptions. Reversely, how and what we perceive with our senses is also shaped by the world. To perceive is to engage in bodily and socio-cultural acts. How does bodily perceptual orientation come about? What does bodily perceptual orientation tell us about conditions of human existence, about the meanings and values experienced and expressed? Pivoting around gender, race, and normalcy we will engage in exploratory movements (not exhaustive accounts) of how bodily and social dimensions of our perceptual existence come to be implicated in and through our bodily existence in the world. In our exploration, I will pick up perceptual concepts with varying degrees of attention. The various engagements we will make together connect to each other, expand and explore each other by adding different angles and weaving in further illustrations or investigations.

Phenomenological Terrains and Traces

It will become clear that no dimension of perception can be understood as distinct or separate from another; rather, each dimension is part of the interrelated dynamic that is our bodily perceptual orientation in the world. Similarly, none of these concepts (gender, race, or normalcy) can be explained solely within the perceptual dimension it is utilized for in this chapter. But via gender, race, and normalcy we will explore concepts such as bodily intentionality, perceptual movement, perceptual habit, and mutual perceptual becomings that make up and shape what I call *bodily perceptual orientations*.

Our movements through perception will be social, personal, historical, and cross-cultural to perform a comparative exploration. If you have ever travelled away from home, you might have experienced your immersion into a different place, a different culture even, as an "onslaught on the senses." We encounter new places in a variety of perceptual dimensions: we perceive the distinct smell of a city made up of exhaust, street food vendors, the types of garbage rotting in the street; we sense a place having a certain "touch" or "feel," the pace of traffic, the bodily proximity of people passing each other, the feel of architecture, clothing and other objects; we are aware of new sounds on every corner, different musical harmonies making up popular local tunes, intonations and gestures in personal communication, car horns, coins clicking, steps on pavement; we taste different foods and drinks, we notice how fruit familiar to us tastes different, and dishes tasted at home are experienced with new flavors. Maybe we even get to stay long enough that certain experiences deemed "exotic" or "strange" to us become familiar, even cease to be the focus of attention of our perceptions and experiences. We might even begin to notice subtleties previously unperceived: the different hues and flavors of chili, the different accents or dialects of a language we still don't understand; we learn to appreciate a culture's music and notice different styles.

Where psychological and philosophical studies have focused on consciousness and epistemology (and have displayed a tendency to universalize the senses), a historical and cultural study of the senses often begins with inquiries into differences in sensory perception.[3] Sensory historians, anthropologists, and ethnographers will serve in my comparative exploration of how bodily perceptual orientations work. Their work can provide us with a more accurate understanding of perception at work in our lives, and of ourselves as sensory constructs and actors.

Our comparative exploration follows two trajectories: The first one has a hermeneutic intent, reading and re-reading phenomenological accounts of gendered, raced, and normalized bodies in conjunction

3. Sensory anthropology as a "re-thought" anthropology has some of its origins in cross-cultural anthropological comparisons of sensory perception, and since the beginning of these inquiries, three decades or so ago, while drawing on interdisciplinary fields, it also increasingly incorporates a critique and contestation of the universality of modern western categorization of the senses. The emphasis on the relationship between the senses, between sensory differences and sensory ideologies, is useful to my concern with bodily perceptual experience and difference. Especially in regard to expanding the attention given previously to highlighting subjective perceptual experiences toward tending more explicitly to communal and social perceptions in various cultural contexts, and cultural differences in perceptual practices, the inquiries undertaken in this field will be useful. Sarah Pink, "The Future of Sensory Anthropology/the Anthropology of the Senses," *Social Anthropology* 18, no. 3 (2010): 331–333. Sarah Pink and David Howes engage in an academic dispute over the contours and trajectories of sensory anthropology/anthropology of the senses. The disagreement between the two is of no significance to my use and appropriation of either scholar's work.

with examples from different historical locations or culturally distinct communities. This will help us understand our own (modern Western) perceptual orientations more complexly by pointing out its non-normativity in other contexts. [4]

The second kind of trajectory has a constructive and supplemental intent, engaging my investigation of bodily perceptual orientation and perceptions of gender, race, and normalcy further. Specifically, it is supplemental in its more complex exploration of the "how" of bodily perceptual orientations, as it adds arguments, distinctions and new illustrations.[5] I will show how some organizing assumptions regarding the aspects of perception and the tools for description employed are universalized conventions not necessarily found across histories or cultures.[6]

4. I want to disaffirm that we may understand both (as in "ours" and "theirs") *fully* or *better*, simply because my understanding and the descriptions of difference I depend on here are still dependent on being articulated in English and within a Euro-Western framework. While I might understand some of what is described, I also want to acknowledge the lack of translatability of certain things that will remain inaccessible to me.

5. Philosophically, it is also supplemental in the Derridian sense. Derrida provides two definitions of "supplement": the surplus addition that enriches the self-sufficient plenitude; and the addition that fills a void, the adjunct which intervenes in-the-place-of. However, as Derrida argues, common to both meanings of supplement is assumption of the marginality of its addition, yet the very fact of its necessity points to the lack of the supposedly complete. It is always the exterior, the outside to which it is supplemented, yet as such it is the condition of possibility of the interior. At the core of the logic of supplementarity is the process of exclusion, the process which establishes exterior and interior and thus establishes the plenitude and the supplement. Jacques Derrida, *Of Grammatology*, trans. Gayatri Chakravorty Spivak (Baltimore, MD: Johns Hopkins University Press, 1976), 144–145, 167. In short, to explore these examples as supplements, I also want to posit them as that which also makes possible our cultural interior by being constituted as the exterior to our self-sufficient knowledge, yet that which is necessary to our own self-understanding.

6. I want to stress again that none of the examples used in this chapter seeks to give a comprehensive account or deliver full knowledge. Readers interested in further elaboration are encouraged to engage in their own comparative travel to my sources. But my intent is not to make my readers more "competent" (as in "knowing more") about differences regarding bodily perceptual orientation (as in

Different times and different contexts embedded bodies in different sensory schematas, some similar or familiar to contemporary experiences, some seemingly strange to us today. The now commonly presumed and utilized organization of perceptual experience into five senses (and four tastes) is not a universal phenomenon. Inquiries into sensory epistemological frameworks shows that the number of senses, their differentiation, interrelation and prioritization, are cultural articulations. It was Aristotle, following Plato's distinction between the mind and the senses, who established five as the number of senses commonly theorized in Western culture, and also established a hierarchy (sight, hearing, smell, taste, touch, descending in epistemological value). Though the numbering of the senses is neither a biological nor universal given, but a philosophical strategy to match and support a relationship between the senses and the five elements identified by Aristotle, Western philosophers remained loyal to this classification and hierarchy up until Hegel.[7] Aristotle's *De Anima* and the psychological theories, problems,

becoming an expert on the bodily perceptual orientation of others). To hold such an aim would be counterproductive to the aim of this project, which is to make a case that bodily perceptual orientation matters, and that if we begin theological analysis with bodily experience, we must be clear about the dynamics of perception which make up our bodily existence. Therefore, the examples used here are neither full case studies nor exhaustive demonstrations of perceptual orientations. But I utilize them to highlight differences in order to explore the limits or "forgotten" horizons of our contemporary Western perceptual habituation.

7. Constance Classen, *Worlds of Sense: Exploring the Senses in History and across Cultures* (New York, NY: Routledge, 1993), 2. Touch, for example, can be broken down into a multitude of specialized perceptions (movement, temperature, pain), which are given a sensory category of their own in different cultures. Moreover, sensory orders are not static, but can change over time with changes in culture and cultural values (Ibid., 3–5). For an overview of Western thinking about sensory perception from Plato and Aristotle to Hegel and Marx, and their connections to epistemological concepts, see Anthony Synnott, "Puzling over the Senses: From Plato to Marx," in *The Variety of Sensory Experience: A Sourcebook in the Anthropology of the Senses*, ed. David Howes (Toronto, Canada: University of Toronto Press, 1991), 61–76. Also Carolyn Korsmeyer, *Making Sense of Taste: Food and Philosophy* (Ithaca, NY: Cornell University Press, 1999), 11–37. The five-fold division in Western sciences also led to the development of cultural theories of the senses, e.g.,

and formulas proposed in it influenced not only discourses in ethics and religion, but also the subsequent thought on the senses (as well as the connection between the senses and the soul), considering sight the highest and touch the basest primary sense.[8] While this Aristotelian five-fold taxonomy of perception is not evident in Christian scriptures, medieval Christianity utilizes it as structural metaphor for the cosmos and as ethical model. It was the senses that led to the fall (the forbidden fruit was pleasing to Eve, and the perceptual enjoyment of it was the sensory dimension of the original sin); redemption of humanity is then acquired through control of sensory impulses, the spiritual mastery of bodily perception within a moral code.[9] Early Christian thinking was already highly visualist, and Aquinas gave theological sanction to an already established philosophical and cultural hegemony of vision.[10]

Marshall McLuhan's oft cited theory of orality or "great divide" theory, which arranges geographical, historical, and cultural spaces into basic sensory groups (oral-aural, chirographic, typographic, electronic). McLuhan's binary theory is sweeping in its claim and significantly depends on Western sensory exclusive divisions and displays a "Euro-forming of Data." Marshall McLuhan, *The Gutenberg Galaxy* (Toronto, Canada: University of Toronto Press, 1962). For critiques of the theory, see Mark M. Smith, *Sensing the Past: Seeing, Hearing, Smelling, Tasting, and Touching in History* (Berkeley, CA: University of California Press, 2007), 8–18. Also David Howes, *Sensual Relations: Engaging the Senses in Culture and Social Theory* (Ann Arbor, MI: University of Michigan Press, 2003), xix–xx. For an account of how the self and the world were sensory-perceptually conceptualized in Western cultures during different historical periods, see Constance Classen, *The Color of Angels: Cosmology, Gender and the Aesthetic Imagination* (New York, NY: Routledge, 1998).

8. Louise Vinge, *The Five Senses: Studies in a Literary Tradition* (Lund, Sweden: LiberLäromedel, 1975), 15–21. For Aristotle, this division was more of a philosophical strategic product to match and support a relationship between the senses and the five elements he identified. Classen, *Worlds of Sense,* 2. Touch and taste involved direct physical contact and were connected to animal pleasures for Aristotle. Sight, hearing and smell were ranked higher as "human" senses. Smith, *Sensing the Past,* 28.

9. Classen, *The Color of Angels,* 3.

10. Smith, *Sensing the Past,* 29. To explore sensory cosmologies is beyond the scope of this chapter, for more detailed descriptions see Classen, *The Color of Angels,*

With the emergence of modernity in the West, perception and knowledge became increasingly tied to an epistemology of visual models and representations which sought to provide viewers with direct access to reality.[11] This perceptual privilege of vision in terms of knowledge has not always been prevalent, as sensory orderings are changeable through time.[12] Pre-modern Western cosmologies were imagined through a variety of sensory symbolism, for example, through touch and smell, and these cosmologies were imbued with and reflected social ideologies. An emerging visualism worked to obscure the sensory imagery of previous eras, and visual imagery—transparency, photographic representation, maps, graphs—became the sensory symbolism underlying

13–60. See also an investigation of the sensorium found in the Hebrew Bible, sensory vocabulary revealing a septasensory model by Yael Avrahami, *The Senses of Scripture: Sensory Perception in the Hebrew Bible* (New York, NY: T&T Clark International, 2012), 1–3 (the Introduction).

11. The *negation* of perceptual capacities as epistemological tools for learning about the world can be traced to Descartes in the 17th century. The exclusivity of sight in philosophical treatises is best connected to 18th century Immanuel Kant (though he should also be understood as thoroughly immersed in the philosophical trends of his time regarding perception). Michel Foucault locates the shift to sight as superior sense in popular Western culture in the 18th century, when semantic shifts in sensory vocabulary occur with the philosophical, cultural, and scientific changes in European space (e.g., the phrase "seeing is believing" emerges, though it is a transformed or shortened version of the previously popular phrase "seeing is believing, touching is the truth"). Avrahami, *The Senses of Scripture,* 5–7. Michel Foucault, *The Birth of the Clinic: An Archaeology of Medical Perception* (London, UK: Tavistock Publications, 1973), 131–152.

12. See, for example, Barbara Maria Stafford's investigation of the epistemological shift to imagery beginning in Europe in the 1700s, a shift she observes in all areas of life (she specifically investigates science and art). Stafford traces how Enlightenment aspirations to perfect experiences (perfect as in untainted revelation about reality), connected to dualistic constructions of the material and the metaphysical, led to a compulsion to find clarity about the metaphysical within the material. Stafford carefully connects visual imagery and its deployment in science and art to the epistemological/pedagogical, that is, she traces how visualization of what is typically unperceivable (from invisible bodily functions and mental/moral experiences to far distant stars) is central to the Enlightenment project, yet significantly, always required the guidance of

modern Western culture, carrying with it an aura of rationality and objectivity.[13]

This privileging has not only led to studying vision scientifically more than the other, considered "lower," senses—which are still very much at work as well—a visualist regime does not imply that our perceptually emerging meanings are effected through sight alone (as I will discuss in more detail subsequently). It also informs our scholarly inquiries into perception, or into any subject for that matter: I take *perspectives* on an issue, seek to *focus* my investigations, *illuminate* a point with *illustrations*, or employ a theoretical *lens*. We investigate an inner world through *introspection, demonstrate* the *scope* of an issue and then provide a *synopsis* or an *exhibit*.[14]

discourse, Logos, or logic, lest the visual appearance deceive the unenlightened/ uneducated mind.

13. Classen, *The Color of Angels*, 1. However, not all cultures in which we find vision to be the highest sense understand vision in the same way in which it emerged in Euro-Western understandings. Among Nepal's Yolmo Buddhist's, for example, one might find more than twenty ways of conceiving of vision, including a form of action and interaction, a means to communicate, a tool for spiritual practice, etc. Vision is not confined to epistemological and physiological purposes, but also includes metaphoric, pragmatic, political, moral purposes and many more. See Robert Desjarlais, *Sensory Biographies: Lives and Deaths among Nepal's Yolmo Buddhists* (Berkeley, CO: University of California Press, 2003), 54–101. Further, even when describing Western orientations as visualist, I do *not* mean to infer a dominant visual order that is singular in structure or universal in scope. For readers interested in the multiplicity and plurality of visual regimes in modern and postmodern Europe, specifically France, see Martin Jay, *Downcast Eyes: The Denigration of Vision in Twentieth-Century French Thought* (Berkeley, CA: University of California Press, 1993), 1–20. For example, Jay suggests a plurality of scopic regimes, e.g., the Cartesian perspectivalism which framed modern epistemology; the detached scientific Baconian empiricism; and the baroque regime which encompasses opacity, surplus images, and bizarre and peculiar visualizations. Jay's significant contribution to understanding the visualism of the West is his pluralization of visualism, in which visual regimes may interact, compete, overlap, and interrelate.

14. Perspective, inspect, introspect, speculate, aspect, circumspect, etc., derive from the Latin *specere*, to look at or observe. Demonstrate comes from Latin *monstrare*, to show, scope from Latin *scopium*, to look at or examine. *Synopsis* is Greek for general view. This project itself does not escape the assistance of visual metaphors

Hence, leaving the familiar sights of our socio-cultural environment will highlight our own bodily perceptual orientations and perhaps even make us feel "strange to ourselves." Even the issue of the body/mind split, the questions guiding this project, might indeed become a strange problem specific to Western theologizing and be nonsensical in a different socio-cultural context. Certain disorientations through historical and cultural examples of different bodily perceptual orientations are the purpose of our explorations. Complete cultural competence may escape us, and we may understand how difference in perceptual orientations may even make it impossible to fully "get it." The subject we have a chance to more fully and complexly understand through exposure to difference is myself: When I became strange to myself, I can begin to notice the ways in which I presume certain sights, scents, sounds, and so on, and my orientations in and through them. To begin, I will describe some "sign posts"—the "what" of bodily perceptual orientation we are out to explore—before moving into the "how" of it.

BODILY PERCEPTUAL ORIENTATION IN THE WORLD AS CONDITION OF BEING

To live is not to live *in* a body, but *as* a body. To exist in this world is to experience the world as body. We bodily perceive, feel, think, will, act. Concepts of the body and the world as mechanical/biological objects and notions of perception as intellectual processes cannot further our

---

to explain a point (and I will discuss language related issues again in the third section), as my explorations in the previous chapter illustrated some bodily perceptual orientations through vision, and some of the examples used might have invoked visual imagery or analogies for the reader. Stafford also notes that visual preferences, especially with the rise of photography, perpetuated an epistemological-perceptual hierarchical division. Scientific inquiries into experience and scientific experimentation, for example, sought to rationally produce knowledge through repeated cause-effect experimentation and deduction; perceptual faculties were divided and ordered, underestimating and neglecting the complexity and intermingling of perceiving, feeling, thinking, understanding, etc.; none is experienced without the other. Barbara Maria Stafford, *Body Criticism: Imagining the Unseen in Enlightenment Art and Medicine* (Cambridge, MA: MIT Press, 1991), 469.

understanding of how the body figures in our experience of ourselves and the world, and how our experiences are our judging and evaluating and thinking about the world. What and how I perceive (in) the world is not caused, but constituted by and embedded in the structure and capacities of my specific embodiment. And because my "body is my point of view of the world,"[15] the minimum condition for my existence is my bodily perceptual orientation in the world. What does this mean?

> We are sitting in the yard, chopping vegetables for a curry. My mother shows me how to cut the ginger into thin slices and the onion she chops brings tears to both our eyes and we giggle. She weaves slices of her life story into her instructions on food preparation. I am savoring the time I have with her, cherishing the experience as I wonder how I am going to tell the story of this moment and explain why it seems special and significant.

I cannot have experiences without embodiment as perceptual being. In other words, I cannot experience cooking with my mother without *living* this experience as body. To explore what this means we need to reorient our questions about our experiences from "What kind of bodily experiences do I have?," to begin asking "What are bodily perceptual experiences?" And "What perceptual experiences *are me*?" or, "Who am I in and through perceptually experiencing?"

BEING IN THE WORLD

BEING PERCEPTUAL

The minimum condition for the subject to exist in the world is not reducible to "I perceive, therefore I am"—since this would return us to a mind deducing this fact from accessing perceptions. Rather, the minimal condition of the subject is "I am perceiving." There is no separation between the conscious "I" and the perceiving body: I am a

15. In other words, I can never have a perspective in and on the world that is not derived from a perspective I first have from my specific bodily incarnation. Merleau-Ponty, *Phenomenology of Perception*, 70. We will explore the implications of this claim in more detail later.

body perceiving. To exist as a human being in this world, I am a living conscious body; I can never be a consciousness without a body or a body without consciousness. Perception is at work in all dimensions of this bodily existence, as we will explore in more detail in what follows. Perceptual processes are body-consciously, worldly, and culturely. In other words, in all aspects of my existence the interconnected and interrelated dimensions of body/mind/world, perception is embedded. As Merleau-Ponty puts it:

> Bodily experience forces us to acknowledge an imposition of meaning which is not the work of a universal constituting consciousness, a meaning which clings to certain contents. My body is that meaningful core which behaves like a general function, and which nevertheless exists, and is susceptible to disease. In it we learn to know that union of essence and existence which we shall find again in perception generally [...].[16]

Perceiving is active. Perception is our bodily *intentionality*, our reaching into the world, our process of structuring or organizing a given sensed environment *for me*, and in this organization of perceptions myself-as-body and the perceived world/objects are constituted.[17] or more precisely, meaning emerges coinciding with the *movements* of the experiencing person(s): As I learn to chop vegetables, it is in experiencing this in a particular place and time with my mother that ginger and onion and the large cutting knife emerge in ways that mean something to me, *because I am experiencing myself in and through* the smell, texture, sound and taste of it all. Meaning emerges through perception, I am experiencing meaning only as perceiving body in a living context, and thus our minimum condition as subjects already demands revision: *I am perceiving meaning in our world.*

The meaning of "ginger" or "mother" does not exist separately from me experiencing the scene described earlier. Their meaning is not

16. Ibid., 147.
17. "The properties of the object and the intentions of the subject ... are not only intermingled; they also constitute a new whole." Maurice Merleau-Ponty, *The Structure of Behavior* (Boston, MA: Beacon Press, 1963), 13.

transmitted between us and received through my perceptual capacities, but it is also not solely an interpretation that takes place in my consciousness.[18] Rather, meaning emerges from the gestalt that is self-world—the perpetually open scene that is always more than just the sum of my home, the garden, my mother and I chopping food. What "ginger" and "mother" means is shared between my body and the world in the same way that pictorial meaning is shared in an image between a figure and its background—the surroundings, context, time, gestures, colors, stories told and invoked take part in what emerges as meaning.[19] Meaning is *in* the situation. Meaning is not imposed from the outside to our sitting and cooking together. My first, most basic experience is always of a whole, with various elements in my experience having a relation to the perceived whole. In other words, I experience a situation as a whole, and the meanings invoked by various elements are in the situation itself. In perceiving, I am transcendent and engage the world as the world engages me.

PERCEPTUAL HABITS

Regarding experience, Merleau-Ponty asserts that

> there is a logic of the world to which my body in its entirety conforms, and through which things of intersensory significance become possible for us ... A thing is, therefore, not actually *given* in perception, rather it is internally taken by us, reconstituted and experienced by us in so far as it is bound up with a world, the basic structures of which we carry with us, and of which it is merely one of many possible concrete forms.[20]

18. "In this primary layer of sense experience which is discovered only provided that we really coincide with the act of perception and break with the critical attitude, I have the living experience of the unity of the subject and the intersensory unity of the thing, and do not conceive them after the fashion of analytical reflection and science." Ibid., 238–239.

19. Watkin, *Phenomenology or Deconstruction?*, 24.

20. Merleau-Ponty, *Phenomenology of Perception*, 326. Emphasis in original.

Meanings I tend to perceive are neither universal nor arbitrary, and my perceptual capacities are not natural givens. Ginger" and "mother"—as they emerge (to me) when my mother and I are preparing food—the meanings then and now are based on human concepts relative to our particular cultures. They are not "given" to me in perception, rather, my body (and therefore my sensory perception) conforms to a logic of the world. Merleau-Ponty calls this the pre-reflective realm of experience, a dimension of our existence that is shaped by the cultural human life-world.[21] This pre-reflective logic to which the world and I conform is neither arbitrary nor independent. There is no a natural material world existing independently from me, a world in which I simply appear.

Meaning emerges in *interrelations* of body and world from within learned *habits*. Our cultural contexts direct our body-world interactions and orient us toward certain specific interpretations thereof. Certain meanings in our experiences appear inescapable because cultural contexts are a depository, the *sediment*, of collected repeatedly emerging meanings. This sedimentation of habits is a condition of our mutual existence, the subtending pre-reflective dimension or terrain of perceptual experience (pre-reflective in the sense in that it subtends my experience without me consciously or reflectively making efforts to connect to it).

Sediment habits are not a fixed, closed system of possible meanings—sedimentation itself is a process open to changes, changes that come with bodily as well as historical and cultural transformations. We are guided and limited in our perceptual potentialities due to the cultural contexts that make up the sediment of perceptual habits. The horizon of possible meanings is delimited, it is specific and only one of many possible culturally delineated horizons, but perception has an indeterminate structure, operating within always to-be-decided customs.[22]

Our exploratory movements therefore require shifting from "*What am I experiencing?*" to the inquiring into conditions that make the

21. Merleau-Ponty, appropriating Gestalt psychology, describes this dimension as horizon/background of perception, a concept that I will not be able to explore fully here.
22. Merleau-Ponty, *The Primacy of Perception and Other Essays*, 12.

emergence of world and perceiving bodies possible:[23] "How did *I* emerge *here* to perceptually experience something?" "How is my arrival in the world also the event in which the world of my perception emerges?" These questions presuppose that my perceptions of and experiences in a cultural, socioeconomic, sexual, raced, religious world *coincide and depend* on my emerging and arriving in the situation as a cultural, economical, social, racial, sexual body. While I might pretend to bracket such qualifiers (e.g., bracketing my gender or race in order to arrive at an "objective" observation of experience), whatever I pretend to bracket is what I arrive with in the first place, and what is in the bracket also shaped that which I am facing, the object of my study. To bracket the background, the cultural habits from which I emerge and which shape my perceptions, is to erase the shaping and coming into being of the object which I am now studying, as if it simply floated in time and space. To bracket my own arrival and history is to bracket the history of the material terrain of my world also, and significantly, it brackets the mutual constitution of me as body and the world and its objects from the *sedimentation of habits*.[24] To bracket my specific embodiment and context is to bracket that ginger is not native to German cooking, and our slicing of this fragrant root in itself is a cultural and culinary disruption (to me) as I learn to cook from my Thai mother for whom ginger is a staple. Ginger is never neutral and never the same. When you taste it, you already come at it as part of your world and you feel it within your

---

23. My phenomenological cues on background, arrival, and orientation is taken from Sara Ahmed, *Queer Phenomenology: Orientations, Objects, Others* (Durham, NC: Duke University Press, 2006), 38. Ahmed, when exploring phenomenology in her work, critiques the oft used bracketing method of Husserl. "Bracketing" as phenomenological method suggests that we can set aside our own presuppositions when observing a phenomenon, set aside that which is familiar to us so that when we suspend all our usual prejudice, we can perceive the world and the object of our attention unbiased, fresh. Ahmed critiques Husserl's bracketing method for failing to account for arrival. In other words, we still rely on that which we pretend to bracket. We pretend that we can set aside our own cultural and practical knowledge and look at, for example, a table as if we had no idea what a table is or what it can or should do. Ibid., 32–39.

24. Ibid.

world on "your" terms (is it a spice, a beneficial nutritional supplement, a symbol of royalty, power, and wealth, is it a medicinal remedy,...?), and ginger and you "come about" in this experience.

Orienting Perceiving

Bracketing the arrival of the perceiving body also relegates to the background that which "performs" our perceptions of the world, namely our bodily perceptual abilities. My *orientation in* this world is fundamentally a bodily sensory alignment *by* the world. I exist as body perceiving and transcend into the world sensorily and the world pulls and pushes my sensing. My extension into and comprehension of the world is not enabled *by* my senses (I do not have senses with which I "do" perception). Rather, my bodily extension in and comprehension of the world *depends on* and *is* my sensory perception.

Bodily perception is not a matter of gathering information but a fundamental dimension of meaning-making, the domain of cultural expression and conceptual *alignments*, the medium of enactment of social values. I am always already perceptually aligned in certain ways: others are always already left, right, front, behind, near, or far in relation to me. And somehow others also already may appear desirable, approachable, graspable, to me. Perceptual orientation is what make bodies and objects emerge in line, aligned with our orientations, and perceptual orientation is how they take shape in space through and for us. Perception is what makes me and you, determines if others are even visible and existing at all (to us). The world and I are oriented toward each other in certain ways, we "line up" in certain arrangements that become compulsory because of the perceptual habits that affect and regulate our perceptual choices: I shape and am shaped by and in a world in which words like "woman," or "family," or "normal" always already place me with-in or with-out alignment of culturally specific meanings. Our environment with others and objects embodying it *is* the space we move into and co-inhabit. I am shaped and oriented by my surroundings and our orientations toward each other.[25]

25. Ibid., 54.

Perceptual experiences are cultural acts, and perceptual differences are not only bodily differences, but also cultural differences, as culture inscribes in movement and *language* how the senses are formed, utilized, and attributed.[26] If meanings are invested and conveyed perceptually, then different ways of perceiving the world also imply different modes of consciousness and knowledge formation.[27] Differences in sensory perceptual ordering in a culture affect a person's (bodily) experiences. Sensory perception varies within and across cultural groups. The "five senses" are not a universal occurrence, quantities and organization of the senses can vary. This has important implications for understanding how meanings are invested and conveyed phenomenologically. The culturally inscribed number and ordering of senses and the interplay of sounds, silence, modes of vision and cultural meanings attached to it, and the language we use to "capture" our perceptions to make sense to and with each other, affect our positioning in and orientation to the world, and thus make up the sensory constitution of the emerging experiencing subject.

The next three chapters are the groundwork exploration for our body theology framework, a survey of *how* perception and experience are embedded within each other. Using gender, I will move us first into *intentionality*, exploring it as bodily perceptual movement, and how we move into and within perceptual orientation through bodily habits and alignments. Race will be the hinge of our discussion of bodily perceptual *habitation* and their *sedimentation*, the subtending terrain of our perceptual orientations. Normalcy will guide our investigation into *interrelations* of body, mind, and world, esp. the emergence of *language* within them.

26. Classen, *Worlds of Sense*, 5. Howes, *Sensual Relations*, iv.
27. Classen, *Worlds of Sense*, 1. Howes, *Sensual Relations*, 245, note 3.

CHAPTER THREE

MOVING THROUGH
EXPERIENCING GENDER

The first significant move to explore bodily perceptual orientation in the world as minimum condition for our existence is to conceive of bodily existence and bodily structures as *intentional*.

BODILY INTENTIONALITY AND MOVEMENT

Phenomenology's founder Edmund Husserl famously located intentionality in consciousness: all consciousness is consciousness *of* something.[1] All conscious acts are *of* or *about* something, intending something. Husserl attempted to solve the Cartesian legacy by posing the posing the body/mind split as a false dichotomy and conceptualizing the intentional consciousness.[2] Merleau-Ponty

---

1. It was actually Husserl's mentor, psychologist Franz Bretano, who termed the directedness, the about-ness of consciousness, "intentionality." But it was Husserl who began using this term to challenge Cartesian conceptions of the mind. Taylor Carman and Mark B. N. Hansen, "Introduction," in *The Cambridge Companion to Merleau-Ponty*, ed. Taylor Carman and Mark B. N. Hansen (Cambridge, UK: Cambridge University Press, 2005), 5.

2. Husserl's phenomenological conception of consciousness as intentional then implies that perception is not solely an interior event; rather, it is essentially transcended and open to the perceived world. In regard to perception, intentionality (the sensing *of* or *about* something) implies that the existence of the perceived object does not depend on the sense experience of the subject. Rather, its existence goes beyond what is perceived; it transcends the consciousness of the self. Moreover, meaning then is neither solely in the consciousness of the perceiver, nor inherent in the object; meaning is always located in the perceptual interaction.

considered Husserl's proposal a continuation of Cartesian dual-isms, and situates intentionality of perception in our incarnated bodiliness.[3] Bodily experience is intentional: Intentionality is that which grounds my relationship with the world. As irreducible body-consciousness I am always already experiencing of/toward/about something, and it is in bodily experience that the world and I are mutually constituted.[4]

Theorized like this, perception cannot be access or apprehension. Now, perception "indicates a *direction* rather than a primitive func-tion,"[5] and perception presupposes situatedness and implies position-ing: As perceiving subject I am specifically located as body in time and space, always *facing* something, and always perceiving in refer-ence to my body.[6] We need to explore then how bodily intentionality is my bodily extension through perception, my sense of situatedness through experiencing "my ownness" and belonging, of relationship and participation.[7]

In perception, references are bodily and charged with signifi-cance: something is up or down, to the left or right, appears large or small, appears to precede me; something is graspable; it is some-thing for me; it is something I can reach from here; it is something

Edmund Husserl, *Logical Investigations*, trans. J. N. Finley, new ed., 2 vols., vol. 2 (New York, NY: Routledge, 2001; reprint, 1921), 77–93.

3. Merleau-Ponty asserts that Husserl maintains the "I" as foundation for all knowledge and then turns to intersubjectivity to explain the "I." To Merleau-Ponty, this is simply a modern version of Cartesianism. Merleau-Ponty, *Phenomenology of Perception*, viii–xxi.

4. Paul Rodaway, *Sensuous Geographies: Body, Sense and Place* (New York, NY: Routledge, 1994), 18.

5. Merleau-Ponty, *Phenomenology of Perception*, 12.

6. Ahmed, *Queer Phenomenology*, 27. Given my Euro-Western cultural context, using the metaphor of "facing something" is easily read analogous to visually fac-ing it as in "seeing something." This is not an implication I would like to infer. I will discuss a variety of ways other than seeing in which we can perceptually face something later.

7. Paul Rodaway, *Sensuous Geographies: Body, Sense and Place* (New York, NY: Routledge, 1994), 8.

I want.[8] Perception positions me towards possible tasks and towards possible ways of achieving my objectives. In perceiving something, I am already perceptually directed towards it and towards perceiving it a certain way. This also implies that what is perceived is already posited as some*thing*, something other than me which I perceptually grasp with inherent meaning *for* me.[9] My sensory perceptions of objects in the world contain projections, apprehensions—significances of perceived objects that "speak" to my body, to the ways in which I can project my body in relation to objects and movement within the world.[10]

This directedness, this perceiving of what is in front of me with significance and meaning, comes about through my bodily intentionality. My bodily existence is inherently transcendent, an openness to the world because of my perception: I bodily exist with a perceptual reach into the world. Perception *is an outward meaningful movement*, an active engagement through which a world appears. Even when I stand still to observe my environment, my gaze is a spatial outward movement of my body into the world, and my perception also entails a temporal movement, since perception is always temporally spread out.

Sensory perception is always intentional and meaningful, because it *brings forth movement and meaning*: in perception I am always reaching outside of my bodily self into the world and reach towards significances, possible tasks and possible ways of achieving my objectives. And reversely, intentionality and meaning are *in* bodily sensory perception.[11] In that sense, perception is *projection of movement and*

---

8. Merleau-Ponty, *Phenomenology of Perception*, 138. The "I" of this understanding is pre-reflective (a concept we will explore later), what Merleau-Ponty coins the *tacit cogito*. Ibid., 369–409.

9. I will discuss and make clear in more detail in what follows that this perceptual grasp does not imply a strict subject-object divide, but rather a mutual implication and interrelation.

10. Merleau-Ponty, *Phenomenology of Perception*, 153. Langer, *Merleau-Ponty's Phenomenology of Perception*, 44.

11. Merleau-Ponty argues the point by looking at learning bodily habits, such as driving a car or playing an instrument: I can steer a car through a street or play

meaning: Perception as bodily intentionality is mediated by knowledge of how sensory information would change if or when a particular path of exploratory perceptual movement is pursued.

For example: When I walk my dog in the morning, I navigate the neighborhood and the path I am taking through it with a certain perceptual understanding of how I can move in my environment, which elements feature as obstacles, as openings, as indications for me (in my specific embodiment and for me in my connection to a dog on a leash), which environmental features will be open to me, which might be treacherous, which might be inaccessible, or which might induce apprehension, fear, or desire. This is a tacit knowledge mediating my bodily perception of my environment and my bodily extensions into it—I might be thinking about what to make for breakfast or how to edit this chapter while I am moving through the neighborhood which holds bodily meaning and significances for me as I walk. Or when I join my mother in the kitchen and she directs me to sit down and watch her, I can sit down on a chair without having to make an effort to register and compare perceptual information with the location and movement of my body without charting a plan to achieve my sitting. Rather, I simply move to sit down, because I perceive the kitchen as my environment, and I perceive my mother, the stove, the chairs, already/always in relation to my body: I am facing my environment and perceive the chair to my left as a sitting opportunity for me, and as I am facing my mother in the kitchen, other areas of the house remain out of focus yet on the periphery of my perception (I might hear my sister talking on the phone in another room or marginally perceive my father through the window as he works in the garden). Further, in my perception, my environment is already emerging with a certain significance: It is a certain chair

an instrument without constantly having to analyze sensory data comparing the width of my vehicle with the street, or the position of my fingers in relation to the instrument. Thus, my perception and movements are not that of a body in a geometrical, cartographical space, but of a body relating practically and in movement to/in what Merleau-Ponty calls "practical" space—a space correlating to my bodily perceptual movements. Merleau-Ponty, *Phenomenology of Perception*, 141–146.

I desire to sit on, and I know I will be able to sit on a chair and rest my arm on the table because I can project certain bodily movements into my environment.

Bodily intentionality is my perceptual extension as an "I can." In other words, my basic experience is not that of "I think," but a sense of "I can" in my world, a sense of grasping perceptually how I can extend and move in the world.[12] Iris Marion Young's famous essay *Throwing like a Girl* describes how female bodies are shaped perceptually because bodily intentionality is gendered. Bodily intentionality, the sensory perceptual projection or apprehension of significances of my environment that relate to my specific embodiment, implies possibilities of movement and expression, but also opacities, resistances, and limits resulting in inhibitions or hesitancies in expressive bodily intentions.[13] For example, while boys might be encouraged to engage in rough play, a girl in this situation might be warned to not get herself hurt or dirty. To get dirty or hurt during play can result in disapproval, disapproval which signals the failure of extending and moving like a girl, the failure of being a girl "correctly." It is a failure of acquiring "acceptable" bodily extensions as a girl, *as well as* the failure to achieve the perception or the status of being a boy.[14]

For women, Young argues, bodily intentionality, the tacit understanding of "I can" is also an "I cannot," an inhibited and ambivalent bodily intentionality, grounded in the situation of women (not in their anatomy or physiology) as condition by sexist oppression.[15] This "I cannot" is not *in place* of the "I can"; it is not female intentionality in

12. "Consciousness is in the first place not a matter of 'I think that' but of 'I can.'" Ibid., 136.
13. Iris Marion Young, *On Female Body Experience: "Throwing Like a Girl" and Other Essays*, Studies in Feminist Philosophy (New York, NY: Oxford University Press, 2005), 42.
14. Gail Weiss, *Body Images: Embodiment as Intercorporality* (New York, NY: Routledge, 1999), 45.
15. Young, *On Female Body Experience*, 42. Specifically, she observes particularly gendered modalities of movement when throwing a ball, noting restrictions in movement in girls. Ibid., 27–45.

place of male "I can" bodily intentionality. Rather, it is a co-existing "I cannot" with the "I can" of "'someone,' and not truly *her* possibilities."[16] This gender difference in bodily intentionality, this gendered self-transcendence, is a gendered bodily perceptual orientation that is both an effect of gendered differences as well as a mechanism for their reproduction.[17]

How we perceptually extend into the world (and thereby experience, know, and order our world) is not universal, neither historically nor culturally. Modern Western culture is a visual culture, and more often than not, our first orientation in a situation and tacit knowledge of others today is visually based: To become familiar with a new situation we "take a look around," or "scope it out." But neither did we always perceptually extend in this fashion, nor are all cultures today tuned into vision as a dominant sense.

Gendered intentionalities in medieval Europe were encoded along differentiations of and within gendered perceptual capacities. Sight and hearing were typically male senses and classified as distance senses, whereas smell, taste and touch were female senses and senses of proximity. Men were typically associated with what was understood as the nobler quality of the sense (e.g., employing it for intellectual and public activities), women with the more ignoble (looking around for sensual and selfish ends). For example, speech as a sense "belonging" to both men and women, manifest properly in gendered intentionalities: speech was a more appropriate extension of men; women may use it, but their proper aural extension ought to be controlled, well, by silence. Speech as bodily extension had gendered possibilities and purposefulness. Aurality extended women, though the quality of their perceptual grasp was gendered, associated with either seduction or nagging (limiting women's perceptual reach to the proximate, domestic realm and towards sensual/selfish desires). In that sense, for a woman to extend through speech "properly" was impossible, an oxymoron, since proper

16. Ibid., 37. Emphasis in original.
17. Ahmed, *Queer Phenomenology*, 60.

speech was restricted to rational—male—discourse, and the best female aural "I can" was to not move aurally at all.[18]

Eve having failed in the Garden of Eden because of her unrestrained appetite was the model women for medieval sensory typing of taste as the "original" female sense. Connected to speech via orality, it fell on women to extend themselves tasteful by properly controlling and restricting their gustatory movements. Holding her tongue and restricting her output and input (fasting from speech and food) were the proper tacit knowledges of how to move into the world in/as her body. Failing to do so risked a double failure—the "proper" failure of male orality as well as the failure to properly extend like a woman. Such a double failure was the "I can" of witches and hags. The social policing and shaping of women's sensory movements found particularly gruesome manifestation in witch hunts, when improper perceptual extensions (of female speech, touch, smell, etc.) threatened male occupation of "higher" sensory realms and associated power.[19]

The gendered social realm—men in the public sphere and women in the domestic realm—was also perceptually constructed, as for example, the ideal sensory realm for women was of proximity to her body, and her "natural' inclination was restricted motility in her smelling, tasting and touching to fulfill domestic duties.[20]

Across cultures, we find with the Ongee in Southeast Asia a world perceptually inhabited through olfactory intentionalities. The identifying characteristic of life force to reside in smell. Smell is *the* fundamental cosmic principle; time is conceived of as cycles of smell, and the calendar is a calendar of scents. References to the self are made through pointing at the nose, as the identity of every living being is composed of smells, and disruptions in bodily functions (e.g., illness) are conceived

18. Classen, *Color of Angels*, 74–75.
19. Ibid., 78. The 15th century Malleus Maleficarum, a witch hunting manual, reads like a guidebook to the gendered manifestation of the senses and associated classifications. It went through more than 30 editions in the 200 years after its first publication.
20. Ibid., 65–66.

as imbalances of odor, with death being the loss of personal odor. Personal growth is marked and symbolized through olfactory development, and social relations are expressed and limited through customs and rituals concerning odor control/flow.[21]

For the Ongee, odor is not an elusive, intangible sensation, but rather bodily movement that has a weight and must be regulated. Monitoring of olfactory bodily intentionality is done through different sexed/gendered bodily techniques. Women's bodily capacity for menstruation is a natural means of odor-weight regulation, whereas men are more prone to olfactory imbalances.[22] Again, gendered bodily perceptual orientation is not a visual extension, though a visualist observer very likely notices gendered patterns of bodily decoration in Ongee clay body paint and interprets these bodily perceptual practices as images and visual symbols of social status. But rather, Ongee clay paint body "decoration" is an odor control act connected to olfactory movement: application of clay paint is experienced as regulation of temperature in order to bind smell to the body and also altering particular olfactory bodily extension.[23]

These are bodily perceptual orientations, not superstitions or pseudo-theories that can be dismissed as not "true." Ongee bodily perceptual orientations are different and complex experiences and responses to the world. It might be difficult for us to "see" this from a hypervisual cultural standpoint, but as noted before, through time even our own

21. Classen, *Worlds of Sense*, 126–130. Vishvajit Pandya, *In the Forest: Visual and Material Worlds of Andamanese History (1858–2006)* (Lanham, MD: University Press of America, 2009), 36–47.
22. Vishvajit Pandya, *Above the Forest: A Study of Andamanese Ethnoanemology, Cosmology, and the Power of Ritual* (New York, NY: Oxford University Press, 1993), 120–122.
23. This is important, for example, in bodily movements when hunting, where tracking, hunting, and interactions between animal and human are conceived of as variables of movement and smell. The smell emitted from a body is described as moving slowly or like a snake. White paint cools the body, inhibiting the release of smell from that particular bodily location, with red clay paint experienced the opposite way. Pandya, *In the Forest*, 109–115.

Western perceptual coordinations changed, and with them, the tacit knowledges regarding how to be as bodies.

RELATIONS OF INTENTIONALITY

Our bodily intentionality is not unidirectional, we are part of *relations of intentionality* between body and world.[24] Relations of intentionality are at least two-fold: I exist as body in an environment and perceptually extend into the world. My intentionality is not a separate consciousness directing outward movement. A kitchen cabinet is high *for me*, a napkin is out of line on the table *for me;* the world is there *towards* and *for* me. This about-me-ness of the world affects my perceptual experience and the meaning of my environment in ways I do not consciously choose—my environment always appears as inevitably meaning something (i.e., the for-me-ness appears to me as meaning inherent in the object). My perceptions, and thereby my experiences and conduct, are affected by this relation of body and world toward/about each other.[25]

Relations of intentionality also exist between conscious intentions and pre-reflective bodily intentions, relations which orient me towards the world and my concerns in and with it:[26] When my mother teaches me how to cook a dish, I already move into this experience perceptually. It is not my mind utilizing my senses to access the situation. I move into the situation bodily by seeing, touching, smelling, hearing, remembering, asking questions, and so forth. When my mother instructs me to get up from the chair and stir the food on the stove, I do not have to direct my perceptual attention to my hand to intentionally guide it, or figure out how exactly to hold the

24. Merleau-Ponty, *The Structure of Behavior,* 220.
25. "Everything is both manufactured and natural in man, as it were, in the sense that there is not a word, not a form of behavior which does not owe something to purely biological being—and which at the same time does not elude the simplicity of animal life, and cause forms of vital behavior to deviate from their pre-ordained direction, through a sort of leakage and through a genius for ambiguity which might serve to define man." Merleau-Ponty, *Phenomenology of Perception,* 189.
26. Ibid., 189, 440.

spoon. I just move to stir the food. I move around the kitchen without consciously giving myself instructions on where and how to move my body. I intuitively reach for a footstool to access items on a shelf otherwise beyond my reach. Unless there is a problem—an item I did not see blocking my access to the stove, the spoon greasy and slipping out of my grip—I am a body moving without having to think about it. I might ponder a shopping list, listen to my mother share the next step of the meal preparation, or absentmindedly gaze out the window. I do not think about stirring food to then execute a plan for it. I have a perceptual understanding of how my body can move in this situation, and what certain objects in my environment mean to me, how my environment *is* for me. I am not explicitly aware of how my body reaches for the spoon and how my hand anticipates the spoon by taking up a receptive gesture. I have a conscious intention, to stir the food in the pot.

My bodily intentionality that is my sensory perception directs my extension and movement into my environment, it orients me by bestowing meaning and significances to my surroundings, specifically in regard to my particular embodiment and capacities. My bodily movements are intentional but do not necessarily occupy my conscious awareness. This is what Merleau-Ponty calls "motor intentionality," the movements of my body within which my body "disappears," the ways in which my body operates without my conscious activation of it because I tacitly know how to move in my world.[27]

Bodily perception is movement and movement is bodily perception.[28] This interrelation is significant: movement brings about meaning; meaning is sited in movement; and because perception is embedded with movement, meaning is embedded with perceptual processes. Movement is at play in *all* sensory perception. Even vision, for example, which in contemporary Western culture is often understood

27. Ibid., 106.
28. "Motility is the primary sphere in which initially the meaning of all significances (*der Sinn aller Signifikationen*) is engendered ..." Ibid., 142.

as passive reception, is effected and affected through movement.[29] Sensorimotor movement affects and effects visual perception, or more generally, the relation between stimuli and motility constitutes perception.

Take color, for example: Visual perception of color does not just relate to, but requires eye movements: seeing colors such as red depends on the structure of the changes occurring when movement occurs (movement of the perceiver or the perceived).[30] The *motor* significance to color must be understood in terms of an embodied dialectic, that is, bodily movement brings about acts of evaluation which reveal the motor values of color.[31] This dialectic implicates sensation and movement in mutual transformation. In other words, the relation between sensory perception and embodied movement does not cohere to physical laws, but is a situation which is eternally open to its own development.[32] For example, the association of colors with qualities (e.g., "warm" and "cool") is an acquired association, not a precise determinate one. Once we see color in a certain way, once we learned to move in certain visual manners, it is not only the color that changed "for us," but we changed with it—the quality of the color is now something enacted by me, a part of what my perceptual experience.[33]

29. Conceiving of the visual gaze as passive is not a historical or universal notion. See Wade, *A Natural History of Vision.*

30. Marratto, *The Intercorporeal Self,* 25–27. Marratto uses research by cognitive scientists O'Regan and Noë.

31. "Thus, before becoming an objective spectacle, quality is revealed by a type of behaviour which is directed toward it in its essence, and this is why my body has no sooner adopted the attitude of blue than I am vouchsafed a quasi-presence of blue. We must therefore stop wondering how and why red signifies effort or violence, green restfulness and peace; we must rediscover how to live these colours as our body does, that is, as peace or violence in concrete form ... red, by its texture as followed and adhered to by our gaze, is already the amplification of our motor being." Merleau-Ponty, *Phenomenology of Perception,* 211.

32. Ibid., 210.

33. Marratto, *The Intercorporeal Self,* 67–68.

Each of my specific and contextually contingent involvements with a color (e.g., the red of the chili peppers on the kitchen table, the red of the grape juice served during a Christian communion ritual) reconfigures my sensorimotor bodily perceptions in following encounters with that color, that is, opens up new possibilities or manners of perceiving this color when I am confronted with it again. And each future encounter with that color (the red of chili sauce in an American Thai restaurant, red of my blood when I cut my finger, the red of the American flag hoisted on the university grounds) involves a further articulation of the history of my involvement with red. This implies that perceptual relations or "laws" (like the perception of red connected to a certain length of light waves) are also contingent to historical, cultural, and individual contexts:[34] The association of specific colors with perceptual and social values is neither static nor universal. In Ancient Rome, blue was associated with hostile Otherness, a barbaric and suspicious color to be avoided. German poet Goethe published the 1810 *Theory of Color*, describing blue as active, warm, luminous (reflecting the socio-cultural perceptual formation of Romanticism).[35]

The Western gendered color association of feminine, delicate, sweet looking pink for girls and blue for boys is a fairly recent one (it was reversed before, with pink as a shade of red signaling vitality for boys, blue symbolizing the daintiness of girls), and the relationship between children's sex and corresponding color as gender signifier itself is also modern (different from the more practical—bleachable—white of previous decades of children's clothing).[36] Red is never *just red*, and red never just *is*. Is it always the red of the shirt I am wearing today as I am typing in my office, or the red of the paper flower in the card from my parents that I remember receiving

34. We will explore these contingencies further subsequently.
35. Michel Pastoureau, *Blue: The History of a Color*, trans. Markus I. Cruse (Princeton, NJ: Princeton University Press, 2001), 26, 138.
36. See Jo B. Paoletti, *Pink and Blue: Telling the Boys from the Girls in America* (Bloomington, IN: Indiana University Press, 2012), 85–99.

in the mail yesterday, the red of my cultural repertoire that speaks of "seeing red" or receiving the "red carpet treatment;" the red of the spine chakra or the yang energy of red on the other hand, may not "be" for me.[37]

BODY SCHEMA AND TACIT KNOWLEDGES

> I understand my body-self as unified whole in movement. I am an expressive unity which we can learn to know only by actively taking it up, this structure will be passed on to the sensible world. The theory of the body schema is, implicitly, a theory of perception.[38]

Merleau-Ponty's concept of *body schema* may be understood as something like a blueprint that configures my specific way of being as body in a given environment: body schema structures perceptions and sense of self and/in relation to environment; it configures my movements and postures.[39] The body schema is a set of enduring dispositions and

37. See also, for example, Michel Pastoureau's history of the color blue in Europe, in which he investigates blue as complex cultural construct, as social phenomenon. Pastoureau, *Blue: The History of a Color*. Idiomatic uses of color also demonstrate differences, e.g., "feeling blue" in English expresses something different that "being blue" in German (referring to being drunk), or to "being голубой/light blue" in Russian (referring to being gay).

38. Merleau-Ponty, *Phenomenology of Perception*, 205–206. While this quote is lifted out of Smith's 1962 translation, I maintain my preference for "schema" over "image" (Smith uses "image").

39. Merleau-Ponty's *schéma corporel* is translated as "body image" in the Colin Smith's widely used English translation of *Phenomenology of Perception*, but I prefer the term "body schema." "Body image" can be misleading because of prevalent uses in psychology (the early use, the habitual account of images accompanying various impressions and bodily movements; the adjusted use, the image of a universal body and the awareness of general functions; nowadays the use in psychology to refer to perceptions of one's own body along social and aesthetic dimensions). Merleau-Ponty understands "body schema" to be not an image and more than just an understanding of the location of body parts. The body schema is a nonrepresentational structure of the body: My body is what embeds me in and directs me toward the world; my body schema informs my sense of perception and perceptual agency in a specific environment at a specific time. Ibid., 100–101.

capacities responsible for our enduring sense of bodily position and possibility.[40] Put differently, the

> body schema is that in virtue of which a bodily movement is a finely coordinated ensemble of motions intentionally organized in advance toward targets that are to be meaningfully moved.[41]

When reaching for a bowl in the kitchen, I do not make separate, distinct movements with different body parts; rather, I reach for it as a bodily unit with coordinated movements. When reaching for the bowl, I already prepare to grasp it tightly, in a different anticipation from how I might tacitly prepare to grasp the (perceived as wet) kitchen sponge. Perhaps the bowl is covered with a cloth and it looks full and heavy to me, so I prepare to lift it with strength, but in fact it is empty and I now yank it off the table because my bodily movements were schemed for a heavy object. The body schema, my tacit awareness of my bodily self as unit, enables this coordination or perception and bodily movement in and toward my environment.[42]

A body schema is crucial to my self-perception as bodily whole as well as to my perception of my environment and the unity of perceived

40. Using "blue print" or "enduring dispositions" might lead to a misconception of the body schema as a fixed entity or a perceptual faculty. As I hope to show in what follows, the body schema is a fluid, or moving schema of perception. It is dependent on the body-world interrelation, which continuously evolves. For an in depth philosophical exploration of what a moving body schema entails, see David Morris, *The Sense of Space*, ed. Dennis J. Schmidt, Suny Series in Contemporary Continental Philosophy (Albany, NY: State University of New York Press, 2004), 53–80. For a complex investigation into the coming about and workings of the body schema (though she uses the term "body image") as well their ethical dimensions, see Weiss, *Body Images: Embodiment as Intercorporality*, 7–37, 129–164.
41. David Morris, "Body," in *Merleau-Ponty: Key Concepts*, ed. Rosalyn Diprose and Jack Reynolds (Stocksfield, UK: Acumen, 2008), 116.
42. Carman, *Merleau-Ponty*, 231. For example, through the body schema, I know how I can move from a standing position toward a chair, and if a chair's surface will accommodate my desired sitting position. Merleau-Ponty, *Phenomenology of Perception*, 1962, p. 98 ff.

things: I interpret myself as more than just a conglomerate image of my body parts and my experiences with/of the body. It is in bodily movement that I experience myself moving as bodily unit: I sit down in the kitchen chair in what I experience as a fluid movement from standing to sitting; I move as a bodily unit rather than different body parts making separate motions. Perception and movement here are embedded with each other. Only because of my perceptual capacities can I move into and in the world, and only because of my movement can I perceive myself as bodily unit and project and "do" my movements.

Similarly, this sense of bodily unity supports the unity of embodied perceptual processes: Because any bodily movement is a synthesized assembly of various motions involving various body parts affecting a sense of bodily unit, any bodily movement also affects a synthesis of perceptually received data toward perception of something whole, a unified object. For example, when rolling a piece of dough between my fingers, I do not need to spend conscious effort to synthesize my fingers into a unit (hand), nor do I perceive several lumps of dough (one for each digit making contact), but I am perceiving a single, spherical object in my hand. This is not merely either a cognitively or mechanically achieved synthesis. This synthesis is effected by the structure of myself as conscious moving body: like movement effects a bodily sense of unity, so movement effects perceptual unity—unity of perceptual collaboration and contingencies.

Importantly, this knowledge of myself and my projection into my world is tacit, or pre-reflective, in that it does not depend on the actual execution of exploratory movement; rather, it is a tacit sense of an open-ended range of sensori-motor actions and correlated sensory information.[43]

PERCEPTUAL HABITUATION

Habits are patterns of movement, ways of moving, closely connected to our understanding of ourselves-as-bodies seen in our body schema.

---

43. Marratto, *The Intercorporeal Self*, 25.

A habit is always both motor and perceptual; a habit is to tacitly understand what is given to me in my bodily capacities as well as what is given to me in my environment. For example, to know how to type is to have acquired the habit of typing, to have a "knowledge in the hands" of what my hands can do, of where the keys on the keyboard are, and to experience an agreement between what I aim to type and what is given to me to achieve this, to experience the harmony between intention and performance.[44]

I am experiencing in bodily movements that are bodily habits. Bodily perceptual movements and habits are neither universal nor natural. The fact that I can learn to type, change my ways of typing, adjust to different keyboards or adjust to changing manual capacities demonstrates that. There is a bodily biological dimension of habit: my bodily capacity to acquire habitual movements through repetition. In moving and in learning to move, I have a bodily capacity for habit, and habits are embedded in bodily dimensions. Acquiring habits is not simply memorizing a bodily task in order to avoid discontinuities in our experience: I do not always figure out anew how to eat with a spoon, I do not always create new ways holding myself up and swinging my arms as I walk, nor do I have to figure out my walking movements in different but similar (say, level or sloping) environments.

We are again at a crucial point in our exploration where we could carelessly invoke a body/mind dualism: If we mistake bodily acquisition of habits with memorizing movement, we install a consciousness that controls bodily functions and movements. If we conceive of acquiring bodily habits as automatic mechanical movements, we frame our habits as simply a sum of mechanically linked reflexes. Our careful exploration is important if we want to avoid relegating observable gendered habits as a matter of "mind-ful" cultural influence disconnected from the matter of sexed bodies, and also avoid essentializing gendered movements as biological-bodily-mechanical reflexes of a sexed body (which would naturalize a connection between sex and gendered movement/habit).

44. Merleau-Ponty, *Phenomenology of Perception*, 143–145.

My habits are embodied knowledge, they are the bodily and practical know-how of possible ways to adhere to my environment manifest in my actions, my possible inhabitations of space. The bodily dimension of habit becomes evident in my ability to make bodily perceptual adjustments and changes in habit, such as improvisation when playing an instrument, or transferring bodily habits such as eating with the fork in the right hand instead of the left, or quickly adjusting to a different size keyboard. Without being a body, I could not acquire habits, and habits would not appear as such without the bodily dimension embodying them. To acquire bodily habits is to grasp and incorporate tacit and practical principles, principles which are only ever expressed in the actions to which they belong, and which are always principles acquired within my own body schema and within my pre-reflective relation to my environment.[45] This is most evident in learning a new skill, such as playing an instrument, a skill which I can only acquire by doing, by incorporating or absorbing new bodily competencies and understandings into my body schema. This in turn transforms my way of perceiving and acting in the world: A guitar transforms from *a* musical instrument to *mine*, now a familiar extension of my body, something I can pick up in a certain way and produce my musical performance with. A group of musicians transforms from providing external sound to extending an invitation to bodily move: to join the round of other Yoruba women and their ritual movements around the *opa sooro* and open up to be mounted by a spirit; to join the other hetero-paired dancers on the floor and take up the "lady's part" in a waltz.[46]

Merleau-Ponty's states that "habit expresses our power of dilating our being in the world, or changing our existence by appropriating

---

45. Merleau-Ponty, *Phenomenology of Perception*, 144. Nick Crossley, *The Social Body: Habit, Identity and Desire* (Thousand Oaks, CA: Sage Publications Inc, 2001), 127.
46. Even intellectual learnings, such as reading, are still bodily activities and/or presuppose a competence in bodily activity (such as reading, or engaging in language games which allow me to incorporate linguistic principles as habits into my corporeal schema). Crossley, *The Social Body*, 128.

fresh instruments."[47] He not only points to the acquisition of skills through acquiring habits; rather, he claims that a change in habit, a change "in our patterns of movement, is a change to *our way of being in the world*—a claim that would be utterly extraordinary if we were not already pursuing the problem of how meaning is engendered within bodily movement."[48] My bodily movements are inherently infused with habits, and my ways of moving, habitual, are what give me a body schema, an "I can," a bodily blue-print that configures my specific way of being in my body in a given environment. My acquisition of habits is realized in bodily intentionality, in my self-transcendence, in the ways I perceptually move and express myself, project myself into my environment, in the ways I act and re-act, re-work my movements toward an anticipated and perceived environment.

Yet habits are social as much as they are biological, and though these two dimensions need to be distinguished, they are not separate or reducible to each other. My bodily habits are more than mere adaptive instincts; a feature of my life as human is that of being a socio-cultural being, in other words, I do not simply adapt to my environment, but I can also adapt my environment through the construction of material culture, through the settling of my bodily habits into nature (i.e., I do not simply exist in my environment detachedly, but my bodily habits "settle" through constructing houses, roads, villages, churches, tools, musical instruments, etc.).[49]

This physical transformation of the world only functions as culture to the extent that it is used by persons, and used according to the meaning socially associated to it. A kitchen is only a kitchen in its specific socio-cultural construction as long as people are disposed to prepare foods in this kind of structure and habitually refer to it as kitchen. This kind of social habit (cooking in a kitchen) presupposes that the meaning of "kitchen" has been incorporated within my body schema. And significantly, my movements in a kitchen and incorporation of kitchen

47. Merleau-Ponty, *Phenomenology of Perception*, 143.
48. Morris, "Body," 117. Emphasis in original.
49. Merleau-Ponty, *Phenomenology of Perception*, 346.

objects into my habitual movements effect a further and crucial trans-formation of my way of being in and experiencing the world, for exam-ple, kitchen tools may become an extension of me as body as I cook.

Many of my habits are acquired from what I see performed around me and am able to copy from a social collective pool.[50] The social habit of cooking in a kitchen is a habit socially shaped for gendered bodies in the context of my childhood environment (familial and social). Thus social mechanisms controlling and enforcing bodily movements also encourage a female "I can" in the specific cultural constructions of this space: As woman, I am not out of place in a private kitchen, but rather my bodily intentionality can tap into a social pool of female bodily habit, and kitchen gadgets may become incorporated into my body schema. For a gendered male body, kitchen utensils might come to be perceived as objects to be utilized (rather than bodily extensions of the self) in a space where bodily movements have not necessarily been acquired as bodily habits—and if they have been, it is something to be noted ("your husband cooks?").

The meaning perceptually emerging between body and world is inherently tied to the perception of gendered bodies and their move-ments. Perceiving myself and my mother in the kitchen emerges with bodily and social meanings related to cooking, provision of food and nurture; perceiving my father entering the kitchen emerges with bodily and social meanings invoking perhaps the entering women's space to receive a meal. These perceptions of bodily movements emerge out of the interplay between bodily habits and social habits, the interrelation between social deposits of habit and incorporation of those habits by gendered bodies, and the transformation of our ways of being and experiencing the world: In my family we take up gendered roles; my mother, sister, and I incorporate gendered social habits and emerge in socially gendered space within gendered social roles, which transforms our being and experience in the world. As women, we enter the kitchen

50. Crossley, *The Social Body*, 129. I will discuss this social collective pool further via creativity/innovation and habituation in regard to social and bodily habits, particularly language.

of our home as extension of our bodily space and tacitly know how to be and move in this space. The meanings emerging between body and world as we move in the kitchen might be different from those emerging between the body of my father and the world/kitchen. My father, incorporating male gendered social habits takes up movements through which the world perceptually emerges differently, might be bodily and socially out of place and not bodily habituated to a kitchen as cultural space for his body-self.[51]

Gendered habits, habitually acquired gendered movements, display how bodily experience constitutes a gendered world, and how in turn gendered bodily experiences are constituted by the world.[52] My movements constitute my world and what the world means for me in my own idiosyncratic physiological and psychical constitution. But I am also constituted by a world acting upon me; my bodily habits, subtended by my body schema, always already reflect the particularities and generalities of a given situation in which social habits (or better: habits

51. Christopher Carrington, in his study of lesbigay families and embodiments of domesticity, also points out that cooking as gendered habituation of feeding is more than simply an act of food preparation, but involves planning, shopping, preparation, and management of meals. It presumes a variety of knowledges about food, about the household, about cultural rules and practices, about management of related household activities, etc., and the cooking/feeding habituations are also informed by class, ethnicity, and other socio-structural factors. Carrington finds that feeding work plays significantly into the construction of lesbian or gay families, complexly structuring the gendered and spatial movements and connected meanings emerging within the household. Christopher Carrington, *No Place Like Home: Relationships and Family Life among Lesbians and Gay Men* (Chicago, IL: Chicago University Press, 1999), 29–65.

52. See also Simone de Beauvoir's works for a sexed/gendered phenomenology of experience. De Beauvoir critiques male philosophers, her contemporary Merleau-Ponty included, for their systematic bias toward male experience. "Woman, like man, *is* her body; but her body is something else than she is." Emphasis original. Simone de Beauvoir, *The Second Sex*, trans. H. M. Parshley (Harmondsworth, UK: Penguin, 1953), 67. For an analysis of how de Beauvoir's work is more akin to and in critical conversation with Merleau-Ponty (and even eclipsing him regarding matters of difference) than the often assumed philosophical indebtedness to Sartre, see Sara Heinämaa, *Toward a Phenomenology of Sexual Difference* (Lanham, MD: Rowman & Littlefield Publishers, Inc., 2003).

shaped and "moved" by social values) bear on my bodily movements:[53] Throwing like a girl, playing like a boy, sitting like a woman, talking like a man, and so on, are ways in which gendered bodies constitute the world and the movement of bodies in it, of the meaning and movements with objects and within space. And this in turn constitutes the meaning of the gendered body, and how a body and bodily movement are gendered by the world acting upon it.[54]

PERCEPTUAL GENDER LINES

The gendered subject emerges with sensory perception habitually referring to her gendered female body. I am directed and placed along perceptual lines in a gendered grid, lines that are like traces of what is perceptually possible—movements that I-as-female can follow and in my following, the gender grid itself disappears in my movements while I get stuck in line and as the line through my habitual movements.[55] "Myself-as-her" and my environment have gendered significances: What is large or small, what is graspable, what is achievable, what is something I want or desire, is oriented for me along gendered lines. I emerge as female body extending through specific gestures, postures, perceptual acts (like speech, vision, or tactile movements), and perceive the world habitually as gendered, aligned with being female and with what is for females, namely what perceptually within reach, up for grabs, in-sync *for me-her*.

Gendered perceptual orientations do not cause gendered differences nor are they simply given. But within sexing and gendering perceptual norms, bodies and world emerge differently and are perceived

---

53. Weiss, *Body Images: Embodiment as Intercorporality*, 11.

54. See also Gayle Salamon's original investigation into bodily experiences of transgender persons, accounting for the construction of transsexual selves using an intersubjectively produced body schema, the felt sense of a trans(itioning) body, a body that might not "be" one's material substance. Gayle Salamon, *Assuming a Body: Transgender and Rhetorics of Materiality* (New York, NY: Columbia University Press, 2010).

55. Ahmed, *Queer Phenomenology*, 57, 66.

differently. The perceived differences in gendered bodily shaping are a sign of perceptual orientations these bodies have taken, toward themselves and toward the world. Bodily perceptual orientations involve inhabiting the world and occupying the world with objects in certain bodily perceptual ways: Walking, speaking, looking, sitting, dressing, scenting, and so forth. In turn, bodies are shaped by the objects they take up and by *how* we take them up to extend into the world, which positions and gestures we trace and align with to inhabit our environment.[56]

In medieval Europe, the science of temperature provided a grid to perceptually align bodies as gendered: Drawn by ancient authorities like Aristotle and supported by contemporary scholarship and folklore were contrasting lines of "cold" women and "hot" men. These medieval perceptions of body parts or bodily interiors perceptually aligned gendered intentionality through temperature. Male bodies perceptually extended through movement of heat, as perceived by the outward extension of genitals and the evidence of baldness in males (lack of hair was a sign that the excessive heat in men tended to burn up their hair). Women's innate coldness and moistness (due to being "half-baked," insufficiently gestated males) inhibited their bodily movement, since coldness was associated with inactivity. It also framed female bodily movement as inwardly directed; rather than burning up food, women stored it, in order to bodily move inward for processes of pregnancy and nourishment of children.[57]

Scientific theories on temperature also functioned to align social bodily intentionality and divisions. Bodily perceptual intentionality, movement, was perceived and structured through temperature: "acting like a woman" was perceived as refraining from vigorous physical body-temperature raising activity (it used up the internally stored heat and burned up their fat and menstrual blood, preventing pregnancy). Visual perceptions of gender transgressions—such as women with male genitals or external female genitals of a size larger than "normal," facial hair,

56. Ibid., 59.
57. Ibid., 64–65.

lower voices, broader shoulders—were perceived according to and as effect of transgression of perceptual alignments in terms of perceptual overextension of temperature (generation and outward movement of too much heat).[58]

The medieval gendered female body also emerged by extending in specifically scented ways, and is perceptually recognized through alignments of odor. These olfactory extensions and productions are both an effect of gendered differences (body-specific fluids involved in sexual arousal, menstruation, and childbirth have particular odors, though the association, meaning, and value associated is variable) as well as a mechanism for their reproduction (e.g., medical science employs olfactory technologies such as scents to move body parts, perfuming as perceptually significant act).

The science and lore about the womb sketched out the traces for bodily olfactory movements that body functions perceptually aligned with. Rooted in pagan lore and classical philosophy which described the uterus as a kind of animal with the power to move and a sense of smell, women's bodily intentionality was perceptually aligned with a scented womb capable of olfaction. In other words, women's outward bodily movements were connected with movements of the womb which could smell (in both meanings of the word) and move about the body. Thus, body technologies to perceptually align female bodies included scented treatments, such as encouraging a displaced womb (a case of her sex getting to her head) through administering scents to lure it back into place.[59] Women were perceived as particularly productive of odor, and perceptual constitutions aligned women in general with malodor, most often associated with the functions of a female womb. Repetitive association of perceptual productions (smells) with gendered bodies

58. Ibid., 65. Perceptual meaning and assigned values could shift, such as heat symbolizing racial perceptions with the beginning of the renaissance. The thermal scheme now aligned non-Europeans, particularly Africans, South Americans, and Indians with heat, representing feminine sensuality and indolence in contrast to "cold" European masculine rationality, industry, and order. Classen, *The Color of Angels*, 67.

59. Ibid., 69.

and bodily functions then also served as perceptual orienting lines of morality. For example, sexual activity was considered to particularly increase the odor production of the womb. Virgin maidens perceptually emerged as fragrant, with pleasant aroma; a malodorous woman was aligned with lesser virtue: since women of bad character gave off the worst smells, malodor was perceptual proof of sexual licentiousness.[60]

Sensory orientation lines have social significance. Medieval Euro-Western class ideologies and distinctions and concepts of the self-aligned bodies and sensory perceptions of bodies, paralleling gender sensory symbolism. Aligned with the lower senses of taste, touch and smell, and orientated toward "class-perceiving," "lower" class bodies were perceived as foul-smelling, preoccupied with their bellies (food and drink consumption) and sexual satisfaction. Olfactory alignments allowed some bodies with certain scents or lacking others to achieve or access certain objects or spaces in line or lined up for them, while being "holding lines" for others. For example, since odors were considered to affect and penetrate body and brain directly, public health regulations regarding occupation of public spaces effectively segregated public spaces along class lines. Male priests extended through the fragrance of rose garlands and incense (scents associated with and obtainable by the divine, restricted to male); the dead bodies of saints (male and female) extended fragrant scents aligning them with holiness; rich families buried their deceased with spices and herbs to effect the alignment with sanctity over against malodorous moral corruption; women can effect redemption through emptying themselves of ill odors (e.g., fasting to repress menstruation) and being divinely infused with sacred fragrance.[61]

The significance of class and selfhood as social concepts in 18th and 19th century urbanization and industrialization of Europe sketched new traces for sensory perceptions and alignments. Ideas about selfhood

---

60. Ibid., 51.
61. Constance Classen, David Howes, and Anthony Synott, *Aroma: The Cultural History of Smell* (New York, NY: Routledge, 1994), 52–54. Classen, *The Color of Angels*, 70–71.

were linked to class formation, which was aligned along olfactory perceptions. Laboring classes were aligned with reeking bad scents, perceptually emerging as foul and dangerous smelling. The bourgeoisie "disappeared" scent-wise behind these olfactory alignments and emerged perceptually as inodorate, without bad scents, thus able to re-emerge as individual selves through individuated smells and habits of perfuming.[62]

These kinds of perceptual alignments of gendered motility extend to perceptions of interior bodily/biological functions as well as conceptual or cultural movements continue today. For example, social habits of perception along gendered alignments of movement (such as passive/receptive femininity and active/aggressive masculinity) shape perception in research on human conception. The descriptive language used betrays the perceptual alignments. Scientific narratives describe "objectively" along gendered perceptual alignments, for example, when the female egg is dependent in its inhibited motility, drifting along the fallopian tube and perceptually emerging as passively awaiting the arrival of the fastest male sperm with the strongest thrust which will penetrate it.[63]

PERCEIVING ALIGNED SEXUALITIES AND PERVERSIONS

Our bodily intentionality orients us toward gendered objects and desires, so that our bodies "have" a sexual orientation—we are bodily *directed and placed in relation to each other* a certain way. Sexuality

---

62. Smith, *Sensing the Past*, 67.
63. Martin, "The Egg and the Sperm." Martin also points out that when scientific observations acknowledge a more active role of the egg in the fertilization process (such as discovering that the egg actively takes in the sperm which by its own movement would not be capable of entering through the egg's membrane), these observations are either still aligned with the given frame of gendered motility mentioned previously, or framed within other cultural stereotypes, albeit negative, such as the egg as female aggressor luring and capturing the sperm like a devouring spider.

and sexual desire are a facing and moving toward an object of sexual desire, and sexual embodiment in Western culture seeks to habituate hetero-directional perceptual orientation.[64] This reinforces and maintains the already discussed gendered bodily intentionality: To be placed directionally and relationally is to be encouraged or limited in wherefrom and where-to and how I can bodily perceptually extend and move.

The contemporary concept of "gender performativity" can be mapped in our explorations. Judith Butler advanced gender identity as performative, explaining how gender identity emerges from repeated accomplished performances.[65] There is no ontologically "natural" sex or gender; rather, gender is accomplished by repeating certain intelligible performances—intelligible because they already conform to sexual norms regulating and legitimating certain gender perceptions and appearances (and undermining those different from the circumscribed).[66] When we conceive of sexuality as bodily intentionality, then sexuality (as identity and as behavior) is a manifestation of bodily perceptual movement that shows how we are not simply oriented toward, or transcend toward something, but how our bodily perceptual orientation in the world is a bodily dialectic. The body in its sexual intentionality, the body that transcends into the world, perceives the proximity of other bodies around it and moves along bodily perceptual gendered orientations with other bodies into and within the world.[67]

64. Ahmed, *Queer Phenomenology*, 66–68.
65. Butler, *Gender Trouble: Feminism and the Subversion of Identity*.
66. Ibid., 25.
67. Merleau-Ponty considers sexual existence to investigate the dialectic of intentionality in body-world experiences, when intentionality of body and world come together so that body and world come to exist and to mean something for each other together. However, Judith Butler notes a heterosexual norm at work in Merleau-Ponty's account of sexed embodiment and bodily intentionality, with bodily perceptual orientations aligned with heterosexual desire. Furthermore, Butler points to an alignment in Merleau-Ponty between male sexuality and a specific perceptual movement, namely the gaze, which in gendered bodily perceptual orientations emerges as a disembodied gaze that objectifies what it observes. Judith Butler, "Sexual Ideology and Phenomenological Description: A Feminist Critique of Merleau-Ponty's *Phenomenology of Perception*," in *Thinking Muse: Feminism and*

Differently sexed bodies are put into *alignment* with differently gendered bodily perceptual movements (performances), setting the stage for gendered bodily perceptual orientations to be directed toward the other sex/gender. Thus it is not simply that desire as bodily intentionality orients me in a certain direction, toward the other-body of my desire, but the *direction* my bodily perceptual orientation is lined up as makes some bodies available for desire and leaves others un-desirable, unavailable for bodily perceptual orientation and intentional movement of desire and connected sexual habits.[68]

Modern bodily perceptual orientations align gender and sex with identity. To display a certain bodily perceptual orientation in sexual desire is to *be* that desire, as in "being a heterosexual" or being a homosexual."[69] Sexed bodies become gendered along heteronormative lines through bodily perceptual orientation and habitual intentionality, as sex and bodily intentionality become aligned: being a man is to be bodily perceptually oriented and to move toward (desire) a woman through acquired gendered habits, and being a woman is to be bodily perceptually oriented and to move toward (desire) a man through acquired gendered habits. Bodily perceptual orientations toward sexual others then confirm and establish the meaning of what I am as a body (woman) by directing my bodily intentionality toward what I am not (man).[70] Sexed bodies are aligned with gendered motility, as well as with other bodies along heterosexual orientations to line up sex and gender, regulating perceptual movements (desire).

Modern French Philosophy, ed. Jeffner Allen and Iris Marion Young (Bloomington, IN: Indiana University Press, 1989), 86.

68. Ahmed, *Queer Phenomenology*, 70.

69. See the work of Michel Foucault to trace the idea of sexuality and sexual identity, particularly in regard to subjectivity. Michel Foucault, *The History of Sexuality: An Introduction*, trans. Robert Hurley (New York, NY: Vintage Books, 1978).

70. Judith Butler, *The Psychic Life of Power: Theories in Subjection* (Stanford, CA: Stanford University Press, 1997), 23.

Bodily perceptual orientations of gendered sexual desire have been explored through perceptual symbolism that privileges sight, like the Freudian Oedipus complex or Lacan's mirror image. In the Ongee world, attraction and desire include bodily adorning and ornamental practices, but they are experienced in olfactory ways: body paint and adornments are manipulations of scent to establish, align, control, and regulate odors. This is of course not to indicate that odor is the *only* bodily perceptual extension regulating Ongee life. Sensory perceptions intermingle and interact, though perceptual orientations may be formed with hierarchies, or better, preferences of one/some perceptual ability informing others (we will explore this more later on).

Ongee olfactory alignment orients toward preferred couplings between the two principal groups of their society, turtle hunters (associated with the seaside and its smells) and pig hunters (associated with the forest and its odors). Turtle hunters are those perceptually extending with keen eye sight, pig hunters are aligned with superiority of hearing. Marriages between these two groups are preferred to establish a union of sight and hearing, the alignment of these perceptual capacities following olfactory divisions of land and sea. The marriage ceremony is a ritual of body painting—again aligning bodies through aligning mutual olfactory desire, penetration and release of scent, if you will.[71]

Sexual identities and erotic desires that make some bodies available for desire and others undesirable are oriented through aligned identities as pig hunters and turtle hunters. Recognition and identification as sexual subject follows bodily olfactory motilities and is directed along olfactory lines—habitually learned facing of the hetero-scented group. This is not to imply that there are no gender divisions or no technologies to ensure heterosexual couplings (in the sense of heterosexuality as perceived identity and bodily orientation). Marriage is bodily movement of a man out of his clan's territory into that of the woman's clan, but the meaning emerging is that of "hetero-odorous" couples, if you will.[72]

71. Ibid., 115–127.
72. Pandya, *Above the Forest*, 21–24.

We can connect here two earlier observations, namely that our patterns of movement, our habitual intentionality, are a way of being in
the world (and implicitly, that a change in movement is a change of our
way of *being*), and that our bodily intentionality is a form of movement within which my body disappears. While the later observation
was made by Merleau-Ponty to highlight the ways in which I move my
body without consciously activating different bodily parts, this extends
to the ways in which gendered bodily intentionalities are movements
within which gendered bodies and the gendering work/habituation/
circumscribed performances disappear by way of making heterosexual desire the "normal" bodily perceptual orientation of bodies, the
"natural" way of being in the world. In other words, sexual bodily
perceptual orientations become habituated in a way to make certain
directions of (sexual) movement/desire normal (lined up "right"), and
it is changes in those movements, such as turning from a heterosexual
alignment, that make this way of being appear different, not aligned,
out of line, not straight, not normal.

To exemplify: I perceive another or myself bodily as "lesbian,"
because my bodily perceptual orientation directs me in certain ways
that "lesbian" stands out against those bodies falling in and disappear-
ing behind a heteronormative line. This body stands out to me because
it fails to align with and follow gendered bodily motility, such as lines
of desire that direct a female body (physically, sexually, emotionally,
visually) toward a male body; it stands out to me because I perceive
a bodily intentionality that moves in the presence, but not in the face
of (as in perceptually directed toward) male bodies, and thus fails to
maintain gendered movements along established perceptual orientations. Thus my bodily perceptual orientations and dis-orientations lead
to recognitions and identifications as "lesbian" because I perceive that
the sexual orientation—my bodily movement and sexual desire toward
another body—turns away from what I habitually learned to face.

I do remember noticing the gendering of my perception and bodily
intentionality, from "yeah, I can do that" to "I cannot do that because
I am a girl," when my carefree movements and oral/aural extension into
the world changed to unconsciously guarded postures and monitored

speech. And I remember when my habitual, implicit perception of myself as "straight" (my bodily perceptual orientation aligned to desire male bodies) changed to perceiving myself as lesbian (my bodily intentionality turning from condoned gendered habits to being directed toward female bodies, my bodily perceptual orientation aligning with a "deviant" object of desire). This alignment with a lesbian bodily perceptual orientation is only possible because "lesbian" is already a perceptual line, namely one that crosses those heteronormative orientations established in the first place, one that turns from the lines maintained as "straight."

The figure of speech "coming out of the closet" is another example of conceptual alignment of movement. Disclosing of a lesbian, gay, bisexual, or transgender identity (remember the previously discussed alignment between bodily orientations of desire and identity) invokes a bodily movement from invisibility or hiding toward visibility and social disclosure of sexual preferences toward specific sexed or gendered bodies not typically aligned with one's own perceived sex and gender. Significant here is that this kind of bodily movement is perceptually assigned to those bodies that are not falling in line with the socially habituated heteronormative orientations of sexual desire ("straight" bodies do not need to disclose their heterosexuality and "come out"). This movement of disclosure toward bodily perception as non-heterosexually desiring body is a bodily motility assigned and required of bodies whose desires are not able or willing to maintain heteronormative alignments. In other words, only bodies conforming to social habits of alignments have the privilege of maintaining their invisibility; bodies crossing lines of orientation make movements that bring them into perceptual focus. "Coming out" is a bodily movement which effects bodily transformations regarding bodily intentionality, habits, and bodily experience in the world.

Orientations and alignments do not just constitute bodies. Bodies performing out of line, against certain orientations, bodies out of place can also re-orient and reshape space and other bodies.[73] The world,

---

73. Ahmed gives the example of the kitchen regarding changing of designs as well as bodies performing in this space. Ahmed, *Queer Phenomenology*, 61.

the environment, space, inhabits bodies and is inhabited by bodies; it extends bodies and is extended by bodies. This makes subversions possible through the bodily activities performed in spaces that are oriented to not support certain bodily alignments and orientations. I am thinking, for example, of bodily perceptual subversions in spaces such as pulpits inhabited by gendered female bodies aligned with certain offices held until then by male bodies only. Or bodies performing marriage rites against and out of line with heteronormative orientations to re-orient and reshape the space of familial homes as public alignments (such as performing woman-man marriage across gender roles orientations, or performing same sex marriage in a church commonly associated with heteronormatively aligned ritual orientations). Bodies and spaces can change through changes in inhabitation, through changes in bodily intentionality/perceptual movement, through re-orientation of bodily motility and alignments. And bodies can change through traveling and traversing space, moving into spaces which are not oriented in ways that a body "knows."

To inquire into possible subversions of social hierarchies, such as gendered alignments of status or moral capacities, we must take into account the bodily perceptual orientations that are work. For example, in a cosmology ordered by smell, the stench of hell and sweet scents of heaven were perceived as in bodily and worldly realms in the context contemporary to Hildegard von Bingen. The abbess of a Benedictine convent is known for her medical writings, liturgical music compositions, and is most famous for her recorded mystical visions. Her scholarly productions already strike historians and theologians as subversive for a woman regarding her socio-cultural world, and often her ability to gain theological credibility is traced to her embracing the mystical and therefore sensory realm, rather than what was considered the scholarly rational pursuit of theology proper reserved for men. But significant here is also that it was through her bodily perceptual emergence that she could extend and move intellectually the way she did: She perceptually emerged exhaling the *odor* of sanctity, aligning her emergence with the divine in ways women commonly could not; and because in her socio-cultural world, to smell was to know, this perceptual emergence aligned her with authority (a female body exhaling divine knowledge) to subvert gendered spiritual and theological hierarchies.[74]

SENSORY INTERRELATIONS AND DIFFERENCES

Our exploration has differentiated and discussed discrete bodily senses, nevertheless we always perceive within an interplay of perceptual processes: I smell what I see what I might touch and hear. Our sensory capacities are not separable or distinct functions but are always interrelated and implicated in each other in our bodily perceptual orientations. This is synaesthesia, a certain intermingling of the senses which does not conflate different perceptual capacities, but highlights the implication and interplay of the senses (e.g., we always see a color as the color of a surface with a texture, or we "see" the coldness of an icicle).[75]

We have seen thus far in our exploration how different perceptual intentionalities (like temperature and odor) were gendered bodily movements which brought about meaning emerging with bodies and bodily functions. Gendered intentionality, like the co-existing "I cannot" with the general "I can" of someone, for European medieval or nineteenth century women, had thermal, tactile and/or olfactory dimensions not easily grasped today (though not completely without connections to, and thus conceptual understanding within, our current perceptual orientations). For example, female self-perception as effect and mechanism of perceptually produced gender differences includes a female bodily intentionality in which a body schema is shaped into a gendered body image which contains an "I cannot bodily extend through

74. Classen, *Worlds of Sense*, 47–48, 59. Crossing bodily alignments of gender perception did not necessarily result in subversions and attaining of respect or sainthood, as in Hildegard von Bingen's case. More often than not, crossing perceptual alignments in medieval Europe, such as taking up public speech or unabated visual extension, led to perceptual alignments with evil and witchcraft, a perceptual crossing of alignments violently punished. Classen, *Worlds of Sense*, 78–82.
75. Merleau-Ponty, *The Visible and the Invisible*, 134.

my smell, or my touch through _____ or other than _____" because it crosses lines of bodily intentionality which orient male subjectivity or threatens the bodily perceptual extension of bodily possibilities, of an "I can" reserved for male bodies.

Female subjects in pre-modern times emerge as bodies more than just visually extending into space through recognized physical bodily movements. For example, embodied olfactory habits are acquired knowledges "in the nose," tacit understandings of what odors are given to me, what scents my body is capable of, and tacit knowledges about my environment and others according to olfactory emergences. The body schema, the blueprint informing and configuring specific ways of being in the world, involves ways of knowing herself as a body with certain odors and temperatures which affect her being in the world, and the meaning of her movements in/as her body and in her environment. The perceptual grid aligning bodies with gender and morality as well as social status includes olfactory, tactile, and thermal orienting lines guiding bodily movements and creating bodily connections.[76] Different alignments may work together to orient us to variations in sensory symbolisms, yet without significantly disrupting gender hierarchies: a male laborer might be associated with the tactility of his work, which is still public, while an upper class lady might have been able to read and write, though it was considered to be more suitable for her to do domestic handiwork.[77]

We already have conceptual tools for this perceptual interrelation. As we have explored, my body schema, the tacit sense of my bodily

---

76. Medieval Christian rituals returned to incense (after rejecting it for its alignment with Pagan practices) and associated it with knowledge of God, in an interesting connection between cognitive-sensory, material-spiritual life. Pre-Enlightenment gardens displayed roses because of their social olfactory importance, the transformation of visual aesthetic trumping (though not replacing) scent came with the Reformation and Enlightenment. Gardens as enclosed scented spaces were also places of regulation of personal encounters and regulated gendered movements. Classen, Howes, and Synott, *Aroma: The Cultural History of Smell*, 51–92.
77. Ibid., 67–69.

"I can," comes about through bodily perceptual movement. My bodily intentionality and body schema always situate me as a bodily unit. I experience as body-unit because my bodily movements are coordinated so that my various bodily parts cohere. And since my perceptual capacities are bodily movements, I perceive as body-unit with cohering and interrelating perceptual capacities (as well as perceptual capacities interrelating with other bodily functions and abilities).

Put differently again, my bodily perceptual schema, to which my perceptions cohere and within which they are coordinated, functions as a perceptual unit. To imagine this through illustrations: I see snow and have a tacit sense of its coldness; I hear the soup on the stove come to a boil and tacitly sense its heat; I hear a loud, low voice behind me and tacitly feel where it may come from and tacitly "see" a large man behind me (and it is in disconfirmation, not confirmation, of these tacit perceptual schemata that something appears surprising to me).

We can explore interrelated gendered perceptual alignments and their subversions and crossings in 19th century European perceptual orientations of gender and smoking. Smoking as male bodily movement, a visual, tactile, oral, and olfactory perceptual extension, was a bourgeois male social habit, a way of being a man and *with* men in the world. Extending male bodies through smoke was a bodily movement grounded by tacit knowledges of masculine assertiveness and supporting emerging meaning regarding male vitality. Women who took up smoking were perceived and described to "smoke like a man," or if a wife was found smelling of smoke, she was perceived as crossing female wifely perceptual alignments and accused of marital unfaithfulness (to smell like smoke indicating a woman must have been penetrated olfactorily and bodily by another man; or to take up smoking behind the husband's back would indicate crossing gendered and sexed lines of habituation). Smoking as a bodily habit involving touching, inhaling/exhaling, smelling, and visually extending through smoking projectiles was not only a way to depict and represent sexuality (with advertisements and literary productions depicting sexual meanings through depictions of smoking), but actually involved complex and interrelated bodily perceptual movements along alignments of gender and sexuality.[78]

In mid-18th through 19th century France, smell segregated public and private domains and also significantly supported the emerging of modern identity and notions of the self. Individuated fragrances allowed for persons of a certain class to perceive their own body-self differently than before, a change in bodily olfactory movement, new patterns of perceptual intentionality changing one's way of being in the world (even inaugurating new kinds of narcissism and sexual desires/alignments). The "I can" of a perfumed bourgeoisie male is olfactorily, tactilely, and visually very different from, for example, that of a lower class housemaid, whose "I cannot" smell or dress a certain way is experienced in conjunction with the "I can smell and dress like *myself*" of someone other.[79] The emergence of an individual self in Europe then can be more complexly understood when taking into consideration the kind of individualized and individualizing perceptual movements in modern Euro-Western cultures to stand out against malodorous, coarse, visually uniform "others" and to perceptually appear as discrete individual.[80]

It is also important to recognize that the structure and the *how* of perceptual interrelations is not a universal given: We have pivoted around gender, which is often a subsuming concept structuring our personal relations and socio-cultural relations. Yet it might not be in other cultural contexts.

For example, the Tzotzil of the Chiapas highlands of Mexico experience through thermal bodily orientations. Heat is the basic force of the universe, ordering space and time. For example, the six directions

78. Dolores Mitchell, "Women and Nineteenth-Century Images of Smoking," in *Smoke: A Global History of Smoking*, ed. Sander L. Gilman and Zhou Xun (London, UK: Reaktion Books, 2004), 294–303.

79. Alain Corbin, *The Foul and the Fragrant: Odor and the French Social Imagination* (Cambridge, MA: Harvard University Press, 1986), 55, 143–147.

80. David Howes, "Olfaction and Transition," in *The Varieties of Sensory Experience*, ed. David Howes (Toronto, Canada: University of Toronto Press, 1991), 145.

have thermal signifiers (e.g., "emergent heat"), and times of day are named according to heat perceptions ("half-heat" is the middle of the day).[81] Heat as a concept and as "major" sense dominates bodily perceptual orientation and alignments, and we need to re-align or disorient our exploration: Our Western habituated perceptions orient our narrative to describe a Tzotzil world in which men possess more heat than women, public spheres are male dominated and land ownership is aligned patrilinearly. But in a thermal cosmology, deeply embedded tacit knowledges about the world is oriented thermally first.

Women and female powers are associated with beginnings, endings, and chief agents in transitional and critical moments in the life cycle and historical cycles. Yet these cycles (daily, seasonally, yearly), while displaying gender valences, are thermal cosmologies forming the pre-reflective, deeply embedded decision-making schema, the tacit knowledges from which present actions emerge and are accounted for.[82] Thermal lines pervade all areas of life such as food, education, gendered relations, communal architecture, infrastructure, and political structures. Everything from rocks, plants, foods, animals, and humans to ceremonies, rituals and symbols possesses a degree of heat, the basic force of the universe. Newborns of either gender possess little innate heat and are bathed in warm water, wrapped in blankets and presented with "hot" peppers until they have acquired enough life/heat of their own to survive. Heat is felt throughout the Tzotzil body: as the dominant perceptual orientation, it structures bodily orientations toward specific foods (imbued with different thermal values) and social relations (exchanges of heat).[83]

Bodily perceptual intentionality aligns bodies that are thermal, and then thereby gendered: women sitting on the (cold) earth, walking barefoot, men sitting elevated, closer to the heat-force in the sky, and wearing sandals, to maintain thermal alignments. Occupying the world

81. Classen, *Worlds of Sense*, 122–123.
82. Gary H. Gossen, *Telling Maya Tales: Tzotzil Identities in Modern Mexico* (New York, NY: Routledge, 1999), 170–178.
83. Classen, *Worlds of Sense*, 123–125.

in thermal ways like this displays a gendered occupation of space. The thermal value of objects or meaning of bodily intentionality is not aligned with gender first and then repeated through thermal perceptual orientations. Rather, thermal schemas run through the environment, connect bodies and world, and align bodies and objects in ways that structure and gender bodily intentionalities. Heat and gender are not reducible to each other; women do not sit on the floor because they are women, but their bodies are thermally aligned with the earth and from that alignment they perceptually emerge as cold/woman.

As visualist travelers, oriented to visual hierarchies (e.g., up over down), at first sight we might perceive meaning emerging according to our pre-reflective perceptual orientation: We might perceive women as valued less than men as we observe social habits. However, meanings emerging for the Tzotzil (and possibly perceivable in our imagination now) align earth, darkness, waning heat, with the feminine as creative force, with reproductive capacity. The bodily positioning of women emerges perceptually in alignment with certain seasons and creative and revitalizing periods in a life or community's history.[84]

Thermal perception, as perceptual intentionality—bodily movement extending us into the world—is a culturally different perceptual orientation than that of Western knowledge of heat as a proximal perception aligned with touch. For the Tzotzil, thermal perception is a sense extended through the whole body (not just parts of it), and the heat extended in working, the eating of hot and cold foods, the movement of temperature throughout the day, the positioning of bodies and objects around heat sources in the home, the movement of heat through the material social body, constitutes the emerging perceived meanings in the world, gendered bodies being one of them. The Tzotzil body schema can be imagined like a blueprint on thermal fabric—the tacit knowledge of how a Tzotzil moves in the world, the sense of bodily unity, the meaning of movement and postures in a given environment, is a tacit sense of thermal dispositions and capacities.

84. Gossen, *Telling Maya Tales*, 172–173.

As a Western subject, my tacit understanding of my own situatedness as/in my body in my environment might be informed by a tacit visual sense. For example, I have a tacit knowledge of how I may navigate through a building with various kinds of doors and winding hallways, because I have a tacit visual and interrelated physical-tactile sense of what this navigation might entail (I know if I will fit through a door and how). This might even include bodily extensions, so when I carry a backpack, hold an umbrella, or walk my dog on a leash, I have a tacit sense of how to chart a path to reach my goal, and how to adjust my bodily posture to, for example, enter through a door.

I may find it difficult to conceive, possibly because of my tacit knowledge dominated by visual perception, how a Tzotzil might be oriented to the world through tacit bodily perceptual knowledges. I do not have a dominant tacit thermal sense or any habituated movements which allow me to know myself and the world through temperature, how I as body-heat move and extend, am obstructed or challenged; I have no innate understanding of thermally inhabiting my environment and the thermal meanings emerging in and with my environment.

In relation to the larger project, to understand gender in and as experience, we can now grasp how our senses structure experience—and through it, a world—that is gendered, and how our perceptions are shaped and structured so that gendered experiences emerge. Bodily perception then is shaping and shaped by a socio-cultural world in which meaning and values emerge with gendered connotations. Some of the examples given, while they might appear alien to us, should also offer us some understanding into our own bodily perceptual orientations and the perceptual interplays at work. While I might be habituated to recognize gender visually, I might also experience that certain aural extensions might "throw me off" or change the perceived gendered meaning (e.g., speech patterns might change my perception of a masculine man and the meaning emerging now is that of an effeminate gay man). Or I catch a scent as I move around the hall corner and expect to see a man, yet it is a woman extending in perfumed ways usually aligned with men and men's scent products. Modern Western perceptual orientations toward gender are aligned in a myriad of perceptual ways and interrelations, though we tend to "forget" and only "remember" when we perceive things "out of line" with the given dominant sense in our meaning-making.

In our exploration so far we moved through bodily intentionality, body schema, bodily habits, perceptual alignments, subversions, and interrelations, and via gender deepened our understanding of what bodily perceptual orientation is. We moved close to something like a common terrain or dimension from which perceptions emerge or stand out from. In the next chapter, our explorations will return to habits and their sedimentation via perceptual experiences of "race."

CHAPTER FOUR

SEDIMENTATION OF HABITS AND ORIENTING EXPERIENCES

I can perceive a world and be perceived by the world because, and only because, body and world are already attuned. And because body and world are already embedded with each other, bodily sensory experience can be what it inherently is: a communion with the world, a *living in* the world: "In order to perceive things, we need to live them."[1] This brings us back to a theoretical assertion I made previously referring to a pre-reflective terrain, the condition by which I appear and am perceived in the world and perceive the world always already as a body emerging as gendered, raced, and normally able. My perceptions, what and how I perceptually experience myself, the world, and things in it, are conditioned by this pre-reflective dimension in which I as perceiving body am situated and immersed. How and where I am situated in this terrain and how I emerge from it (arrive in the context of my experience) is also significant to my perceptual experience, as we have already explored somewhat in terms of directionality of perceptual orientation.

My exploration of a "pre-reflective" terrain is *not* about a sort of perceptual layer "below" our conscious reflections. This pre-reflective dimension is like a layer of sound, a vibration, or current running through our experiences *with* our bodily experiences that we are more easily attuned to. Rather than something to unearth or dig up, it is a supporting note implicated in the sounds and pulsating vibrations that

1. Merleau-Ponty, *Phenomenology of Perception*, 325.

make up our being alive, that make up our bodily perceptual orientations in the world (though not inherently creating or implying harmony
or disharmony). Or put differently, it is like a current that "floats our
boat of experience," like currents in an ocean which give a vessel direction and movement, even when this movement is not felt. I prefer to use
the terms terrain and dimension interchangeably in this exploration:
Terrain indicates a ground, a specific placement, of our perceptions
(rather than an abstract unmarked space), a material world with particular features that influence our movements and directions, neither
universally the same, independent of us, nor unchanging. Dimension
allows me to invoke the pervasive, seemingly concealed sphere of our
existence, which also is neither universal, exclusively other, nor static.[2]

When meaning emerges between body and world, then the emergence of meaning in the perceptual interaction is never taking place in

2. In what follows, I actually draw somewhat on Merleau-Ponty's conception of
background/horizon. I will digress from his concepts of pre-reflective dimension and
background/horizon, but make use of the latter in order to more complexly explore
the significance of the former, and to remain within the already sketched frame
of perceptual orientations and habits. Merleau-Ponty inherits the terms "background" and "horizon" from the two different schools he is merging in his thought,
phenomenology and Gestalt psychology. Both terms function similarly (though not
identically) in Merleau-Ponty's work, connoting an indeterminate and ambiguous
background or horizon against which a figure comes into perceptual focus. The
configuration of this horizon or background is always changing, depending on context and perceptual focus: gathered background changes, and as perceptual focus
or orientation changes, what is determinate as figure becomes indeterminate and
relegated to the background, and what was indeterminate becomes determinate
as it emerges as figure from previously being in the background. There is a difference, however, in the suggestions invoked by the terms: A "background" in some
ways, though it is presented to me as I am facing the figure, also connotes a certain
temporal dimension, a past, a gathering which led to an arrival of a figure; and a
spatial dimension of what is gathered behind, what supports yet is hidden by the
perceptual arrival of the figure. The term "horizon," though, appeals (also spatially
and temporarily) to a futurity, possibilities, an open-ended range that moves on as
we move toward it. As already mentioned, I prefer to remain with the notion of
dimension, partially also in order to elicit an imagery that allows us to conceive of
the dynamics explored in this chapter as concurrent and embedded with each other,
rather than evoking spatial or even temporal distance.

a void, it always emerges from sediment habits. These habits though, the social collective pool of bodily habits and perceptual meanings are not my fate, they do not determine my experiences as body, rather, they are the "constant atmosphere of my present."[3] For example, my bodily experience as woman and socially acquired habits of being familiar with a kitchen as a space supporting my bodily movements as woman emerges in a terrain of sediment habits of social bodies before me, a dimension which is not easily ignored or experienced "against" through conscious reflection and decision. In other words, just reflecting on the sexist and patriarchal division of home spaces and deciding that the kitchen indeed is not *the* place for a woman does not dismiss or destroy the many dimensions of my bodily experiences when moving into my mother's kitchen (e.g., the emotional and physical familiarity connected to bodily habits and tacit knowledges of how to move, how to cook, how to *be*).

The pre-reflective dimension of my bodily experience is the dimension in which habits sediment into a pre-reflective terrain of bodily experiences, into a landscape or current in which habits join into a "natural" flow. The bodily habits I acquire are already such that they are in reference to the specific features and character of my perceptual terrain, my appropriation of habits is as much individual as it is my "going with the flow." There is a powerful, sometimes even violent dynamic inherent: Our "coming to be" in these habitual currents, in this perceptual terrain shaped by cultural and historical contexts, allows a signaling of possibilities and change, possibilities for turning the tide or ripples emerging, seeming impossibilities of hardened gestures or impassable cliffs of separation, of different involvements and significances in the lay of the land to emerge. It implies that my arrival as experiencing body infers a being surrounded, being immersed in, and being supported by certain perceptual terrains or currents of experience which dominate the conditions of my arrival in a space already perceptually emerging as female or male, straight or gay or queer, able or disabled, white or brown or black body.

3. Merleau-Ponty, *Phenomenology of Perception*, 442.

Habituation, or sedimentation of habits, is "work," bodily and social efforts which can violently sweep up bodies to align them along socio-cultural ideologies. This "work" of/in the pre-reflective dimension might be obscured though, so that it might appear ethereal or inconsequential to the here-and-now of my experience. Let me explore what I mean by this assertion through investigating the perceptual emergence of racialized bodies. How do I emerge from this pre-reflective terrain, and how is this dimension significant, integral and supportive to my emerging as a perceptual body (a brown woman) and the co-incidental emerging of the perceived (race)?

PERCEPTUAL DIMENSIONS
AND SEDIMENTED HABITS OF PERCEPTION

> My act of perception ... takes advantage of work already done, of a general synthesis constituted once and for all; and this is what I mean when I say that I perceive with my body or my senses, since my body and my senses are precisely this familiarity with the world born of habit, that implicit or sedimentary body of knowledge ... The person who perceives is not spread out before himself as a consciousness must be; he has historical density, he takes up a perceptual tradition and is faced with a present ... [This body] is better informed than we are about the world, and about the motives we have and the means at our disposal for synthesizing it.[4]

Because my immediate perceptual experience is not of sense data but of meanings or structures, or better, meaningfully structured objects and environments, I perceive in the world within an already given logic and language.[5] It is a "logic of the world to which my body in its entirety conforms, and through which things of intersensory significance become possible for us."[6] This logic is bodily in the sense that

4. Ibid., 238.
5. Ibid., 36, 58–62.
6. Ibid., 326.

it is "lived through," in that it is not primarily for a consciousness to account for, but is an imminent meaning that is opaque to itself and is first grasped by the body.[7] To say it differently, our bodily existence in the world is always intelligent, purposeful and skillful. But, this intelligence and intelligibility, this purpose and skillful embodied action, is not derived from a specific act of conscious intellection (prior and/or separate from it).[8] Rather, our embodied existence itself, qua sensory perception, is already and inherently intelligent and purposeful. That is because our bodies and bodily movements emerge from a historical and social (habitual) terrain. Our perceptual experiences take up habitual schemas, or what Merleau-Ponty following Husserl also calls "sedimentations," and deploy them.

Our bodies and the world emerge from this sedimentation of habit and this sedimentation is bodily: the histories in which our bodies and world are immersed are performed bodily, in demeanor, posture, and gesture. Body and world take up sedimented habit, take up historically and socially conventionalized forms of conduct. To clarify, it is not the *content* of perception, the content of the work of general synthesis, which is established once and for all. It is the general synthesis, the reciprocal relationship between body and world,[9] which is constituted once and for all. Put differently, perceptions, bodily experiences and actions, all embodied dimensions of life are open to historical-cultural change, except for the historicity of the body itself. Our bodily perceptual habits may change, but that we are body-creatures of habit (taking up perceptual traditions with

7. Ibid., 48–49.
8. Nick Crossley, "Body-Subject/Body-Power: Agency, Inscription and Control in Foucault and Merleau-Ponty," *Body & Society* 2, no. 2 (1996): 100.
9. Merleau-Ponty later thinks of this as chiasm, or the reversibility of the flesh. He begins to question his own conception of perception, though this conceptual work remained unfinished. He describes the lived world of the flesh, of which body and world are both part, as something like the unfolding and differentiation of flesh, yet flesh that is reversible; that touches and is being touched, sees and is being seen. Merleau-Ponty, *The Visible and the Invisible*.

individual expressions in the present) in a reciprocal relationship with the world does not.[10]

When acting in this world, we are grounded in habitual patterns of behavior, collective layers of experience constituted by myself and others which are taken for granted, traditions or histories of bodily motility and perception. Present perceptual movement and behavior is conditioned to conform to a past, yet it is not bound to it. Sedimentations establish a certain perceptual perspective, certain orientations (as discussed earlier), but does not determine or confine the ultimate content of perception or character of behavior. Choice/creativity is possible, though it depends on habits/sedimentation, and both are necessary to our bodily existence (e.g., I need both, motor habits and the ability to spontaneously re-orient in new situations to drive a car). Put differently, choice is only possible because there is already a cultural repertoire and meaningful engagement with the world so I can choose in reflection what might be meaningful to me—otherwise this ability to choose amounts to random indeterminacy.[11]

For example, habituated gendered expressions precede me; I am already born into the terrain of a world in which my geo-socio-cultural group embodies gender roles in a certain way (socially, institutionally, individually). To embody choice in my gender expression, I must already make reference to the gendered habitual system in place; already engage purposefully and meaningfully in socio-cultural and bodily relation with others in my environment. Within my bodily capacities, I then can enact a choice as to creative transformation or change in gendered habit, such as choosing only to wear pants, or shaking hands with a firm grip. This choice can sediment as habit, so that my wearing

---

10. Crossley, "Body-Subject/Body-Power: Agency, Inscription and Control in Foucault and Merleau-Ponty," *Body & Society* 2, no. 2 (1996): 103–104.
11. Connected to this then is that choice is not a choice itself. The ability to choose is connected to our inherent embeddedness in a world of bodily and cultural habits. Crossley, *The Social Body: Habit, Identity and Desire*, 134. See also Stephen Priest, *Merleau-Ponty*, ed. Ted Honderich, The Arguments of the Philosophers (New York, NY: Routledge, 1998), 150–165.

pants is part of a pre-reflective dimension of my experience (I do not always reflect on my bodily movements and habits as I am wearing pants), or so that firm handshakes extended by women is a sediment habit that is taken up by more women in a social group. These habitual schemata can be understood by remembering the concepts of the body schema, the tacit knowledge of my bodily capacities in a given environment: Like body schemata, habitual schemata are tacit knowledges concerning social habits, socially meaningful, conforming, and communicative bodily movements.

Body and world are dependent upon cultural repertoires and perceptual skills, and just as much reproduce them; bodies "tend to do things" and the world "tends to be things." Sediment habits, historical and social continuities of bodily intentionalities and movements, form the pre-reflective current in which our perceptual experiences take place; sediments are histories as well as possibilities (in the linking of significances or creating of historical/social intersensory connections). Attending to the currents of sediment history via repetitive bodily action allows cultural theorists to analyze bodily expression within the possibilities and constraints inherent in the dimensions of social habitus or body-power.[12]

---

12. Habitus is Pierre Bourdieu's term. It refers to systems of durable, transposable dispositions that integrate past experiences through the very matrix of perceptions, appreciations, and actions that are necessary to accomplish infinitely diversified tasks. Bourdieu, cited in Ahmed, *Queer Phenomenology*, 56. Body-power is Michel Foucault's term, the power of social and political orders to control, direct, delimit and co-opt actions of the body. Michel Foucault, *Discipline and Punish: The Birth of the Prison*, trans. Alan Sheridan, 2nd, reprint, illustrated ed. (New York, NY: Vintage Books, 1995). Whether social order is explained via disciplinary technologies, symbolic medium of rituals, habituated etiquette, or internalized restraints, social factors of order, structure, and control depend on bodies, albeit an active one (many theories on the processes of social order depend on a passive conception of the body). Bodily control, conformity and transgression, are possible because bodily experiences can be habituated to conform (and conformity making transgression possible), but it is also through bodies that agents may assert control over the social institutions that they have bodily created and maintained. In other words, habituated bodily movements are created through social structures, and social structures can be rehabituated, reshaped in bodily movement. See Simon J.

Significant to my argument here, our bodies and the world take the shape of certain habituated repetitions, or appropriating Ahmed, habituated perceptual orientations. "Orientations shape what bodies do, while bodies are shaped by orientations they already have, as effects of the work that must take place for a body to arrive where it does"[13] and, I would add, *how* it does. Concepts such as sex, gender, normalcy, race, and sexuality are not originary concepts or experiences. They must be understood as the effects of repetitions, repetitions that are not neutral, but perceptual repetitions that shape bodies in certain ways, and significantly, orient bodies perceptually in certain ways so that in the moment of perceptual recognition, the work of bodily repetition disappears as sediment. Put differently, the pre-reflective terrain of our perception is never "just there," but is the effect of the work of habituating and orienting perceptual experience; they are the currents directing our bodily perceptual orientation.[14] Perceptual orientations are effected habits, open to continuity through repetition and open to change through re-orientations.

PERCEPTUAL EXPERIENCE OF RACE/PERCEPTUALLY EXPERIENCING AS RACIALIZED

For example, I also remember a shift in my own bodily orientations regarding race and nationality. My body was a nationalized body when growing up in Germany. Because of the reading of my skin color, it was often demanded that I hyphenate myself, through questions like, You are German and . . .? I often refused to claim a hyphenated identity as German-Thai in favor of labeling my parents with different nationalities.[15] Looking back, I somehow "knew" through my bodily perceptual

Williams and Gillian Bendelow, *The Lived Body: Sociological Themes, Embodied Issues* (New York, NY: Routledge, 1998), 48–66.

13. Ahmed, *Queer Phenomenology*, 58.

14. Ibid., 55–57.

15. The identity of Thai-German also never emerged in my bodily perceptual orientations, since Thai was a national identity aligned with mother, but not with me. My passport, language, and geographical bodily perceptions oriented me spatially,

orientations that I could not fully extend into space as a German "only," yet that I indeed was also not German-Thai. I was not aligned in a way that I could, for example, extend bodily perceptually, linguistically, and culturally as a German-Thai in a Thai context; perceptual orientations by Thais would align me as foreigner. Differences in exposure to food and culinary preferences did not make me a hyphenated German-Thai. Perceptual orientations allowed me to be aligned as German citizen though (e.g., through my unmistakably German name, my linguistic skills, my passport, my geographic-spatial origins), as long as I would not *visually* extend into a space, as long as my inhabitation of space was not *visually* perceived. Because skin color in Germany is oriented along national identity lines, my skin color demanded identification along national orientations.[16]

It was not until I moved to the United States that my body became a racialized body, and it took me a while to be disoriented to the ways in which bodies are perceptually shaped (from) within US national (body) borders.[17] Skin color in the United States is most often aligned along racial and ethnic orientations first. This, of course, has a history,

culturally, and even emotionally in ways so that Thai hardly emerged as meaningful in a way to be signified by ordering my identity as Thai-German.

16. For this kind of self-analysis I am indebted to Mita Banerjee, "The Hipness of Mediation: A Hyphenated German Existence," in *This Bridge We Call Home*, ed. Gloria E. Anzaldúa and Analouise Keating (New York, NY: Routledge, 2002), 117–125.

17. I am leaning here on the differentiation made by Sara Ahmed, who describes racialization as a process, an investment of meaning in skin color. Race is an effect of racialization, not the cause. "Racialization involves the production of 'the racial' body through knowledge, as well as the constitution of both social and bodily space in the everyday encounters we have with others." Sara Ahmed, "Racialized Bodies," in *Real Bodies: A Sociological Introduction*, ed. Mary Evans and Ellie Lee (New York, NY: Palgrave, 2002), 47. I will investigate these processes and everyday encounters. For essays inquiring into the meaning of skin and other bodily surfaces and their manipulation in spaces of contestation, liminality, and reconfigurations of identity, see Adeline Masquelier (Ed.), *Dirt, Undress, and Difference: Critical Perspectives on the Body's Surface* (Bloomington, IN: Indiana University Press, 2005).

a sedimentation of bodily habits and activities, from which the perception of bodies and world as raced emerges, and bodies and world take on meanings specific to the spatial and temporal terrain of sediment habits.[18]

Colonization, as global bodily movements, shaped and aligned bodies through the movements these bodies took toward each other. Racial alignments of bodies was not *caused* by white and black bodies meeting in space, rather, in a sense, bodies with different hues of skin pigmentation meeting in space already arrived with sediment history, from which bodily motility and with it bodily alignments emerged.[19] Whiteness is the orienting line which shapes and arranges the emerging bodies and perceptual orientations so that bodies became oriented and aligned as raced. Bodies emerged as raced in a race-specific terrain, a terrain shaped by currents through which raced bodily orientations aligned movements in space and with space, and which supported how certain racially perceived bodies could move/be swept up in space along certain lines, or were perceived out of line, out of currency.

By virtue of being pre-reflective, this terrain supporting our racial perceptions is the condition by which raced bodies appear, the condition which mutually constitutes my emergence as brown body in a

18. Terrain, currents, or dimensions are often imagined spatially, as in the current of a spatially confined river, as the water running through a landscape demarking opposing sides. But they are also temporal in two ways: Terrains are shaped and shift with the passing of time; dimensions are temporal like the past that is necessary to the arrival and shape and age of the person or object perceived in the present, or the currents of histories, genealogies that shape the emergence or arrival of something that appears to be present now. And terrains/currents/dimensions are temporal in that they are changeable precisely because of the changing temporal situatedness of the present. In a way terrains/currents/dimensions accumulate histories and genealogies, and these can be inherited as well as consciously and subversively gathered. Ahmed, *Queer Phenomenology*, 38, 137, 143, 185n.8.

19. See, for example, Comaroff's analysis of the interrelated emerging of biomedical science, colonialism, Christian mission healing, and racial perceptions. Jean Comaroff, "The Diseased Heart of Africa: Medicine, Colonialism, and the Black Body," in *Knowledge, Power, and Practice: The Anthropology of Medicine and Everyday Life*, ed. Shirley Lindenbaum and Margaret Lock (Berkeley, CA: University of California Press, 1993), 305–329.

world with raced bodies and power and privilege predominately in the grasp of white bodies. I do not have to reflect consciously about my bodily skin tone or connect my perception of skin color to the person embodying it: I walk through my neighborhood and see a Hispanic man tending to a garden. "*His* race" is not a natural material bodily condition, but sedimented habits of racialization, racial taxonomies and bodily alignments is the terrain I am navigating, is the current running through my bodily experience. So when I walk through my neighborhood, I already perceive a Hispanic man according to my social habituation, before I might consciously reflect and ponder why and how his brown skin featured into my perception and the emerging meaning (e.g., I begin to wonder why my tacit bodily experience aligned him as out of place in the neighborhood, or perhaps in line with social habits of yard work, but out of line with home ownership in this space).

Orienting lines that map out the repetitions and aligning performances which allow for habits to sediment disappear through their work, and they also occlude the presence and force of this pre-reflective dimension by orienting our perception to what emerges: in this case, raced bodies. The pre-reflective current in which bodies and meanings emerge is not necessarily *what* is repeated, what orienting *device* is at work. But it supports the *directionality* of perception that is generated (the product of effort that becomes effortless through its own repetition and work, the work that disappears as such through its repetitious enactment), supports the movement of our bodily perceptions as we face "race" through the force of gathered sediment, force determined through acts of habitual repetition.

When we see a boat floating down a river, the alignment, directionality and movement of the boat appear "natural," though its stability, speed, and floating itself are determined by the amount and force of the moving water. Transferring this image to our discussion of racial perception, raced bodies do not appear as figures in perceptual focus because they emerge from a sea of whiteness and blackness. Racial perceptions or racialization of bodies (what is repeated), the fantasy of racial hierarchy (an orientation device), and blackness as well as whiteness (the orienting lines along which bodies are perceived and aligned) are already supported by pre-reflective currents, currents supporting the repetition of racial perceptions, generating a directionality of perception (in this example, racialism), aided by the ideological notions of racial hierarchies, establishing racial orienting lines. Specific gathering currents, the terrain which supports specific kinds of arrivals, sweeps up and positions bodies so that they emerge perceptually as raced, might be the political-economic project of colonialism, or the orientalism of objective science.[20] Racialism as a naturalized orienting line, as natural perceptual directionality in which the repetitious work establishing racial perception disappears, occludes from focus the driving currents of bodily perceptions and orientations containing sedimented habits.

One example for a forceful current of sedimented habit supporting and running through the perceptual emergence of race might be nation and citizenship: At the end of the 19th century, the US Census Bureau announced the end of the continuous westward expansion. But with the frontier declared closed, the work of establishing the meaning of the American nation and citizenship continued. The sedimented social habits of nation-building bodily movements "floated the boat" of racial ideologies manifesting in laws and classification systems by which races are invented, defined, characterized, aligned and hierarchically organized.

The work to establish a centering anthropological image for the American citizen to define nationhood plays out in the repetition of racialized bodily perceptions, generating a directionality of perception, thus establishing lines of perception in which raced bodies emerge, but which simultaneously aligns citizens and non-citizens. Social Darwinism, which applies biological principles to social development, becomes one of the orienting devices to building racial ideologies. Efforts of repetition in immigration laws generate directionality of perception which establishes the American citizen as white. The American nation as racially white appears as a "natural" directionality

20. Frantz Fanon, *The Wretched of the Earth* (New York, NY: Grove Press, 1968). Sara Ahmed engages Fanon in her discussion of orientation in "Orient" and "Orientalism," Ahmed, *Queer Phenomenology*.

of perception, so that we perceive inhabitants of "American" space as racial bodies.

The pre-reflective terrain for bodily movements that perform "nation" gains force through habits and transformation of habits, for example, legal habituation and changing legal habits through acquisition of immigration laws guided by racialized perceptual orientations. Legal alignment of bodily and social habits regarding movement in or as citizen of a nation sediments social habits, which add to the particular force of the current running through racial perceptual emergences.

More specifically: Immigration legislation, for example, the Naturalization Act of 1790 and those following, up to the immigration act of 1924, established immigration and naturalization along racial lines, though not necessarily maintaining a focus on race. By 1882, regulation at the borders put laws in effect that allowed only healthy and self-supporting persons in, refusing the poor, physically and mentally ill, criminals and moral delinquents.

Medically and morally oriented perceptions aligned immigrant bodies, as certain groups were associated with certain ailments. For example, Asians were screened specifically for worms, Mexicans for lice, Jews for tuberculosis, Italians for criminal behavior. Thus the perceptual orientation to raced bodies was aligned through, for example, medical orienting devices, and race and ethnicity were visually aligned by perceptions of health and economic ability (medical exclusions increased from 3% in 1898 to 69% 1917). For example, a Romanian family is described by an officer as looking forlorn and frail, typical of the poor class. They stood in contrast to immigrants from Scandinavia described as fine looking and healthy persons.[21]

---

21. See Martha Mabie Gardner, *The Qualities of a Citizen: Women, Immigration, and Citizenship, 1870–1965* (Princeton, NJ: Princeton University Press, 2005). Compare this also with Barbara Welter's famous exploration of the Cult of True Womanhood, the establishment of the female citizen shaped by purity, piety, domesticity, and submissiveness, which emerges out of and maintains the American nation by perceptual alignments along class, race, and gender lines. Barbara Welter, *Dimity Convictions: The American Woman in the Nineteenth Century* (Athens, OH: Ohio University Press, 1976). Another investigative comparison

Thus, only certain bodies can successfully navigate this terrain to inherit or gather the kind of habitual schema which aligns their bodily emergence within reach of objects of privilege (e.g., citizenship, marriage, employment). Whiteness as a line of orientation aligns bodies just so in a space that is oriented around a privileged kind of embodiment; certain bodies can more easily take up social habits aligned with/ aligning them with privilege. And consequently, all others in this space become aligned and oriented in a way that the habitual schemata available for bodily habits and movements leave certain things hard to/ out of reach, or leave their bodies out of line, even rendering certain bodies (non-white, non-heterosexual, non-citizen) objects rather than subjects.[22] The orienting lines of whiteness also serve as vertical and horizontal lines of coherence, allowing certain bodies to move up or reach across spatial, institutional, educational, and economical lines.

Bodies can also "disappear" behind certain perceptual lines such as whiteness,[23] for example, when the sediment habit of perceiving

could be drawn from the racial and religious orientations of immigrant bodies in social gospeller Rev. Josiah Strong, the reports of the Dillingham commission on immigration, or Jane Addams' writings about Hull house and her work on the Americanization of immigrants. Josiah Strong, *Our Country: Its Possible Future and Its Present Crisis*, reprint ed. (Bibliobazaar, 2010). William Paul Dillingham, *Reports of the Immigration Commission: Statements and Recommendations Submitted by Societies and Organizations Interested in the Subject of Immigration* (Washington, DC: Government Printing Office, 1911). Jane Addams, *Twenty Years at Hull House: With Autobiographical Notes* (New York, NY: The Macmillan Company, 1911). Of course, "nation" is not the only current, but rather one of genealogical dimensions gathering sediment. The "West"/Occident or "civilization" are other sediments in our pre-reflective current. And race is not the only perceptual orientation establishing the grid of national alignments; class, gender, and religion are among other perceptual orientations and orienting lines drawn, and any of these can also serve as sediment from which other orientations can emerge. See, for example, Foucault's tracing of the emergence of "sexual identity," which in this framework can be understood as emerging partially from a background of "modern democratic society" which requires regulation of social bodies, "sexuality" turning into one of the political technologies, or orienting devices, along which to perceive and align social and political bodies.

22. Ahmed, *Queer Phenomenology*, 112–113, 159.
23. Ibid., 136–137.

citizenship leads to perceptual orientations of American bodies as white bodies, bringing to focus those bodies differently raced. This allows white bodies to disappear, or perceptually emerge race-less, while racially perceived bodies—those with darker skin hues—emerge incoherent from the sediment habitual schema regarding citizenship. For example, a social bodily habit regarding legal enforcement of immigration, aligned through devices such as the 2012 Arizona law provision known as "show me your papers" (allowing Arizona law enforcement officers to demand proof of citizenship/immigration status of people suspected of residing on US soil without proper legal documentation) emerges along perceptual lines which allow bodies raced as white to appear in line with citizenship, whereas bodies perceptually emerging as questionable in regard to citizenship/residency are bodies racialized. The tacit knowledge concerning nationhood and citizen bodies supports and is supported by perceptual orientations to race.

To stress an image presented previously again: pre-reflective dimensions of bodily experience are not simply deeply buried layers, barely impacting our perceptual orientations. As illustrated earlier, it is the particular terrain in which our bodies move, the currents implicated in and fed by our bodily and social habits, supporting and supported by repetitive bodily movements which allow for acquisition of habits which again sediment and gather in a current to be taken up, repeated, and/or transformed.

To give another example, as a culturally Euro-Western woman, I might walk down the street in a city. When a black male comes toward me, I unreflectively reach for my wallet, to assure it is safely tucked away and out of reach from the passerby. I am not consciously aware of doing this, though on a pre-reflexive level of bodily experience my behavior is intentional and meaningful. When called to attention, I may be surprised at my bodily movement and my orientation of intentionality. Through critical inquiry and reflection I would be able to account for the meaning of this act through an account of its historical dimension: Perhaps I have been mugged before, and any approaching man is perceptually apprehended as a threat; the securing of my wallet aligns certain objects outside of the bodily perceptual reach of the other. I may not have been robbed before, but my bodily perceptual orientations are gathered in a current of cultural and historical sediment, such as the criminalization, vilification, outlawing, and violent extermination of black male bodily intentionality and motility, the extension of black male bodies in space.[24]

This history and social sediment is contained now in my lived bodily perceptual experience, it is the current from which my body and the other body emerge as raced: a brown female body, curiously aligned now along lines of whiteness, mutually emerges with a black male body, now perceived as criminal threat, and with that, the meaning of our bodies moving in our shared environment emerges also. The history which I now inhabit as I inhabit the colonized territory called United States of America sediments in bodily gestures, bodily intentionality. I may reflect on the meaning and significance of bodily perceptual orientations by attending to the sedimentations of habits, and discover that in the pre-reflective dimension I find a gathering of relations supporting my perceptions (such as socio-historical and cultural stereotypical images circumscribing my perception of a black body as criminal) as well as an indeterminate current gathering perceptual possibilities (such as socio-cultural and historical bodily gestures like conquest, slavery, abjection of black bodies, which turn the focus of my perception on the habitual gestures that sediment these alignments and possibly even turn the focus on orienting lines such as whiteness and white heteronormative patriarchy allowing for perceptual re-orientations in the face of black male bodies).

But nation and citizenship remain a perceptual dimension which supports perceptions of raced bodies, even when not-perceived bodies-out-of-space may come to be perceived as bodily perceptual orientations shift. For example, abject bodies denied citizenship and denied bodily extension in the nation as spatial community, such as invisibilized undocumented domestic workers, may perceptually emerge as either "illegal" or "undocumented" workers. But they may still be perceived

24. See, for example, Tina G. Patel and David Tyrer, *Race, Crime and Resistance* (Thousand Oaks, CA: Sage Publications, 2011).

along racial and ethnic lines (brown bodies aligned with illegal immigration), and these orienting lines are supported by and reinforce the pre-reflective current whose force divides who will be part of the nation and lined up on a path to citizenship and who will be deported and aligned behind national lines/border fences.

Sensory Interdependencies/Interplays in Perceiving Raced Bodies

Pre-modern and modern articulations of racial differences were not simply cast visually, associating the darkness of skin color with the supposed "darkness" of human nature in the racially different person. Mark Smith's sensory history of race in the United States shows how racial identities have been mediated and articulated through sound, smell, taste and touch, not only before, but *especially with* the emergence of modern racial stereotypes. Increase in racially mixed populations began in the colonial period and made clearly defined racial identities unstable, and one could no longer rely on modern eyes to verify visual racial identities. The preference for visual detection of race is as much a socio-cultural construction as race itself, and as visual orienting lines of white/black lost their potency, the techniques and work of perceptual repetitions of race needed to transform to maintain the mediation and articulation of racial meaning.[25]

Racial constructions and identifications increasingly relied on other senses as detector of racial identifiers: perceived innate body odor, animalistic sound and noises, tactile differences and ascribed blindness to moral offenses. The aforementioned Aristotelian taxonomy and ranking of the senses guided the perceptual encounter of colonial elite whites with black slaves, aligning black bodies with the lower senses: Black bodies were perceived as emerging perceptually through the lower senses of smell, sound, and touch; they were aligned with

---

25. Mark M. Smith, *How Race Is Made: Slavery, Segregation, and the Senses* (Chapel Hill, NC: University of North Carolina Press, 2006), 3–7.

those senses in regard to their bodily intentionality, that is, they smelled different but also had a keener sense of smell.[26]

Because perceptual hierarchies are also employed in the emerging of class, one of the complications in racial perception is the approximate material conditions—similar oppressive and exploitative working conditions—of poor whites. The ensuing crisis demanded "buffers,"[27] which were bodily perceptually installed. Poor whites, too, were aligned with, for example, malodor and poor taste on perceptual grids, but orienting lines were dominated by the prevailing need for racial distinctions, thus perceptual values and meanings were sensory interplays of vision and smell/sound/touch which maintained racially segregated perceptual orientations. Put differently, while both might emit the smell of a laboring person, poor whites still smelled, sounded, and sensed differently from black slaves.

This material-perceptual segregation was partially accomplished through the alignment of certain bodies with the power to suspend or cross perceptual orientation lines. White bodies were aligned with the power to cross racial lines and sound or look like a black body, and to act on the desire for black bodies by suspending prohibitions of touch (a power more often than not embodied through brutal violence).[28] But where visual alignments of whiteness and blackness were challenged or subverted by black slaves "passing" as white, aural markers were important interrelated perceptual extensions; to pass visually as white, one needed to also pass with "white sounds" in order to be seen as white.[29]

The pre-reflective terrain of racial perception shifted, in this case, for example, from an industrialized agricultural economy and political assemblages of a union of states encountering an abolitionist threat to national unity to a postbellum nation under reconstruction

26. Ibid., 11–12.
27. Jennifer Harvey, *Whiteness and Morality: Pursuing Racial Justice through Reparations and Sovereignty* (New York, NY: Palgrave Macmillan, 2007), 67–69.
28. Smith, *How Race Is Made: Slavery, Segregation, and the Senses*, 24–26.
29. Ibid., 34.

and struggling with waves of immigration. This terrain collected and arranged the sedimentation of habits so that bodily movements and alignments of perception and movement emerged with racial meanings. Sediment history and sediment bodily socio-cultural habits established perceptual perspectives, which are open to change and choice as they are feeding into conventionalized forms of conduct, such as racial perceptions and alignments. The end of slavery, then, did not initiate an end to perceptual segregation; rather, physical/sensory intimacy of racial bodies was regulated through fluid perceptual alignments (not consistently following a strict logic), with the power and authority to draw orienting lines in the perceptual grasp of white bodies.[30]

Racial perception emerging from a terrain of political desire for nationhood or economic expansion, for example, is already perceptually aligned and socially meaningful. However, while certain perceptual habits and alignments might come to be dominant orientations of a dominant social group, it does not follow that these habits, alignments, or resulting perceptual emergences are also uncritically transferred to those dominated and oppressed by these perceptual orientations. Mark Smith, for example, finds little evidence that black slaves in the colonial

30. Ibid., 48–52. Smith also argues that it is exactly the failure of visual perception to clearly align racial bodies that increased racial anxiety and led to legal definitions such as the "one-drop-rule" (any parentage or ancestry of non-white origin, no matter how far removed, automatically assigned a person's identity to the social group with lower status). Ibid., 41. This adds a "legal" and "pedigree-oriented" eye to the perceptual repertoire, preparing the way for racial perceptions in modern genetic science and eugenics. Miscegenation became aligned with criminality, as it was scientifically perceived to produce biologically flawed human bodies. For the influential voice presenting arguments in favor of racial eugenics, see Madison Grant, *The Passing of the Great Race: Or, the Racial Basis of European History* (New York, NY: Charles Scribner's Sons, 1922). For a contemporary discussion of the politics and perception of genetics, see Anne Kerr and Tom Shakespeare, *Genetic Politics: From Eugenics to Genome* (Cheltenham, UK: New Clarion Press, 2002). Lennard J. Davis, "Constructing Normalcy," in *The Disability Studies Reader*, ed. Lennard J. Davis (New York, NY: Routledge, 2010), 15. Mark Sherry, "(Post)Colonizing Disability," in *The Disability Studies Reader*, ed. Lennard J. Davis (New York, NY: Routledge, 2010), 101.

and antebellum South perceived whiteness similarly aligned as the perceptual construction of blackness. Exploring Olaudah Equiano's narrative, we see him countering white stereotypes of blackness without applying ethnological stereotypes to whites. While Equiano resists and refutes perceptual orientations of blackness (stressing habits of cleanliness, good taste), he does not present ethnological arguments by describing perceptual evaluation of white bodies (loose hair, red faces) as/with innate traits.[31]

The instability of perceptual meaning, then, can also allow for not just individual choice or expression, but changing sediment habits regarding perceptual movements. When visual alignments of racial bodies led to increased ambiguous emergences—such as interracial coupling producing a variety of skin hues—other perceptual capacities and mechanisms may support or replace the perceptual "deficiency" of vision to maintain racial alignments. In other words, when vision fails to support meaningful emergence of race, touch, odor, and sound may become the perceptual habits to conform to sedimented social habits and tacit knowledges. The meaning emerging perceptually is indeterminate and ambiguous in two ways: The perceived meaning of hair (e.g., texture, style), sound of speech, or body odor is indeterminate and may allow for emergence of a classed or raced body; or the emerging perception of, for example, a raced body might be tacitly known through a perceptual extension previously "insensitive" or "not sensing" of race.[32]

The currents supporting orienting lines of modern racial segregation, then, up to the contemporary industrial prison complex segregating racial bodies, are the products of repetitive and adjustable perceptual alignments and bodily movements, perceptual orientation of our attention to say, crime and/or violence (the perceived moral inferiority

---

31. Smith, *How Race Is Made*, 29–32. Olaudah Equiano lived in the 18th century. Kidnapped as a child and sold into slavery, he later bought his freedom and became a involved in the abolitionist movement. James Walvin, *An African's Life, 1745–1797: The Life and Times of Olaudah Equiano* (New York, NY: Continuum, 2000).
32. Ibid., 40–41.

of a racialized group).[33] The orienting lines of race may be violently enforced, though again, crossing perceptual lines was also a perceptual control and extension of power: threats and acts of lynching enforced racial orienting lines by prohibiting a black man crossing perceptually by touching a white woman (or being perceived to have touched her); the act of lynching itself was a violent suspension of rules regulating sensory proximity and alignments. Gender differences were also significant in this complex perceptual alignment, as interracial touch was permissible between men in organized violent encounters such as boxing; white men could rape black female bodies without legal consequence, but black male bodies perceived as touching a white woman embodied a manifold transgression into the perceptual domain of touch inhabited by white males.[34]

The repetitions of racial perceptions played out in various sensory realms, though the perceptual orientation directing bodies to perceive raced meanings occludes the thickening sedimentations of white supremacists' heteronormative patriarchy, a terrain which supports efforts to align economic, political, social, cultural, and religious capital and desire along racial lines "naturally." Sediment perceptual habits

33. For a discussion of the industrial prison complex, criminalization of racial bodies, and legal discrimination against "criminals," see Michelle Alexander, *The New Jim Crow* (New York, NY: The New Press, 2012). Since the original draft of this manuscript was created, the Black Lives Matter Movement emerged in response to, using the terms of this work, the aggressive, violent, and deadly habit of "putting black bodies in line" by armed civilians and militarized police alike. Our response to perceiving the many audio-visual experiences shared with us emerges out of our own bodily perceptual orientations—who do we align with? To whom does our sympathy extend? Which gut reactions and questions emerge for us? What is the immediate meaning making in which our bodies and experiences are implicated?
34. Ibid., 58–61. The perceived transgression of forbidden touch between black and white, esp. when extending from black men to white women, could then be violently suspended in lynching, the violent touching of black flesh being put to death by white bodies. The bodily perceptual experiences of lynching were then extended through the dismemberment and sale of body parts, the taking and mailing of photographs. These were visual, tactile, and olfactory (through the smell of burnt flesh or fibers) extensions, the suspension of segregation through the cradling of blackness in the hands of whites, perceptual reminders of white power.

then worked to give rise to alignments of social interactions, as segregation, legal decisions and social activities were ordered using perceptual qualifications that were racially aligned: segregating railroad cars aligning bodies socially through haptic, olfactory, and auditory orientations. For example, lower class railroad cars emerged as having stench, being coarse, and dirty, aligned with the bodies meant to inhabit them. Black bodies and poor bodies perceptually emerge out of reach of the softer, quieter, sweeter-smelling material spaces of upper class whites. The assignment of places was up to the railroad conductor, who used his perceptual capacities of sight, smell, and touch.[35]

The example of smoking can also illustrate again the power of bodily perceptual orientations and sediment habits regarding difference: Spanish Jews, who had been expulsed from Spain in 1492, were visible outsiders to the European cities to which they migrated and had a positive association with smoking by way of the Spanish trade of still exotic tobacco. Jewish acculturation and unstable visible perceptual identifiers, however, necessitated new perceptual habits to support racial orienting lines. The alleged connection between smoking and Jewishness was supported by sedimenting social habits of racialization, the racial essence of Jewishness perceptually emerging through the sensory qualities of tobacco consumption. The racialized pathologizing in Anti-Semite discourse of modern Europe sedimented in part as social bodily habit *after* communal desegregation, so that smoking aligned perception of innate physically and psychologically different Jewish bodies. Passing as a "good Jew" prompted Western Jews to contribute to the sedimentation perceiving Jews as social misfits through their tobacco use, assigning the perceptual alignment of Jewishness with smoking to Eastern Jews. This kind of bodily perceptual orientation and bodily movement to perceptually disappear as Jewish body over against othered Jewish bodies, though, only strengthened the pre-reflective current to racial perception of Jews. The West-East alignments as social habit only joined (though not seamlessly) the sediment

35. Smith, *How Race Is Made*, 59–62, 79–87.

of other perceptual habits regarding Jewishness as race, such as perceptual alignments with mental and physical ailments.[36]

The sensory aspects of smoking also highlight the interplay of perceptual capacities, and that an interrelation of sensory impressions and values may be conflictual or contradictory within perceptual habits, effecting reordering and changing in perceptual interrelations and meanings. If a person passes as white but doesn't sound "right" or smell/look "right," perceptual habits can change and be reordered so that aural, olfactory or tactile perceptions guide or dominate bodily perceptual orientations toward certain bodies' emerging.

In underestimating the bodily perceptual orientations to, for example, race so thoroughly sedimented in the contemporary context of US social habits, we risk missing the force of Paul Gilroy's argument of the "continuing dangers of race-thinking," or as I may put it inelegantly, race-sense-knowing. Gilroy, like Smith, shows that the powerful appeal of "occult, militaristic, and essentialist theories that are currently so popular, should be seen as symptoms of a loss of certainty around 'race.'"[37] While we might assert that in 21st century US society "race biology" seems more unstable than ever, bodily perceptual orientations to race still operate, for example, in biomedical sciences, perceiving and seeking to confirm genetics through visual racial alignments, employing a gaze penetrating raced skin to align raced bodies on microscopic and molecular levels (though increasingly confirming the opposite, namely the inability to uphold racial patterns in genetic alignments).[38]

"There is no raw, untrained perception dwelling in the body. The human sensorium has had to be educated to the appreciation of racial differences. When it comes to the visualization of discrete racial groups, a great deal of fine-tuning has been required."[39] This education, as

36. Sander L. Gilman, "Jews and Smoking," in *Smoke: A Global History of Smoking*, ed. Sanders L. Gilman and Zhou Xun (London, UK: Reaktion Books, 2004), 278–285.
37. Paul Gilroy, *Against Race: Imagining Political Culture Beyond the Color Line* (Cambridge, MA: Harvard University Press, 2000), 8.
38. Ibid., 48, 217–218.
39. Ibid., 42.

Mark Smith's work shows, has a long sediment history of social habits training bodily perceptual orientations beyond visual imagery, including a full-body sensorium. To come to terms with the persistence of racial imaginations is to heed the perceptual construction of race and otherness in multi-perceptual dimensions.

Sensory Interdependencies/Interplays and Differences in "Racial" Perception

Critical race theorists theorize race as social construction, dynamic and fluid, and racial grouping as binding together social groups of people loosely sharing historically contingent, socially significant elements of geography, morphology and/or ancestry.[40] Race appears as a dynamic and fluid meaning, attaching to a group of people sharing socially significant elements of amongst other things, morphology, ancestry, and geography.

To understand more deeply the dynamics and differences in bodily perceptual orientations toward sameness and otherness, we need to explore how bodily markers may be perceived through means other than visual means: Morphology, ancestry, and geography may be perceived olfactorily or aurally rather than being visually mapped or textualized, and may depend on cultural habituation rather than genetic tracing. We explored earlier that the modern concept of race worked in the visible realm, but needed support from or transformation through other perceptual realms when visual perception alone was not sufficient in upholding the stabilization of indeterminate racial categories. Non-visual perceptual capacities are interrelated with it and supported recognition of emerging black or Jewish bodies.

However, as might have become clear, it is not by accident that race and visual perception emerge together. The meaning of race aligned

---

40. Ian F. Haney Lopez, "White by Law," in *Critical Race Theory: The Cutting Edge*, 2nd ed. (Philadelphia: Temple University Press, 2000), 626–634. Michael Omi and Howard Winant, *Racial Formations in the United States* (New York, NY: Routledge, 1994).

with visual markers of skin hues emerged when currents of rationalism, Enlightenment philosophies, scientific objectivism, and colonial expansion sedimented perceptual schema. The bodily emergence of race and its meaning therefore could not but emerge as a Western visually-dominated perceptual habit. Cartography and other scientific tools of measuring and recording were perceptual tools sedimenting vision (and images, photography, textuality) as intellectual, civilized, and "white" perceptual activities. And while vision might have been and continue to be the culturally prominent sensory field, it operated interactively with other perceptual domains, not least to map out and test the "lower" senses of "primitive" people, their olfactory, tactile, and aural capacities.[41]

Cross-cultural comparisons will aid our understanding of these dynamics regarding tacit knowledges of racial otherness and sedimented habits regarding racial perception. To do this beneficially, I must shift my language here and explore the perception of sociocultural "others" in order to gain a more complex understanding of what perception of others within a differently ordered structure of bodily perceptual orientations might show us.[42] How might otherness be perceived if it is not something that hits the insider's eye?[43]

To bring up a comparison through olfaction again, a culturally different example can be found in the Tukano-speaking tribes in the

41. The data gained from hierarchical sensory investigations was often inconclusive in European exploration of "savage" peoples, though it was interpreted to support the perceptual orientations in place. Howes, *Sensual Relations*, 4–6. See also Anne McClintock, *Imperial Leather: Race, Gender and Sexuality in the Colonial Contest* (New York, NY: Routledge, Inc., 1995), 49–61.

42. Especially when taking into account Omi and Winant's racial formation theory, which highlights that race, rather than a biological and universal concept, is a field of social conflict, political organization, and cultural meaning. While race operates in individual and social dimensions, and as concept is deeply embedded in modern Western consciousness, it is not a universal or a historical phenomenon. Rather, it becomes a social habit, a tacit knowledge of bodily perception, or a "common sense" idea about and orientation in the world. Omi and Winant, *Racial Formations in the United States*, 52–62, 106.

43. I do not wish to imply, however, that in order to shed the prejudices inherent in a visualist emphasis of Western epistemology we need to dismiss sight and take an

Amazon, which show a complex perceptual order and hierarchy. Cosmology and social life are structured through interrelations of color, odor, temperature, and flavor. Odor, for example, is a combination of color and temperature and makes up perceptual alignments of people, animals, and plants, for example, different odors function as a marker of tribal identity and territory. All members of a tribe are understood to share the same general body odor, the word for which can be translated into *sympathy* or *tribal feeling*. This shared body odor is considered to be caused by the different food customs and to mark territorial boundaries through distinct odor trails. The different odors also have specific symbolic associations which serve to order intertribal relations.[44]

Olfactory identifications and divisions may also be found among the Dassanetch of Southwestern Ethiopia. Bodily orientations to odor include that humans, who are considered naturally inodorate, acquire their particular smell through inhabitation of particular environments, thus Dassanetch social groups are identified with the odor of the species of animals a respective group depends on (fish or cattle). Odors of fish and associated scents then not only emerge as malodorous to pastoralists, but fish and fishermen emerge as alien, foreign to the community, outside of cycles of creation and community life.[45]

Soundscapes (sounds arising in a specific environment) in Israel create networks of belonging and identity, socially shaped sounds which serve for perceptual movements and meanings of group identification.[46] Publically performed sounds collect certain people around common

"antivisualist" approach, as this might make us prone to dismiss sight in culturally different epistemologies. While a culture might be olfactory or oral, sight might still be an important avenue for knowledge, though its role and nature might be conceived of and embodied differently. See Classen, *Worlds of Sense*, 135–137.

44. Ibid., 81. Classen, Howes, and Synott, *Aroma*, 98.

45. Classen, *Worlds of Sense*, 84–85.

46. Devorah Kalekin-Fishman, "Sounds That Unite, Sounds That Divide: Pervasive Rituals in Middle Eastern Society," in *Everyday Life in Asia: Social Perspectives on the Senses*, ed. Devorah Kalekin-Fishman and Kelvin E.Y. Low (Burlington, VT: Ashgate, 2010), 19–39.

interests and highlight cultural and political differentiation: popular radio music on Jewish radio stations invokes not only nostalgia,
but traces origin through Slavic melodies and seeks to unite Jewish
identity as it also perceptually excludes the ancestry of half the Jewish
population from African and Near Eastern countries; sirens signaling emergencies and alien hostilities direct and require a homogenous
and ritualized performance of a unified national population (all are
threatened, all act out protective measures, strengthening performance
of state and citizenship); Muslim prayers offered in mosques and via
loudspeakers are aural and bodily movements uniting the participants
and aligning Muslim identity, sounds which to others might emerge as
noise, disturbance, and potential perceptual signal of mobilizing political action against the state.[47]

Bodily perceptual orientations and habituated ways of perceiving
are our epistemological schemata, our ways of thinking and knowing.
Knowing difference differently, or knowing what is same and other differently, can help us conceive of ways in which otherness or strangeness
may be aligned in ways strange to visual determinations of otherness.

By focusing on the content of our perception, rather than the *processes* of bodily perceptual orientations, we are oriented to overlook
the subtending terrains which provide the conditions for our habits,
their sedimentation, as well as the conditions for new habit acquisi-
tions. But it also occludes differences from our perception, things that
are out of line: for example, it occludes how our discoveries about race
are dependent on the creation and perpetuation of this very category
itself. Just like terrains and currents are shifting and indeterminate,
so are the relations between sediment habit and perceptual orienting
lines or devices. For example, an orienting line such as whiteness can
provide the habitual schema supporting perceptions of gender, femi-
nizing the racial other or denying the racialized female body alignments with femininity.[48] Sedimented habits regarding perception of

47. Ibid., 26–34.
48. For those studying postcolonial theory, none of the arguments I just very super-
ficially traced appear new, in fact, they might remind us of works of Frantz Fanon,

nationhood can become an orienting device, aligning perceptual orientation toward religious bodies (as seen, for example, in perceptual orientations toward Persian men aligned with emerging meanings of Islamic fundamentalist religiosity, which then contribute again toward sedimentation of bodily habits—emotional, legal, cultural—toward these bodies, as in fear, incarceration, wars against terror, and so forth).

Understanding our orientations and perspectives on the world as fundamentally embedded in and emerging from our bodily manner of existence then allows us to begin grasping how it is not reason or intellectual reflection alone that effects and therefore can address perceptual alignments which might appear problematic to us (such as perceptual alignments of female bodies as submissive, queer bodies as deviant, or black bodies as criminal). Rather, as we have explored thus far, habits and socio-cultural practices are not simply matters of belief or conviction held in a disembodied mind, but are embedded within our bodily perceptual orientation as conditions of our existence. Only from this perspective can we understand more complexly how mechanisms of perception lead to prejudice and oppression of bodies perceived as different, mechanisms so powerful that appeals to intellect or mindfulness fail to prevent violence against bodies perceived a certain way.

Relating back to the larger aim of this project, to develop a robust understanding of experience for body theology, we can now understand how experiences of race (or racialized/racializing experiences) come about in visceral ways, that is, involving all our senses and the bodily ways in which we use them or are "used by" them. To interrogate bodily perceptual orientation in order to usefully and complexly

Black Skin, White Masks (New York, NY: Grove Press, 1962). Edward W. Said, *Orientalism* (New York, NY: Vintage Books, 1979). Ward Churchill, *Fantasies of the Master Race: Literature, Cinema and the Colonization of American Indians* (San Francisco, CA: City Lights Publishers, 1998).

1998). Stephen Greenblatt, *Marvelous Possessions: The Wonder of the New World* (Chicago: University of Chicago Press, 1991). Meyda Yeğenoğlu, *Colonial Fantasies: Towards a Feminist Reading of Orientalism* (New York, NY: Cambridge University Press, 1998).

understand bodily experience is to heed perceptual orientation as that through which one comes to terms with meanings (such as race, skin color, other bodily markers) in the world, and it is to heed perceptual orientations not as structures of consciousness, but as bodily experience, bodily expression, bodily motivations, bodily intentions, bodily behaviors, bodily styles, and bodily rhythms. These orientations are not firstly and fundamentally expressed at the level of thought, but give rise to thought, thought that embodies the precision and nuances of bodily perceptual orientations.[49] The next chapter will conclude our theoretical exploration, investigating the notion of thought, more specifically in connection to language as habit and perception of normalcy.

49. Here I am appropriating again Charles Long's definition of religion: "Religion will mean orientation—orientation in the ultimate sense, that is, how one comes to terms with the ultimate significance of one's place in the world." And in the following paragraph, he further clarifies: "The religion of any people is more than a structure of thought; it is experience, expression, motivations, intentions, behaviors, styles, and rhythms. Its first and fundamental expression is not at the level of thought. It gives rise to thought, but a form of thought that embodies the precision and nuances of its source." Charles H. Long, *Significations: Signs, Symbols and Images in the Interpretation of Religion* (Aurora, CO: The Davies Group Publishers, 1996), 7. Long shows how specific orientations in and of the world give rise to the creation of knowledge. To put his definition to work, the modern Enlightenment project framed the experience, expressions, motivations, intentions, behaviors, styles, and rhythms of the bodies in the Western world in specific ways as these bodies expand into a world "other" to them. And the origins of the study of religion, just like the category of religion, cannot be fully understood without acknowledging and accounting for these bodily and conceptual orientations which gave and give rise to thought and knowledge productions. While Long defines religion here, I hope that my argumentation thus far has already demonstrated that religion is but one dimension and alignment of bodily perceptual orientation, like race or gender. Long points out the specific configurations and lines of orientation in the study of religion, the way history was invented, constructed, and oriented, if you will. Religion as a concept oriented the European colonization, documentation, and categorization of those conquered and subjugated in "other" worlds. Ibid., 106–108. I am elaborating on the connection between Long's religion as orientation and Ahmed's investigation of orientation more specifically in Heike Peckruhn, "Bodies as Orientation in/to the World—Bodies in Queer Phenomenology and Religious Studies," presented at the *American Academy of Religion Annual Meeting* (Chicago, IL: 2012).

CHAPTER FIVE

LANGUAGE AND PERCEPTION OF NORMALCY

So far we have explored how it is that our being in the world is fundamentally grounded in bodily perceptual orientation. There is still room left to posit interior conscious processes, such as a conscious subject directing recognition of different bodies along cultural schemata through interior mental acts, disconnected from bodily experience and engagement in the world. At stake in misunderstanding our processes of perceptual orientation as interior mental acts is that we might mistake the pre-reflective dimension conditioning, our "take on the world" (how I come to interpret and assign meaning around me), simply as a set of thoughts or beliefs rather than a complex, internally heterogonous set of perceptual orientations embodied through me.[1] If the former were so, if our takes on the world, our views on race, gender, and normalcy were simply a matter of internal thought, then changing those beliefs emerging out of thought in accordance with "rationally" pursued knowledge should affect our perceptions and embodied experiences in some ways so as to be in alignment with our intellectual convictions.

For example, if I know "in my mind" that skin color makes no difference in regard to the value or intellectual capability of a person, then my bodily experiences should follow my intellectual convictions,

1. Linda Martín Alcoff, *Visible Identities: Race, Gender, and the Self* (New York, NY: Oxford University Press, 2006), 113.

and I should no longer perceive skin color in hierarchical ways, nor should I experience reactions to skin color that have evaluative effects. Yet I do, because there is knowledge tacitly present in my embodied being which orients me toward others, as I have discussed previously. And how is it then, that I can "know in my mind" that my grandmother is still a human being as she is seemingly unresponsive to personal interaction, but I seem to have to keep telling myself that this is indeed so, all the while my visceral response to her betrays a perceptual orientation incongruent with what "I think and know"?

We now need to understand how the corporeal and social dimensions of perception interrelate. When we explore the relationship and dynamic between bodily and social dimensions of our existence through "normalcy" and the role of language, we will find that these dimensions are irreducible to each other and their interrelation paradoxical: Language manifests as bodily perceptual orientation that shapes bodily difference in terms of deviance and/or normalcy and within systems of social, economic, and political empowerment.

LANGUAGE IN/AS BODILY PERCEPTUAL ORIENTATION

To help conceive of language as corporeal and social, of language as inseparably related to body-mind and the world, it is useful to think of language through the previous frame of perception. I have discussed in the previous chapter how separating perception into, for example, bodily sensation, and evaluation and judgment in the mind, is problematic: We experience the seeing or tasting or something not as separate entities of a process (e.g., I do not experience stimulation on my retina, which I then evaluate as distinct information regarding light, and then make a judgment as to what I perceive as "person in front of me"), but rather, I see a friend coming through the office door. This is because perception is always bodily (I have physical capacities in my bodily functions, the interplay of my organs, and neural system), consciously (perception extends me into the world, it is an engagement with the world that is more than just bodily reception of sense data, perception makes sense of my world and how I bodily "fit"), and worldly (the way I bodily perceive and which meanings emerge is also influenced by the world, the social contexts, meaning systems, and bodily alignments into which I am born and which shape my acquisition of perceptual habits).

Exploring language, we can grasp different components at work for language to emerge, components which are irreducible to each other, but nevertheless inseparable. I have a bodily capacity for articulation and voice; I use my lungs for a certain kind of breathing, which, coupled with my vocal cords, produces sound; with my tongue, teeth, lips, and force of breath, I make speech sounds. I can use my bodily capacity for voice to express myself, as form of communication. This extends me into the world and is a form of engagement with the world, it involves conscious acts of using voice and articulation intentionally, about something, toward a purpose. And the world is also involved; without a world, there would be nothing to use voice and articulation in reference to, and/or nothing to express myself for. My social context also provides the socially shared rules, the sediment habit of linguistic rules such as grammar, a meaning system within which I can use speech to communicate.[2]

In regard to understanding language as corporeal and social, none of the listed aspects can be separated from the other. While I might not be able to use my vocal cords in ways to use my voice, I can nevertheless "speak" with my body, through bodily gestures forming signs and even

---

2. Swiss Linguist Ferdinand de Saussure defined language as *langue* + *parole*: *Langue* is the language system, the sedimented system of signs of the community in which we learn to speak; *parole* is the act of speaking by a person, the social activity of using words to speak or write to communicate something in a specific context. There is an interdependency between *langue* and *parole*; *parole* develops *langue*, but *langue* is also implied by *parole*. Language as the sum of the two then also incorporates the bodily capacity to speak. Ferdinand de Saussure, Albert Sechehaye Charles Bally, and Albert Riedlinger, *Course in General Linguistics*, trans. Wade Baskin (LaSalle, IL: Open Court, 1986).

"tonality" through gestural emphasis (as we can see in sign language, which is not a translation of spoken language, but has its own grammar, rules, and system).[3]

Research into language acquisition and cognitive development shows that phonology (organization of sound), morphology (formation and structure of words), and syntax (arrangement of words) indeed are acquired through neural mechanisms in the brain. By way of cognitive development, we can observe timetables of linguistic maturation connected to physical, biochemical, and neural development. By way of pathology we can observe absence of capacity to organize sounds considered proper in a given language, or an inability to arrange words according to cultural rules of syntax connected to injury or disease affecting the brain. Yet the learning of words itself is not reducible to a biological capacity. Cognitive linguistic research shows that it is rather a rich and complex system of conceptual representations, capacities to infer the intention of others, and perceptual sensitivities to cues given regarding meaning in the speech and gestures of others.[4]

3. I do appreciate Elaine Scarry's argument regarding the undoing of language in extreme pain and suffering; extreme physical pain (as in torture) is inexpressible in the given cultural vocabulary. Yet her argument is based in conceiving of language mainly as linguistic expression, while I would conceive of her world-making activities such as artistic and cultural creations also as dimensions of bodily language. In the end, however, our conceptions might turn out to complement each other, as the kinds of extreme pain she describes might be accounted for in my framework as experience with no readily available/emerging meaning, unmaking orientations and alignments we are habituated to. See Elaine Scarry, *The Body in Pain: The Making and Unmaking of the World* (New York, NY: Oxford University Press, 1985). Sonia Kruks also comments that while pain might be difficult to represent discursively, it does not necessarily lack communicability. In fact, pain might be "spoken" through bodies expressing their condition in ways that can be "felt" by others. Sonia Kruks, *Retrieving Experience: Subjectivity and Recognition in Feminist Politics* (Ithaca, NY: Cornell University Press, 2001), 165.
4. Paul Bloom, "Roots of Word Learning," in *Language Acquisition and Conceptual Development*, ed. Melissa Bowerman and Stephen C. Levinson (Cambridge, UK: Cambridge University Press, 2001), 159–181.

Merleau-Ponty's stated that "I think through and with and by means of language."[5] Language is not a property of an independent consciousness, it is not simply the outside to a prior existing interior thought. Rather, thought and language are simultaneously constituted by our bodily capacities and embeddedness in a world—my capacity to think is inherently related to my bodily biochemical capacities, to my bodily intentionality (to extend into the world bodily and consciously), and to my social context.[6] Put differently, because I am a body, because I see, smell, touch, feel, hear things in reference to my body-self, language "makes sense to me" in reference to my situation in the world, and language has sedimented as a result of corporeal reference and habitual meanings, and my bodily and social habituations allow for creative expression, allow for new meanings to emerge.[7] Yet I also "do" language as a living, speaking, perceiving body, which also limits

---

5. Merleau-Ponty, *Phenomenology of Perception*, 389. Merleau-Ponty's conception of language is one he repeatedly returns to, but also repeatedly reformulates and revises. His thoughts on language are not continuous, but transforming with each reiteration in terms of other issues he is articulating. What is most useful to my discussion is that Merleau-Ponty points to parameters within which he places language: the ambiguity of significations (it is always open to more than just a consistent network of significations) and the expression of a style (the achievement of saying something as an expressive gesture, which is bodily intentionality intertwining with the world/being an embodied point of view, making it possible to say something "new"). Hugh J. Silverman, "Merleau-Ponty and the Interrogation of Language," in *Merleau-Ponty: Perception, Structure, Language*, ed. John Sallis (Atlantic Highlands, NJ: Humanities Press, 1981), 123. Linda Singer, "Merleau-Ponty on the Concept of Style," in *The Merleau-Ponty Asthetics Reader: Philosophy and Painting*, ed. Galen Johnson and Michael Smith (Evanston, IL: Northwestern University Press, 1993), 233–244.

6. Within which I learn *langue* and *parole*. See note 2 of this chapter.

7. Merleau-Ponty is not the only or first philosopher to make this observation. See also, for example, Wittgenstein on the biological underpinnings of language, or Polanyi on the tacit reliance upon the body for all forms of knowledge. Ludwig Wittgenstein, *Philosophical Investigations*, trans., G. E. M. Anscombe, 3rd ed. (New York, NY: Macmillan, 1958), 188–189, 280–283. Michael Polyani, *Personal Knowledge: Towards a Post-Critical Philosophy* (Chicago, IL: University of Chicago Press, 1964), 61–66.

"*my* language"; I am limited in/by my bodily capacities, my conscious engagement with the world in language, and the socio-cultural world in which I exist.

For example, my mother's native tongue, Thai, is a tonal language, so that the same string of syllables can make up different signs/words by way of intonating it differently. Thai has five different tonalities: high, middle, low, rising, and falling; and there are regional tonal dialects as well. The syllable *maa*, for example, can signify *dog* if spoken in rising tonal register, but signifies *come* when spoken in the high or middle register—inviting hilarious or offensive misintonations by the tonally non-fluent. Tonality is a bodily capacity to arrange vocal cords and breath to reach the desired sound, yet it is also a bodily habit which needs to be acquired. It is not impossible to learn a tonal language as second language, but for those growing up in language systems in which tonality expresses emotion or takes on grammatical functions (such as shouting when angry, or raising one's voice to signify a question), tonal languages tend to be difficult bodily habits to acquire.

The sounds of *ä*, *ö*, and *ü* are embedded in my native German language system, and I grew up learning to produce, identify, and use diphthong sounds. Yet these bodily capacities and/or habits do not necessarily emerge together. Trying to teach American students German diphthongs, I could teach them how to form *ü* with their lips and tongue, so they could, for example, speak the word *fünf* (five). Yet when asking them if they could hear the difference between *fünf* and *funf*, many of those sounding out *ü* were unable to distinguish it even after much practice.

Another example could be found in Thai language again. The sounds distinguished in English or German as "r" and "l," produced through certain movements of the tongue either in the back or the front of the mouth, are sounds not distinguished in Thai, so that the word for *foreigner* can alternatively be pronounced as *falang* or *farang*. While both soundings are distinguishable to the Thai ear, the meaning signified is not, and both pronunciations may be heard.[8]

8. A similar example can be found among the Kikuyu in Kenya. Members of this tribe tend to mix up "r" and "l" in the English language, the meaning emerging

To engage in language systems is more than just learning linguistic skills. Socio-cultural processes of personal and communal engagements and meanings are also bound up in language, language again understood as corporeal and social. Outsiders in a given context may appear so for their lack of "passing" linguistically. For example, Thai language does not tend to imbue speaking with emotional qualities. Culturally, emotions or emphasis added is not necessarily done in inflections (though not impossible, but it is not the main way to do so). A question, for example, is indicated by an added word, rather than the raising of the voice at the end of a sentence (in English words may be added as in *Where did you go?* or one may simply raise the voice as in *You went there?*). This may make sense when considering that Thai culture puts great value in public presentation, "saving face" through a certain way of performing language, such as measurement in vocalization, but also in the many meanings embedded in a smile.[9] The cultural values of how one presents oneself publicly to others then also sediments in the manner of speech, so that to speak Thai is to be bound to a cultural language system in which measured tonality, voice, and bodily expressions are highly valued.

It appears to us now that language also operates along pre-established perceptual alignments which stabilizes perceived meaning through sedimented habits, while still always being open to new or different perceived meanings. In my speaking, I am dependent upon my bodily

then depending on context (e.g., the Kikuyu politician Mary Wambui spoke in her acceptance speech of having experienced a hard "erection." Official news media outlets would adjust the linguistic sign to match the context—political election—whereas social media maintained the r/l mispronunciation in order to invoke the sexual meaning within the political context). My gratitude to Patience Kamau for bringing this example to my attention.

9. Thailand is often called "the land of a thousand smiles." A smile might suggest a humorous situation, friendliness, or kindness; it may express politeness, forgiveness, readiness to listen, gently expressing one's doubt or opposition; it may indicate defensiveness, even anger or hurt, sadness, or feeling insulted. The Thai practice of smiling eludes my perceptual capacities and linguistic abilities. I might see my mother smile, but I have yet to become "fluent in speaking/hearing/knowing/being Thai smiles."

capacities of word formation, I am dependent on past uses of language in order to convey anything meaningful (in thought, speech, writing, etc.), yet I can say something new or different by fitting and using my linguistic expression into my context. This new speech and associated meaning now takes on a "social life" and may be a part of linguistic sedimentation.[10] The "social power" of this new meaning depends on if and how this meaning sediments through habituation.[11]

I enter into a world in which language is already sedimented. I am born into a pre-existing linguistic terrain within which I learn to think and express my thoughts through words, within which I learn to use my bodily capacities for voice and gestures, for example, to "say something," to make use of my bodily capacities within the conventional signifying system. And while words and rules of grammar and syntax might exist before I bodily-consciously use language, my actual saying something is not a fixed reference. Language is ambiguous and open to bodily change (change in how we pronounce words or intonate them) and new meanings, even new rules and structures.

For example, the English word *dog* and the associated pronunciation already signifies a furry animal of a certain shape which can adapt to living with humans and emits certain barky sounds. Yet there is no necessary univocity or consistency when I use the word *dog*—the meaning emerges in the interrelation between the sedimented language and my taking up language in a speech act: there is no direct and consistent connection between the word dog and the bodily being it signifies. But

10. "Speech is, therefore, that paradoxical operation through which, by using words of a given sense, and already available meanings, we try to follow up an intention which necessarily outstrips, modifies, and itself, in the last analysis, stabilizes the meanings of the words which translate it." Merleau-Ponty, *Phenomenology of Perception*, 389.

11. It should also become clear here then that language is more than expression. While expression or communication are functions of language, language encompasses the social systems of signification within which we express ourselves; the bodily capacities for sound, voice, gesture, and tonality; cognitive capacities of association, learning, and memory; social abilities such as relating physically and emotionally, and more.

neither do I create this meaningful connection anew every time I utter the word. The paradoxical relation between existing linguistic meanings and the not-yet-emergent meaning expressible in the speech act is that present meaning can only emerge because of previously emerged meanings *and* because of the possibility of new meanings. This paradox is what makes creative individual and communal expression possible, it is the relation between speakers, signs (the word as spelled and pronounced), prior language use (socio-cultural sediment) and current speech (my bodily utterance in the moment referring to something).

Context is significant in the use of language: If my saying *dog* actually refers to a *furry barking animal*, or to a *sausage put between a bread bun*, or is a *derogatory reference* to another human person, or is creating a new contextual meaning nevertheless perceivable to others, is only determinable in the situational *and* socio-cultural context while at the same time depending on the dynamics of socio-cultural sediment (the occurrences of linguistic habits forming).

Dog may become a slur only through repetitive derogatory speech acts and habitual sedimentation through social repetitions.[12] But if *dog* emerges as slur depends also on the situational context, including my actual bodily performance of this speech act encompassing other sensory dimensions (such as sound and gestures). As all meaning is ambiguous and indeterminate, so are linguistic signs and meaning open to change: For example, *dog* as derogatory reference to a human person is open to change so that *dawg* (phonetically similar, though visual-textually different) emerges as sign to refer to a close friend in speech acts between two African-American men in an urban US cultural context.

Without bodily and cognitive capacities, and without using these inherited frames of linguistic references, I cannot "accomplish" language,

---

12. Involving the bodily capacity for speech, but also specific intonations that may be habitually aligned with speaking insults, the cognitive capacity to think about ways in which to creatively use words when we wish to insult a person, and the social habit of providing me with linguistic habits so that certain words are recognized as insult, rather than a random act of misplaced reference.

though language is not a fixed system with static reference to meanings.[13] The meaning of linguistic expressions emerge over time, they are dynamic and changeable in new eras and social contexts. Linguistic signs (a word and the associated sound and textual representation) that have sedimented can be taken up and metamorphose anew through a spontaneous speech act: I might call a person a dog and it is understood as insult, not as misrecognition or misspeaking; or I might still misspeak due to bodily perceptual alignments which lead to failure to perform recognized linguistic gestures (e.g., even if I may accomplish speaking *dawg* phonetically, my specific embodied existence might prohibit the intended perception).

Language is not separate from the intertwining of body-mind-world. I speak as body, physically; I speak from my corporeality, in reference to my bodily being; I speak to an embodied world, in reference and communication with world within which meaningful discourse emerges, and within which I am but one of the players in an active and creative process of meaning. In speaking, I speak through my bodily gestures and perceptual capacities—I do not think a thought and then command my body to carry out the thought through language. I think through and with and by means of language as body.

As I have explored through the example of Thai language, language is proper to the body in that my bodily perceptual orientation in the world inscribes the meanings emerging in/through language as bodily perceptual intentionality. Language is not strictly only the words I utter within a grammatical system, but language is bodies in movement, and bodies extending physically and socio-culturally toward others in the world. In other words, I "do" and embody language through being a thinking/gesturing/speaking body (even as I silently type, I do this as body and through my bodily capacities). And the manner in which I emerge via language is embedded in my bodily capacities and habits, my bodily perceptual orientations in and toward the world, and

13. Merleau-Ponty, *Phenomenology of Perception*, 178, 197. Maurice Merleau-Ponty, *The Prose of the World*, trans. John O'Neill (Evanston, IL: Northwestern University Press, 1973), 13.

interacts with socio-cultural sedimented habit (such as specific linguistic habits or culturally informed bodily gestures) in bodily form, in a specific context.

To speak, write, and think is a form of bodily intentionality, to extend into the world through bodily-linguistic movements toward cultural expression (though language, like perception, is always more than this function of expression). This movement takes bodily being beyond biological limitations/capacities, and body and culture become implicated with each other and incorporate each other.[14] Put differently, I can extend into this world and relate to and about my dog—thinking and speaking about it, touching it—because I have a bodily relation and reference to this furry animal. But I am also already moving bodily beyond my biological capacities; I am already extending myself toward and through cultural means. Namely, I use the signifier *dog* and relate to this animal as my pet; I engage in culturally determined social, economical, moral, and individual habits of pet care.[15]

Significant here is that without others, there would be no need and no sediment habit to extend myself (with). Using language is already a relational bodily movement, moving intentionally toward an other; extending linguistic gestures the meaning of which emerges in the relation between me and other. Communication through bodily gestures in relationship takes place in a *reciprocal* perceptual grid or current, where my bodily intentionality and the other's intertwine in order to be meaningfully grasped. In other words, language, gestures, bodily movements, perceptual intentions, need to be part of a sediment habit, repeatable and performable (though not fixed or static), in order to be appropriable in relation between bodies.[16]

14. Silverman, "Merleau-Ponty and the Interrogation of Language," 125.
15. How these are culturally determined bodily expressive intensions becomes more clear when reflecting on other cultures, in which "dog" might emerge within meaning systems where this kind of furry animal is related to as food source. For an investigation of perceptual alignments of animals, see Melanie Joy, *Why We Love Dogs, Eat Pigs, and Wear Cows: An Introduction to Carnism* (San Francisco, CA: Red Wheel/Weiser, 2010).
16. Silverman, "Merleau-Ponty and the Interrogation of Language," 125.

Language and Bodily Perceptual Orientation of/to "Normal"

Language is inscribed in any of the problems we explored previously—be it perception as fundamental to our being in the world, be it gendered perceptual intentionality, be it racialized perceptual alignments—and can help us explore the relational dynamics at work. But language itself is also bound to the knowledge frame in which we undergo these explorations.[17] Just like I can only know about my experiences by experiencing, I can only know about my perceptions in perceiving, and I only know about language by thinking, speaking, writing, and reading. The significances of our experience, perception, and language as bodily movements are manifest *in* our movements.[18] The ground from which meaning and significances emerge is the mutual constituting of space between body-body/body-world through bodily movement (bodily perceptual intentions). In this inherently open bodily relation, meanings are not fixed, but are ambiguous and indeterminate. Therefore our cognitive achievements, even complex and sophisticated ones (such as concept formation and linguistic abstractions, like language and concepts referring to normalcy) are fundamentally grounded in embodied life.[19] Exploring language can point us "back" to the sedimentation of habits from which our bodies and perceptions emerge.[20]

17. Ibid., 122. For example, my using language in this project is already bound to the knowledge frames that tend to separate body and mind, so my thinking and writing about it in some ways binds me to this pre-reflective epistemological frame, and I might have to create ways of speaking about body and mind that appear cumbersome (or even writing about the "problem" of a body/mind dualism, which might not be a problem in a different cultural context where there might not even be differentiating words).

18. Merleau-Ponty, *Phenomenology of Perception*, 394.

19. Marratto, *The Intercorporeal Self*, 19–20.

20. Merleau-Ponty describes this relationship as a phenomenological principle of "foundation," identified by Husserl as the necessary connection which can unconditionally serve as basis for valid inferences and necessary truths. Merleau-Ponty designates this connection as a two-way relationship in which neither originator nor originated can be ordered, because the latter makes manifest the former. For example, the relation of thought to language is a founding term, but a two-way

When it comes to "normal" bodies and minds, I notice how I habitually perceive body and mind as distinct but connected entities: sitting with my grandmother in her still-early stages of Alzheimer's as she appears to be ignorant to the smell of burning milk on the stove, wondering if she is losing her mind ("how can a 'normal' person not respond to this acrid smell?"); or helping my father change her diapers, when "she is losing control" over "normal" bodily functions. Perceptual orientations to "different from normal" may extend meanings between intellectual and physical abilities, for example, a wheelchair user might be perceived as intellectually inferior, or an outstanding athlete might make news because of his intellectual difference.[21]

NORMAL SEDIMENTS

How exactly is the living matter of our bodies connected to perceptual associations with social hierarchies? Cognitive linguists Lakoff and Johnson analyze language and cognitive structures to argue that linguistic metaphors are always essentially rooted in embodied life and embodied structures and in turn structure the world we live in and our experiences of it.[22] Primarily focusing on the embodied nature of

relationship: language is thought as originator and thought presented as originated, yet it is only through thought that language is made manifest. The two cannot be absorbed, their ambiguity not resolved. Merleau-Ponty, *Phenomenology of Perception*, 177–199.

21. For example: James McElwain, a person with autism, became a news sensation after scoring twenty points in four minutes during a high school basketball game. His position was that of team manager, assistant to the coach, though when his team had achieved a significant lead, the coach put McElwain on the court as a thank-you for McElwain's dedication to the team. In news media and Internet platforms such as YouTube, McElwain's "undiscovered" or "unexpected" aptitude continues to circulate as inspirational story for able-bodied and able-minded persons.

22. Johnson and Lakoff argue that embodied schemas, as they arise from our perceptual interactions with the world (our bodily movements, our motile engagements, our bodily perceptual grasp), are crucial for the intelligibility of language. These embodied schemas include, for example, bodily projection (front-back,

metaphors and the embodied effects of linguistic practices still leaves room to argue that language actually does refer to biological "raw materials" given that inherently carry meaning. Were this the case, then dealing with problematic derogatory social associations all we need to do is cease using language with devaluing meaning or re-value language with positive meanings. Simply ceasing to refer to my grandmother as "vegetable" when she seemed cognitively incapable should be enough to change my emotional and behavioral attitude toward her to "rediscover" her inherent meaningfulness as human being. Or imbuing references with positive meaning, as has been done, for example, by reclaiming "crip" in a socio-political act of disability pride should suffice as social and political action to "un-cover" the inherent worth of uncommon bodies.

But linguistic meaning emerging between the biological and social is indeterminate and discontinuous. The sign language of American Deaf communities, particularly the linguistic meaning of "deaf" and related signs illustrate this: The signed phrase A-LITTLE-HARD-OF-HEARING, a phrase in audist cultures referring to someone who is slightly hearing impaired (a little hard-of-hearing), is used in Deaf communities to refer to persons who are *slightly hearing* (but mostly deaf).[23] The signed phrase VERY-HARD-OF-HEARING, a phrase in audist cultures referring to someone who cannot hear well at all (very hard-of-hearing), is used in Deaf communities to refer to persons who can hear well (only a little hearing impaired).

---

near-far, up-down), or force dynamic schemas (push, pull, support, balance, gather), and other schemas less easily categorized (part-whole, cycle, link, contact). Mark Johnson, *The Body in the Mind: The Bodily Basis of Meaning, Imagination, and Reason* (Chicago, IL: University of Chicago Press, 1987), 29–45. George Lakoff and Mark Johnson, *Philosophy in the Flesh: The Embodied Mind and Its Challenge to Western Thought* (New York, NY: Basic Books, 1999), 31–36. See also George Lakoff and Mark Johnson, *Metaphors We Live By* (Chicago, IL: University of Chicago Press, 1980; reprint, 2003).

23. I am following here the habit of capitalizing linguistic signs, which are not spoken, but gestured.

Here we have biological givens (different degrees of auditory abilities) connected to linguistic signs (hard * hearing), yet they are discontinuously aligned. Audist explanations offered trace this back to lack in proper English skills, a case of deaf communities mixing up and failing at "normal" meaning associations. But, as Padden and Humphries demonstrate, this difference in linguistic meanings emerges out of social habit: In Deaf communities, HEARING is the opposite of what Deaf people are. DEAF, not HEARING emerges as dominant bodily habit and socio-cultural value (deaf is normal) in hierarchical perceptual alignments. The sedimented linguistic habit for HARD-OF-HEARING connects this sign to mean deviation of some kind. Bodies align differently in this perceptual grid, so that A-LITTLE-HARD-OF-HEARING means slight bodily deviation from normal-deaf (a little different from deaf, mostly deaf), whereas VERY-HARD-OF-HEARING indicates greater deviation from normal (very different from deaf, mostly hearing).[24]

Disability scholar Rosemarie Garland Thomson remarks:

> Thus, the ways that bodies interact with the socially engineered environment and conform to social expectations determine the varying degrees of disability or able-bodied-ness, of extra-ordinariness or ordinariness. Consequently, the meanings attributed to extraordinary bodies reside not in inherent physical flaws, but in social relationships in which one group is legitimated by possessing valued physical characteristics and maintains its ascendancy and its self-identity by systematically imposing the role of cultural or corporeal inferiority on others.[25]

Meaning is not achieved on the level of thought as an interiorized mental activity. Social ideologies pervading social imagination indeed are

---

24. Carol Padden and Tom Humphries, "Deaf People: A Different Center," in *The Disability Studies Reader*, ed. Lennard J. Davis (New York, NY: Routledge, 2010), 393–402.
25. Rosemarie Garland Thomson, *Extraordinary Bodies: Figuring Physical Disability in American Culture and Literature* (New York, NY: Columbia University Press, 1997), 7.

expressed in and do their work through social gestures, language being *one* of the dimensions of social enactment and habitual repetition.

Language is one of the ways in which normalcy emerges in the interaction between bodies and social world. Language demonstrate the dialectic between bodies and social world, because it is embedded it, and helps us explore bodily perception as immediate and mediated.

Differences in bodily capacities—which influence our bodily perceptual movements—are differences in being in the world. Normalcy as able-bodied-ness, as "not disabled," reveals the linking between bodily difference and cultural and corporeal values made in references and representations.[26] Exploring the corporeal dimensions of language and discourse is crucial. If we do not explore them, we might leave in place a naturalized discursive concept of bodily difference, that is, we may presuppose that bodily differences materialize through production and regulation of hegemonic symbolic orders only. Embodied differences then remain bodies coming to matter and taking shape within discursive productions of values, as materialization of discursive concepts. While materiality is not reducible to the discursive, not exploring the corporeal dimension of language makes it difficult to engage the materiality of bodies beyond discussing cultural constructions within which these bodily differences materialize as such. It might also make

---

26. Discourses on "disability" engage (to use or to deconstruct) the distinctions of the World Health Organization between impairment, disability, and handicap: *impairment* is defined as an abnormality in function, *disability* as not being able to perform an activity considered normal for a human being, and *handicap* as the inability to perform a "normal" social role. While these distinctions are useful when discussing physical or mental difference over against socio-culturally imposed barriers or inaccessibility, these terms still inherently draw on a medical classification system that makes assumptions about normalcy and maintains the focus on the perceived/experienced impairment and solutions to it. This keeps disability within the confines of individualized experiences and bodily difference and its desired normalization, rather than highlighting social and cultural disabling mechanisms. Colin Barnes, "A Brief History of Discrimination and Disabled People," in *The Disability Studies Reader*, ed. Lennard J. Davis (New York, NY: Routledge, 2010), 29.

discourse about bodily difference the originary perceptual experience, privileging cultural concepts over material embodiment even when insisting on their embeddedness. In other words, we make it difficult to engage bodily experiences of a paraplegic, for example, beyond social constructions of disablement by inadvertently positing the discursively constructed meaning of "paraplegic" as originary to this kind of bodily experience.

Merleau-Ponty's body schema reminds us that embodiment is not free from cultural inscriptions. Experiencing and engendering of meanings is a deeply bodily experience where difference is engendered, but not necessarily discursively dominated. Remember that my body schema is my bodily blueprint that structures perceptions and my sense of self and/in relation to my environment. If it configures my movements and postures which also affect my bodily sense of unity, then no matter what body I find myself in, one dimension of bodily experience (which is not separate, or beneath, but concurrent/a co-current with other bodily experiences) is that of myself as a bodily unit.

For example, a person born without limbs holds a complete body schema (her legs have not been severed through perhaps amputation), and her body schema and bodily intentionality (such as her proximal movements) are established according to her tacit understanding of herself as bodily unit. Also, what are usually considered as objects different from bodies might also come to be part of our body schema and bodily extension, for example, a pianist with visual impairment comes to incorporate the piano into his body schema so that the piano is part of the bodily unit that is him, similar to the ways in which a cane can become not an object or tool of a person who is blind, but a tactile bodily organ, part of the unifying/-ied body schema.[27] Bodily

27. Miho Iwakma, "The Body as Embodiment: An Investigation of the Body by Merleau-Ponty," in *Disability/Postmodernity*, ed. Mairian Corker and Tom Shakespeare (New York, NY: Continuum, 2002), 78–81. See also Merleau-Ponty's description of a blind person walking with a cane, the cane being how the person is aware (aware with the cane, not of it). Merleau-Ponty, *Phenomenology of Perception*, 143–146.

perceptual intentionality, my movement in the world, is synthesized in the various motions my body and bodily parts are capable of, and my body schema is that of a whole, unified body.

Being deaf/Deaf might again help to illustrate this point. While common ableist modern perception of this difference in bodily perceptual capacity is that of *deaf* as lack of hearing, the *Deaf* instead see themselves as a distinct cultural group that uses a different language. The culturally Deaf (those considering themselves as part of a linguistic and cultural minority), understand themselves to function as an adequate, self-enclosed, self-defining culture and community, yet a cultural minority which functions in an "audist" society, a society that is biased toward the auditory mode of communication. This is not simply a linguistic redefinition but a bodily perceptual experience and orientation. The bodily experience of a deaf person is not necessarily one that is immediately or solely a materialization of an audist/able-ist conceptual inscription. Rather, the person born deaf extends bodily as a whole unit within and through the bodily capacities of her individual sensory perceptual intentionality, rather than as an incomplete unit, extending with perceptual deficiencies. From this perspective, the absence of hearing is no more a deficiency, abnormality, or disability than the absence of English speaking skills is.[28]

Of course, as both disability and feminist scholars have pointed out, fragmentations of body *image* are not only possible, but a bodily experience shared amongst those subjected to becoming the embodiment of difference.[29] But the body *schema*, this pre-reflective perceptual

28. Deborah Beth Creamer, *Disability and Christian Theology: Embodied Limits and Constructive Possibilities* (New York, NY: Oxford University Press, 2009), 97. Harlan Lane, "Construction of Deafness," in *The Disability Studies Reader* (New York, NY: Routledge, 2010), 86–87.
29. See Lennard J. Davis, "Nude Venuses, Medusa's Body, and Phantom Limbs: Disability and Visuality," in *The Body and Phsyical Difference: Discourses of Disability*, ed. David T. Mitchell and Sharon L. Snyder (Ann Arbor, MI: University of Michigan Press, 1997), 51–70; Jennifer C. James, "Gwendolyn Brooks, World War Ii, and the Politics of Rehabilitation," in *Feminist Disability Studies Reader*, ed. Kim Q. Hall (Bloomington, IN: Indiana University Press, 2011), 153–157. Gail Weiss, *Body Images: Embodiment as Intercorporality* (New York, NY: Routledge,

understanding of my bodily capacities and motility, is an experience in which bodily difference emerges as such. I realize my bodily self-transcendence as/in my body, and my body schema informs how I perform my "I can" in the world.

Now, if I were born without legs, I am not just "compensating" for what others with four limbs might perceive as a lack. My pre-reflexive bodily experience, my tacit knowledge of my ability to extend bodily in a given environment, is not of lacking a certain capacity and then adjusting to this lack. But my body image as impaired, disabled, or abnormal is a concurrent dynamic influencing my bodily experience, not separate and/or following from my body schema entering a social world, but the terrain in which I move and am bodily immersed. My bodily intentionality, my bodily movement toward cultural expression, then takes my bodily being beyond my biological capacities of movement with two limbs, incorporates sediment habits of language ("I have a mobility impairment," "I am disabled," "I cannot walk on legs," "I do not move like a normal person") as I speak of my bodily condition.

All the while my self-experience of myself as fully functioning and capable person in my specific incarnation runs against the currents of sedimented linguistic habits of "normal," taking up words and gestures as expressions in their ambiguity and indeterminacy within cultural schemata, yet I am always "speaking against" concepts of normalcy as I am embodying and speaking through cultural linguistic signifiers of normal: "My different body is normal"—extends expression within the language of normalcy, while seeking to make use of the indeterminate meaning of "normal." My self-perception is immediate—I concurrently can perceive myself as different *and* normal, because the meaning of these words has a corporeal dimension and I *am* those signifiers as much as I *use* them. And meaning is mediated through my body *and* culture, because I understand the meaning of these words in reference to my body but within the cultural habits of understanding them, even as I bodily invoke new meanings.

1999), 50–51. Elizabeth Grosz, *Volatile Bodies: Toward a Corporeal Feminism* (Bloomington and Indianapolis: Indiana University Press, 1994), 44, 141.

Body schema and body image are then not reducible to each other nor are they internally simple. Body schemas, as we have seen, are fluid and can change according to my embodied material condition: I grow older, might lose physical flexibility or experience changes in perceptual capacities; I might learn how to drive, how to drive vehicles of a different kind or size, or learn an instrument; and my body schema, my tacit knowledge of bodily comportment, enables and supports these changes and the acquiring of bodily habits.

Body images are also fluid and changeable, according to the dynamics of social relationships aligning value and meaning to specific bodily emergences and how I move as (changing) body in (changing) contexts. In other words, my bodily perceptual orientation is a dialectic of complex and heterogonous terrains. I extend outward through a tacit body knowledge *and* through socially mediated perceptions of what "there is to know" about my body.

I know how to move into a classroom as an able-bodied woman; my bodily difference is manifest in my bodily comportment (I am physically fit, of a certain height and strength), but my habits also display a certain caution or restrained bodily motility around male students. I perceive interactions with students along gendered lines, which influences my affect and other bodily gestures—I move around the classroom with a range of bodily abilities (I walk around chairs on two legs, write on the whiteboard while listening to my students), but also control my movements in alignment with perceptions of gendered bodies (I approach male students differently aware of my gendered body than I might perceive myself around male friends or female colleagues).

It is not until I experience a back injury which temporarily affects my bodily motility that the terrains of my body schemas and body images might "run through me" differently, though not necessarily harmoniously. I might learn to adjust bodily postures to alleviate pain and compensate for impaired movement; I might still hold a body image of an able-bodied woman who needs to return to able-bodied-ness, but I also might feel social pressure to perform professional femininity *and* able-bodied-ness (out of sync with what I tacitly know my body to be capable of in the moment) in the classroom in order to maintain social power as a teacher through repetitively established perceptual alignments. Put differently, while I hold a tacit or pre-reflective awareness of my-body-self without having access to my body as an object of my awareness (I know where my body is and know how to move my body, but I cannot be aware of *my* body as separate from *me*), I can still be perceptually aware of my-body-self by engaging in a cultural world. "I" as my-body-self am that subject who has taken up the mechanisms of culture and has achieved awareness of myself as normal or different/deviant—within the bounds of my culture.

Sediment cultural habits might precede my subjective individual bodily experience, my habituated patterns of perceptual behavior and consciousness as subject. But I am also embodied in this world with tacit knowledges of my bodily intentionality, I hold a body schema which organizes my movements without conscious attention. And my engaging in language and other bodily expressions as body and as body in a pre-subjective world can show the compelling character of perceptual demands of normalcy within which I find myself recognized and through which I reflect: Perceptual concepts (gender, race, normalcy) might change; my contextual engagement with these concepts might change; the contextual meaning emerging in the corporeal dynamics between bodies and world might change; but the fact that I perceive and emerge as subject with culturally given perceptual concepts does not.

Because I take up perceptual mechanisms of culture, I take up political relations of perception: My perception of normalcy is intertwined with relations of power which align me with certain perceptions of normalcy and otherness that are not neutral or innocent. For example, the persistent body/mind dualism and the cultural hierarchies preferring "mind over matter" in Euro-Western concepts of human existence more often than not instill us with doubt that a life without "normal" cognitive function might be a life worth living. Not only can we not imagine existing without our mental capacities (after all, we are habituated to embrace our imagination as a mental, not a bodily act), but our social value systems idealize the mind and all the control over life we *think* it affords us, for example, as the locus of intention for our actions in the world.

The habitual schema I am immersed in of perceiving preferentially mind-over-matter also has a socio-political force inherent to it. Alzheimer's disease or dementia, for example, emerge as fear-inducing to me because the loss of mental control signals a loss of identity and human agency. An uncontrolled mind is to blame for a body out of control, so that recent socio-political public conversation regarding violence focuses on control of bodily restriction of access to weapons and legal provisions for mental health providers, using language and imagery which frame "normal" people as "reasonable" and "mentally stable" and therefore in charge and empowered to control "crazy" people who are perceived as out of control and bodily violent.

We perceive normally-abled persons because we come to recognize certain bodily and mental capacities as common to human persons, at a time when identification and control of normal bodies and minds is important to the organization and structuring of human bodies in cultural and political space. The bodily perceptual experience of abnormality (deviance from normal) alerts us to the dynamics between body–bodies–social world from which the other body might not emerge as subject analogous to "normal." Because some bodily perceptual movements (gestures, movements, gaze) are socio-culturally not recognizable as "normal" in the field of interaction—or at least not recognized in their specific form (a limp, a slur, the absence of vision) due to perceptual orientations—the *mutual constituting* of space between bodies, the ground from which bodies are perceived, is a dialectic from which *unequal* bodies emerge into perceptual recognition.

Thus, the "abnormality" of bodily function which defines "impairment" is already the transition toward and entering into representational relation to another concept, that of normalcy—so that an impaired body materializes as body image framed within socio-cultural conceptions of normal/abnormal. Yet while these perceptual alignments have real embodied effects, and can produce complex, multiple, and fragmented self-perceptions and body images, bodily difference comes to be matter also in the dimension of body schemas, a terrain in which difference is not necessarily experienced as pathology. The relationship between meanings—specific bodies relating with and through linguistic signs—once reflected on within the parameters outlined in this chapter, is not one of necessity, but rather one of discontinuity. There is no natural or necessary linking between bodily difference and meaning in language (though a linking between the two always *is*), which implies that other meanings and links are possible, especially when remembering the histories and possibilities potentially to be gathered on perceptual backgrounds.

Just like bodily perceptual orientations are aligned to support some perceptions over others and are directing our perceptions to focus on some emergences over others from a supporting pre-reflective dimension, so do our bodily perceptual alignments support a construction of normalcy which invests perceptions of difference with meanings that endow perceptual dialectics with taxonomical, ideological, political, and cultural significance.

HISTORICAL PERCEPTIONS AND HABITUAL SEDIMENTATION OF NORMALCY

Inquiring into the origins of perceiving disabled bodies, Lennard J. Davis advances that "normalcy" as a concept constructed the problem of bodily difference labeled "disability." As a construction, it is not a universally perceived condition but has a history, a social process, a gathered background, which led to the perceptual emergence of disabled bodies in a certain kind of society at a certain time.[30]

Davis describes the emergence of the idea of the "norm," and with this perceptual concept the socio-cultural imperative of "normalcy" in the Euro-Western world. The word "norm" as sign had signified something "perpendicular" with reference to a carpenter's square in the early 19th century. The word "normal" as referring to a conforming to a common type only entered the English language in the mid-1900s. The rise of objective (and objectifying) sciences and industrialization

---

30. Lennard J. Davis, "Constructing Normalcy," in *The Disability Studies Reader*, ed. Lennard J. Davis (New York, NY: Routledge, 2010), 3.

connected perceptual orientations of bodies with generalized notions of normal as imperative through repetitive gestures in various socio-cultural arenas. For example, using medical data compiled in the new field of statistics, generating an "average" body as exemplar of normal life and the normal worker.[31]

Medical, political, and mathematical science, economics and social science, all repeat habitual gestures which sediment "normal" as a concept and as language in reference to bodies, implying the imperative and desirability of normalcy over against the undesirability of difference and deviance: The scientific notion of average or middle develops into a philosophical justification for the mean position of the bourgeoisie in the great order of things;[32] the notion of an average human supports and justifies Marxian theories of average workers and average wages and thus average human value;[33] and the notion of average human capacities supports and justifies the demand, need, and moral

31. Ibid., 4. Though Davis acknowledges the somewhat simplistic chronological division, he usefully points toward preceding notions of the "ideal," for example, an ideal body found in the divine, which no individual human bodies could embody. The grotesque was inversely related to the ideal, but as a signifier of common life, of common humanity, rather than the marginal.

32. And many words are used to support the meaning associated with "normal" in the social imaginary, manifesting in the cultural production of the novel. For a study of disability as a literary trope, see David T. Mitchell and Sharon L. Snyder, *Narrative Prosthesis: Disability and the Dependencies of Discourse* (Ann Arbor, MI: University of Michigan Press, 2000).

33. Marx quotes French statistician Adolphe Quetelet in *Capital* to acknowledge that while individual bodily differences may exist, these "errors" might compensate for one another whenever a certain minimum number of workmen are employed together. Marx's labor theory of value/average wages is thus partly based in his positing the idea of the worker as an average worker. It is only from the idea of an average worker that "abstract labor" may be thought about (as in reflecting on work and wages in relation to what an average—"normal"—worker can be expected to accomplish). Karl Marx, *Capital*, trans., Samuel Moore, vol. 1 (New York, NY: International Publishers, 1970), 323. Davis explores Quetelet's notion of the average human, applying the mathematical "law of error" to physical and moral averages of human attributes, in Davis, "Constructing Normalcy," 5–7.

imperative of surveying, controlling, and eliminating individual deviances for the sake of the normalcy of the community.[34]

Cultural scientific tools such as fingerprinting and genetics embed into these perceptions of corporeal normalcy ideas and concepts such as heredity and identifiable essential differences: bodily perceptions become cues for a coinciding identity located in perceivable bodily differences. Perceived bodies are not identical with a presented identity, and this identity may be unchangeable and indelible. In connection with notions of deviance as undesirable existence against the norm, bodily perceptual orientations aligned irrepressible physical or mental qualities with moral qualities identified and possibly criminalized. Bodily perceptual orientations in the modern industrial West loosely aligned what we now call disability with criminal activity, mental incompetence, and sexual license, a legacy still influencing perceptual emergence of meaning today.[35]

Yet "normal" as *perceptual* habit remains ambiguous and indeterminate, and so is the use of "normal" as linguistic habit: When normal comes to be perceived as "ideal," as the imperative toward which human progress must align, the problems of extremes as well as the apophatic definition (defining normal through its negative, through determining abnormal) of "normalcy" demand supplementation through other notions and demand the continuation of the work of repetition. This leaves "normal" caught up in the evolution of nature and culture. To elaborate: If normal (as in "common" or "average") is the ideal, then

34. Lennard J. Davis, *Bending over Backwards: Disability, Dismodernism, and Other Difficult Positions* (New York, NY: New York University Press, 2002), 102–118.

35. The technologies or embodied effects may change though: Eugenics, for example, was a scientific tool hailed to improve the national body by eliminating unfit individual bodies. Similarly to race, disability or deviance then emerges in perceptual focus against the background of nation/citizenship. Institutionalization of deviant bodies (prison, mental health hospitals) or social control through professionalized fields of care (psychology, social work, police) are of the same aim, namely constructing and upholding the normal by identifying and controlling (or inhibiting) the "spread" of the abnormal. Barnes, "A Brief History of Discrimination and Disabled People."

extreme deviation comes to be undesirable. Yet with notions of prog-ress, human perfectibility, and perceptual preferences already connected to perceptual orientations, processes of ranking supplement the ideol-ogy of normalcy to perceive of the normal as always moving toward one end of the spectrum, not the other. For example, higher than aver-age intelligence is perceived today as preferable to lower than average intelligence, therefore normal is perceptually aligned leaning toward perceiving lower intellectual capacities as deviant abnormal, whereas higher intellectual capacities come to be perceived as desirable hope-fully soon-to-be normal.[36] In conjunction with solving the problem of extremes by substituting ranking for averaging, notions of progress and human perfectibility sediment ideologies of normalcy and produce habits of elimination of deviance in favor of a dominating hegemonic perceptual vision of a normal—"must be"—human body.[37] "Normal" in reference to desirable body types is caught up in how human bodies adjust to changing environments and how cultural images of normal health or beauty transform over time.

The habit of perceiving normalcy is embedded in linguistic habits. For example, a bodily perceptual orientation of a deaf person extends bodily in reference to this individual bodily incarnation and through bodily movements and capacities within the given bodily perceptual capacities and orientation. Yet when the meaning of "normal human body" emerges as a perceptual fully capable body, then the absence of hearing is perceived and linguistically expressed as *lack* of hearing, or as sensory abnormality. Scientific and economic efforts as bodily move-ments then are geared toward "fixing" this abnormality or toward "restoring" *normal* hearing.

The terrain supporting the perception of deaf bodies and the emer-gence of meaning can change, and with it the linguistic signs referring to deafness, and the bodily perceptual orientation to/of deaf bodies. As with gender and race, deafness involves a perceived physical difference, yet the meaning emerging is subject to change and transformation,

36. Davis, "Constructing Normalcy," 9.
37. Ibid., 4–9.

meaning embedded in socio-cultural dynamics as much as corporeal ones. For example, until the middle of the nineteenth century, moral models of personhood defined deafness as a physical condition that isolated the person from the Christian community. Deafness, as affliction and blessing, was a separation from the "light" of the gospel (which needed to be heard), yet was also perceived as an ignorance of the "darkness" of the world. Innocence and ignorance of deafness were compared to virginity and barrenness (the blessing of virginal innocence becomes the curse of barrenness if not lifted from that state). Sign language became the educational (visual gestural) device to perceptually align deaf bodies with the values of a Christian community.[38]

Yet shifting terrains of nationhood and the building of the national body (see also the previous chapter on race and sedimentation of habits) then support the shifting of meanings regarding deafness, aligning the emergence of bodies with national desires. To be deaf then perceptually emerged as a physical impairment (not primarily a moral sign or insufficiency) which cut off the person from English-speaking American culture; the tragedy was no more the loss of salvation via the hearing of the gospel, but the lack of national identity via the participation in the hearing of America.[39]

This change can be traced in the sedimentation of language habits. We have noticed that language has a corporeal dimension and sediments as corporeal reference and habitually established meanings. A change in culturally habituated movements (e.g., nation building),

---

38. Douglas Baynton, "'A Silent Exile on This Earth': The Metaphorical Construction of Deafness in the Nineteenth Century," in *The Disability Studies Reader*, ed. Lennard J. Davis (New York, NY: Routledge, 2010), 38–40. This perceptual orientation is what is framed in disability studies as the "moral model." Social evil is traced to the weakness or deficiency of the individual, reformation of society can only come through moral reform of individual members. A certain duality was at work though, as physical impairment, though located in the individual, would emerge as holding moral meaning for the community, either as affliction or possession by evil forces, or as blessing and divine message. Creamer, *Disability and Christian Theology*, 19.

39. Baynton, "A Silent Exile on This Earth," 33.

then, is a change of a culture's "being" in the world which then effects the emerging meanings between body and world. Let me elaborate: The first schools for deaf people in the United States were established during the Second Great Awakening. Evangelical Protestant reformers established residential schools where deaf children were brought together to receive a Christian education, teachers conducting education via signed language in order to allow for knowledge, salvation and moral messages to be "heard." One significant effect of these residential schools for deaf persons is that it led to the emergence of the Deaf, that is, the alignment of individuals with a cultural and linguistic community. Previously separated individuals now began forming distinct communities, sharing a history and identity, embracing a common language and common experience.[40]

However, as the unity of the national body became an important bodily orientation, the separation and perceived isolation of deaf communities from the life of the nation was increasingly perceived as troublesome, the assimilation into the national body of greatest importance.[41] The change in bodily and social habits regarding education for deaf people was signaled with linguistic expressions referring to "progress" (the same language referred to in the education of immigrants discussed earlier, and in the education of American Indian children, to which I will turn later). Taking Davis' conceptual exploration of "progress" and "normal" into account, to progress as a national body, citizen bodies must become "normal," meaning they must be able to

40. For a more detailed account of what in this project I would call the sedimentation of bodily movement, linguistic expression, and change in bodily habituation as change of being in the world, moving from deaf to Deaf, see Carol Padden and Tom Humphries, *Deaf in America: Voices from a Culture* (Cambridge, MA: Harvard University Press, 1988). And Jack Gannon, *Deaf Heritage: A Narrative History of Deaf America* (Silver Spring, MD: National Association of the Deaf, 1981).
41. Baynton, "A Silent Exile on This Earth," 34. This is the same current which oriented education and immigration to the importance of assimilation of immigrants into the national body, though as just described, mechanisms of alignment also screened out undesirables from crossing national boundaries. Deaf bodies emerging within the nation though demanded different orienting and re-alignment devices, supported by the pre-reflective current of nationalism.

disappear behind perceptual orienting lines of bodily abilities which aligned national citizenship. Progress as a nation was then connected to the assimilation, the perceptual disappearance of deafness into the national body and its sediment bodily and social habits, so that habits changed to lip-reading and audible speech. We can see how differences regarding perceiving normalcy may be observed in historical contexts not too far removed from our context today, and even undergo transformations within a lifetime.[42]

Emerging from this pre-reflective current of nationalism, then, are meanings of deafness signaling an inability to assimilate into the national body. Bodily perceptual orientations regarding hearing as normal were aligned through educational devices and oralist ideologies

42. You might disagree that nationalism and nation as political phenomena have something to do with bodily differences and experiences such as deafness. Yet the issue of a common language—a common, or preferred shared body-mind-world connection—is deeply embedded in the perceptual emergence of a national people. Benedict Anderson, for example, points to the enforcement of a common language through devices such as the printing press and through mechanisms of capitalism (dissemination of printed language through the market); he argues that only a common language was/is able to harness and enforce images of national character, national entities, and national progress. Benedict Anderson, *Imagined Communities: Reflections on the Spread and Origin of Nationalism* (London, UK: Verso, 1983), 45–48. Anderson, though, seems to define language mostly as textual system of words/signs and grammar. But I believe an argument could be made that a common language, with language defined as corporeal and social as I have here— habitual movements of body-mind-world, common associations of bodily referents and habits—may also apply to his argument, perhaps even expand it.

For an example of a different kind of perceptual alignment regarding the emergence of the normal and healthy national body, see Robert Desjarlais, *Shelter Blues: Sanity and Selfhood among the Homeless* (Philadelphia, PA: University of Pennsylvania Press, 1997). Desjarlais discusses the experiences of homeless persons in a facility never completely built, abandoned persons gathered in an abandoned building. Homeless persons suffer abjection from the national body, and Desjarlais describes and analyzes the perceptual alignment of homelessness with grotesque bodies, animality, and incomprehensibility, presenting it over against self-representations, intimate first-person narratives, and favoring non-visual accounts of the complex cultural, political, economic, sensorial, emotional, and physiological experiences of the homeless persons he came to know.

(advocating for purely oral education for deaf people). While sign language as linguistic expression in deaf communities could not be undone, solely manual education (through sign language and writing) was replaced by the early 20th century with nearly 80% of children taught entirely without sign language, being taught through lip reading and speaking.[43]

Deafness as a marker of a community which does not require oral/aural communication challenges the coherence of a national body which moves and extends socially and culturally through a common language, a common bodily habit. Because language itself is a set of congealed bodily and social practices shaping our way of being in the world (as I have argued previously), non-participation in the (national) language system emerges as incoherent with social habits and movements. The meaning emerging is that of misalignment with citizenship and dysfunctionality of bodily sociality. The threat of D/deafness is that it may be unperceivable/invisible: unless a deaf person extends through engagement in language, she does not emerge visually as deaf, engaging in "foreign" language, inheriting a "different" culture, isolated from the "normal" life of the nation.[44] Deaf persons were described as a collective people, inferior, who were unable to exercise their citizenship unless they were made "people of our language" (in reference to English and in support of suppressing sign language). Deaf people were persons "without a country" needing to become members of a community with leaders and rulers, embodying the threat of foreignness, the offense of using another language.[45]

Language as bodily movement and social habit, in this example swept up in the pre-reflective current of nationalism, aligned deafness by the

43. Baynton, "A Silent Exile on This Earth," 34. For a more thorough tracing of the development of deafness as discourse and the material/political significance of sign language, see chapters 2–4 in Lennard J. Davis, *Enforcing Normalcy: Disability, Deafness, and the Body* (New York, NY: Verso, 1995).
44. Davis, *Enforcing Normalcy*, 76–83.
45. Baynton, "A Silent Exile on This Earth," 41–43.

end of the 19th century as a physical condition with social meanings of deviance, a way of being in the world which emerged out of place and in need of correction through social habituation, immersion into the sediment cultural habits of spoken English language. The force of pre-reflective currents supporting the emergence of specific meanings regarding bodily habits (such as perceptually extending through sign language) is evident, for example, in late 19th century proposals of Deaf communities to found a separate state.[46]

What I want to draw our attention to, once more, is the significance of language as corporeal and social. Tacit bodily knowledges and sediment social habits are implicated in thought and language, but meaning (regarding the bodily aspects of the social, and social aspects of the bodily) remains indeterminate and open to change. Language, because of its corporeal and social dimensions, may support orientations to and alignments of, for example, the national body and the movements and expressions of this national body. Pre-reflective currents of nationalism supported bodily perceptual orientations toward bodily capacities along lines of citizenship, and national common language changed alignments of deafness from immorality to abnormality (changing from lack of hearing in reference to access to the gospel to inability to pass as English hearing and speaking citizen). Deaf bodies failed to emerge as properly Christian, but the emergent meaning changed to deaf bodies failing to represent normal nationality. Bodily extensions of Deaf people, supported in the terrain of nationality, then extended through tacit body knowledges regarding their cultural and historical belonging and communicative bodily expressions (Deafness as culture and sedimented habit) *and* through socially mediated perception of nationality

---

46. For example, British Deaf communities suggested founding a deaf state in Canada; American communities proposed forming a deaf state in the western part of the continent. Davis, *Enforcing Normalcy*, 84–85. The kind of movement and land usurpation involved in these ideas would have involved dynamics of nationalistic colonial expansion and intersections with class and race, aspects I cannot fully explore here.

shaping meaning and perceptual habits (deafness as otherness in need of corrective alignment).[47]

DIFFERENT PERCEPTIONS OF WELLNESS/ILLNESS CONNECTED TO "NORMALCY"

We just explored the ways in which perceptual and linguistic habits regarding "normal" may sediment, for example, through medical practices and descriptions. Michel Foucault's investigation of the medical gaze, the perceptual power of the modern medical eye, shows how seeing, and a particular mode of seeing, comes to be a perceptual mechanism of culture, reinforcing perceptual habits of body/mind dualisms.[48] To find comparative clues as to how different bodily perceptual orientations might emerge from differently habituated ways of perceiving features considered common—though not necessarily obligatory, or "normal," as we will discover—let us explore via what is often termed "traditional" (as in, not modern, not scientific or Western, likely inferior in effectiveness) medicine and healing practices.

Modern medicine is a medicine of modernity, meaning that it emerges as social practice habituated to seeing body and illness emerging in a certain way, objectifying the ill body and distancing the medical expert. The sedimentation of the medical gaze in scientific bodily and linguistic habits also sedimented ontological perceptions of human existence (particularly the body as object of medical alteration).[49] Kim

47. For a collection of essays inquiring into differences of hearing (across time, culture) and the different meanings associated with it (e.g., regarding healing or religious devotion), see Veit Erlmann, ed. *Hearing Cultures: Essays on Sound, Listening, and Modernity*, Wenner-Gren International Symposium Series, ed. Richard G. Fox (New York, NY: Berg, 2004).
48. Foucault, *The Birth of the Clinic: An Archaeology of Medical Perception* (London, UK: Tavistock Publications, 1973), 54–63, 107–123.
49. Taewoo Kim, "Medicine without the Medical Gaze: Theory, Practice and Phenomenology in Korean Medicine" (Ph.D.diss., University of New York at Buffalo, 2011). Similarly, Mu Peng highlights embodied knowledge in rural Chinese Master-Apprentice relationships, within which knowledge is transmitted

Taewoo highlights the non-universality of modern Western medicine and its perceptual orientations in his study regarding phenomenological aspects of Korean medicine. The medical practices Kim observes in Korean contexts encompass a centrality of bodily knowing (rather than observation applied to knowledge), a knowing achieved through bodily intentionalities, through experiencing the other's body in/through the body of the medical practitioner. Experiences infer comprehension *as body* which can not necessarily be transmitted verbally.[50]

This approach to Korean medicine makes sense within an Asian habituation to embodiment and health that is embedded in pre-reflective currents of a cosmology that orients the body within the holistic naturalism of an integrated universe, in which human bodies are part of a constantly transforming and relating inorganic-organic-human life space-time relation (e.g., yin yang and Five Phase Theory). Elements, seasons, life phases, and associated colors are stages in a process that ought to be harmoniously arranged to maintain the cosmic order in which everything goes with the natural flow of the Ch'I, the material force in everything. Every phenomenon, bodily matters included, is the result of the interplay of the two alternating interdependent forces of Yin and Yang (signifying dense or dispersed aggregation of energy-matter), and all symptoms and signs are perceived along orienting lines of yin yang. Health makes sense within the terrain of harmony, interrelation of all creation, and being in tune with the continuous flow of cosmic transformation; all

---

not primarily through text or oral education. Rather, pedagogical tools are body learning and sense honing, which are acquired through detailed bodily imitation. Peng Mu, "Imitating Masters: Apprenticeship and Embodied Knowledge in Rural China," in *Everyday Life in Asia: Social Perspectives on the Senses*, ed. Devorah Kalekin-Fishman and Kelvin E. Y. Low (Burlington, VT: Ashgate Publishing Company, 2010), 115–136.

50. Kim, "Medicine without the Medical Gaze," 3,175–179. Medical training then is compared to the Korean linguistic equivalent of "embodiment," which in Korean signifies "knowing by bodily gaining." Learning medicine is done by the body, practicing medicine is a somatic awareness extended toward another, to appreciate the medically meaningful in bodily experience. Ibid, 181.

that is in the world and all stages of matter are interrelated. When out of balance, disharmonious states are perceivable, because of colors different from normal for associated body functions, parts, or stages.[51]

Color perception therefore is an important part of diagnosis in Korean medicine. Skin hues in facial regions indicate the state of functioning of connected organs (e.g., Yellow indicates an issue with the spleen and digestive issues), the bodily experience of the Five Colors is more than a visual grasping, more than a fine-tuning of visual perception to detect changes in color. Rather, it is a bodily experience of being in proximity to a color, a bodily recognition of more than just seeing color, but other visual significances, auditory sensations, and tactile perceptions referring to a disharmony, an imbalance in which patient, doctor, community, and cosmos are all involved in and tuned into. While color as visual perception might indicate a medical objectivist gaze, Kim describes vision as a proximity sense, closely interrelated and significantly connected to other bodily perceptual capacities. In the same trajectory, Blue or Yellow as conditions, then, are not scientifically described or textualized in order to define a diagnosis, they do not match or adhere differentiations in Western scientific taxonomical typologies.

Color as a diagnostic tool in various traditional Korean medicines is a bodily experience to acquire as habit, and these habits, as patterns of movement, perceptually orient the practitioner's body to make use of tacit knowledges in bodily experiencing others. Linguistic references might be used, but do not make up the dominant cultural habit

51. A detailed exploration of this cosmology is beyond the scope of this project. For an exploration of cosmology and medicinal theory in traditional Chinese medicine (which has similar cosmological connections and medical practices), see Friedrich G. Wallner, Fengli Lan, and Martin J. Jandl, eds., *The Way of Thinking in Chinese Medicine: Theory, Methodology and Structure of Chinese Medicine* (Frankfurt, Germany: Peter Lang, 2010); Richard Wilhelm, *The I Ching* (London, UK: Routledge and Kegan Paul, 1967); Robin Wang, *Yinyang: The Way of Heaven and Earth in Chinese Thought and Culture* (Cambridge, UK: Cambridge University Press, 2012).

of describing and defining wellness/illness.[52] Because the experience and emerging meaning of illness is woven in a perceptual terrain of Ch'I, it is not an individual bodily experience with a chronologically cause-effect schema (for illness as well as prescribed cure) which may receive individual medical attention. Rather, illness is an experience of disharmony with the flow of the world, embedded in spatial and communal dimensions. Restoration of harmony may take a variety of personal, communal, and material forms, beyond the treatments catching the curious eye of Western travelers (beyond acupuncture, herbal medicine, and Tai Chi; Feng Shui, I-Ching and other techniques of reading and aligning bodily movements with the flow of the material and social world). To experience disharmony in illness is not experiencing the occurrence of something bad (caused by bad choices or influences) affecting me. Rather, illness is the experience of disharmony with the way world-us-you-me-world are already going and wellness is to bring ourselves into alignment with the current phase of world-us-you-me.

The Anlo-Ewe people in West Africa can provide us with another comparative example of perceiving well-being, one that might help us further understand the complex bodily experience and corporeal/social dimensions of language.[53] Kathryn Geurts' anthropological study among

---

52. Kim, "Medicine without the Medical Gaze," 181–183. Remember here also my elaboration of Merleau-Ponty on color perception in chapter 3.

53. That language classified by outsiders is not always a representative taxonomical map also becomes evident here. "Anlo is essential to this study of sensoriums and experience, and yet it is not an easy word to translate or define. It identifies a dialect of Ewe, which is a West African language spoken by many of the people who live in southern Togo and the southeastern corner of Ghana. But for many Ewe speakers in Ghana, Anlo denotes a specific group of Ewe people who inhabit the coastal area of the Volta Region, around the Keta Lagoon, and whose traditions and dialect have unfairly been taken (by scholars, missionaries, and other representatives of colonial regimes) to represent Ewe culture as a whole." Kathryn Linn Geurts, *Culture and the Senses: Bodily Ways of Knowing in an African Community* (Berkeley, CA: University of California Press, 2002), 21. Geurts is also careful to highlight that this common language or reference to a people group by no means represents uniform or homogenous social and cultural perceptions.

the Anlo-Ewe revealed that Western linguistic and conceptual classification of sensory perception was clearly an etic taxonomy when observing
perception in an Anlo-Ewe context.[54] Touch, taste, smell, hearing, and
sight revealed themselves clearly as linguistic and conceptual categories
developed largely within a Western European scientific tradition. While
the Anlo-Ewe people use bodily capacities (looking, listening, touching, tasting) to experience and know the world, these perceptual modes
did not sediment in linguistic expressions transferrable to traditional
Western categories. Linguistic signs translated into German or English
as "sensing" do not refer to Western categories of bodily experiences
(e.g., sensing as touching), but rather refer to "thing recognized," "things
that help us to know what is happening (on) to us," or "how you feel in
your body." Undifferentiated linguistic signs do not infer undifferentiated
bodily experiences; Anlo-Ewe "sensing" encompasses various bodily
experiences with which one can "feel in the body," experiences including
specific physical sensations (e.g., tingling skin), or sensations considered
non-physical, such as heartache, inspiration, and intuition.[55]

Bodily movements, such as walking, are synesthetic and kinesthetic
movements, emerging as bodily-emotional extensions indicating morality. "Lugulugu," for example, a swaying bodily movement, may be a signifier for a person's character or the manner of movement a road directs.
To move lugulugu-ly is to experience the sensations of lugulugu-ness, to
embody lugulugu ways, think lugulugu-ly, and become a lugulugu person, which is then again bodily experienced by others who perceive the
lugulugu walk. Lugulugu is not experienced and thus categorizable in
separate spheres of language, cognition, sensation, perception, culture,
but in a synesthetic mode of knowing. The bodily perceptual orientation

54. Etic and emic are terms used in anthropological studies: Etic refers to the use
of categories, distinctions, and concepts derived from the outsider's point of view,
emic refers to the use of categories, rules, and concepts meaningful to people within
a particular cultural tradition. Clifford Geertz, *Local Knowledge: Further Essays in
Interpretive Anthropology* (New York, NY: Basic Books, 1983), 56–57.
55. Ibid., 38–41. Geurts' study is also an interesting investigation of cultures which
do not conceive of body/mind splits in ontological, epistemological, and phenomenological dimensions.

of Anlo-Ewe people is that of moving and perceiving and knowing as deeply intertwined bodily-moral-knowing persons.[56]

Another example of different conceptualization of normalcy via illness/wellness which highlights the interplay between various perceptual extensions is found in the Massim (indigenous to Papua New Guinea), a complexly structured oral and olfactoral culture. Bodily intentionality is embedded in Massim self-understanding. A person comes to be through exteriorization; identity as such is not who one "is on the inside," but how—and therefore who—one extends to the outside, how one expands from the surface of the body.[57] Identity emerges through this bodily intentionality. Not sight or speech, but smell and sound/hearing are ranked the most important transcendent movements. Odors penetrate bodies and consciousness, and adornment, clothing, and other technologies of bodily intentionality in Massim culture always incorporate an important odorizing element, and it is the fragrant elements of a ritual or other bodily practice which are understood to hold the most potency. As perceptual extension and epistemological venue, smell and sight are understood by the Massim as interrelated, but it is odor, the olfactory expansion of a person's presence, which determines one's appearance; to have a beautiful smell leads to appearing visually handsome.[58]

56. Ibid., 74–76.
57. Howes, *Sensual Relations: Engaging the Senses in Culture and Social Theory* (Ann Arbor, MI: University of Michigan Press, 2003), 72–73. Judith Butler, *Giving an Account of Oneself* (New York, NY: Fordham University Press, 2005), 19–21. Modern Western understandings of the constitution of the self, e.g., in Nietzsche, Foucault, or Laplanche (as utilized in Butler), articulate how a subject comes into being through an internalization of the constitutive outside—responding to an address, internalizing discursive technologies, or being shaped through body power.
58. Howes, *Sensual Relations*, 75–76. Regarding gendered bodily intentionality and perceptual movement, perceptual values manifest in sexual orientations of desire through bodily practices aligned with olfactory orienting lines. The nose, as olfactory site, is an eroticized organ and a site of sexual stimulation, whereas the mouth is an organ of intellect, which explains absence of Western eroticized acts, such as kissing. Social/familial gendered relations are also bodily aligned through the nose, for example, a swollen nose is a sign of blockage between a man and his in-laws. Howes, *Sensual Relations*, 120, 202.

Other bodily perceptual orientations involved in the intentionality of a person and her perceptual movements involve primarily sound (though not language/speech). The objects used as medium for bodily extension (e.g., shells) are valued for the acoustic and kinetic effects they produce (as opposed to visual value). As previously mentioned, it is through expansion that the Massim self perceptually emerges, thus it is in the giving away of valued objects that a Massim person matures and is aligned perceptually with social recognition and status. Objects given away bodily extend a person acoustically, and the value attached to the audio qualities is indicative and constitutive of the value of the person who gave them away.[59] The object's value perceptually emerges via its mobility (sound travels as the object travels), and this relates to how persons become intelligible in Massim culture: Bodily perceptual orientation as condition for the Massim subject manifests in auditory and olfactory extensions in space and time, sounds and odor are superior perceptual movements (as they can travel across distance and/or when vision is obstructed).[60]

To develop normally, or to mature well, is to progress from visual realms to aural realms, to establish oneself as a "name," rather than a visual image, or face. The extent of mobility of a person's sounds determines a person's "existence." In other words, to be visually perceived is "not to be"; only as a "name," as a person who is heard, one emerges in a community, in the ears of the beholders. To further elaborate: What Western eyes may perceive as visual body decorations (such as feather ornamentation or skin treatments with coconut oil) are aural devices which augment the power of a person's speech and sound. The actual speaking (greetings, incantations, spells) is embedded in a language system in which bodily capacities for speech involve bodily habits of *sounding* speech. Onomatopoeic expressions (e.g., "tudududu" for "roll of thunder"), when sounded out, bring about material and perceptual transformations (e.g., an object is transformed into a sound). But where Western interpretations of this phrase explained *tudududu* as metaphorical use of language, an aural perspective can help us

59. Ibid.,79.
60. Ibid., 112.

understand that it is not in metaphorical meaning, but in acoustic amplification, in aural performance, that language is employed.[61]

Wellness and illness then need to be understood within these bodily perceptual orientations in the world. Bodily perceptual extensions through sounds and smell are not only ways to emerge "larger than life"—to intensify a person's presence and increase social value—they also align perceptions of a person's social competence and alignment with community values. Inability to hear, bodily or metaphorically, is to be unable to be socialized and align with the oral extensions of family; it is to go mad or insane.[62]

Because for Massim, bodily perception is conceived of as production of effects in others (rather than the reception of incoming stimuli from others), to not hear others is to not be in line with the expansion of family and community. Insanity is linguistically signified with a word also translatable as "deaf," though hearing does not equate knowing. Again, because social values are aligned with bodily perceptual extensions, the intellect, the seat of the "mind" is located in the throat, the bodily organ from which one speaks. For something to be known, even by oneself, it must be voiced and heard; to think and understand involves speaking and hearing oneself talk. To be incapable of social knowledges then is to be incapable of hearing and/or speaking; but not as Western prejudice regarding a person deaf or mute would have it, inferring an incapability to think from inabilities to voice thought or hear others speak their thoughts. Rather, thinking is sound-thinking, the intake of noise-force (knowledge) *and* the ability to extend it outward again (because to "keep something inside" is just as anti-social and "insane" as being unable to connect with others' oral or olfactory extensions).[63]

The importance of understanding differences in the corporeal and social dimensions of language, such as those provided in the examples

---

61. Ibid., 78–88. This would go against a structuralist/Saussurian conception of language, in which onomatopoeias merely illustrate the arbitrariness of linguistic signs. But rather than simply a special instance of language, the actual sound, the bodily linguistic production of the sign, is of significance.
62. Ibid., 114.
63. Ibid., 116–117.

here, is to understand that these different bodily social habits (experiencing the color of a patient, complex communally oriented experiences of bodily illness, the descriptions of insanity in oral/aural/olfactory cultures) are habits which are not simply intellectual conceptions, but deep-seated ways of being in the world. I move, feel, see, and think through and with and by means of language; I move bodily into the world through linguistic gestures; my extension through language is my motile engagement through which I and the world appear; my "living" of/through language is a cultural act of bringing forth meaning and movement. Language as a bodily habit and bodily extension through embodied cultural habit is incorporated within my body schema, within my tacit knowledge of myself and the world.

To learn a new language is not simply to learn new signifiers, it is to learn a new way of bodily being in the world. George "Tink" Tinker's investigation of colonizing missionary activities such as American Indian "boarding schools" highlights the importance of not underestimating this interrelation of bodily experience and the role of perception and language. Tinker describes how educational policies forcefully removed American Indian children from their communal homes and gathered them in institutions of re-education, where they were severely punished when caught speaking their native language. The enforcement of the colonizer's language as common social and political language (remember the exploration of common language in the previous section) then enforced alignment with the dominant socio-cultural bodily habits and communal values. This alignment brought about loss of bodily perceptual orientations, which again, were more than merely changes in speaking, but enforced and policed changes of deep-seated ways of being in the world, including bodily social habits such as family structures, values, dietary habits, communal organization, tacit knowledges regarding the world and one's place in it. We need to regard this not just as "only" enforced political control, but rather must more aptly label this violently enforced bodily perceptual re-orientation as genocide.[64]

64. George E. (Tink) Tinker, "Missionary Conquest: The Gospel and Native American Cultural Genocide," (1993): 49–50. George E. Tinker, *American Indian*

Language, then, is a bodily *and* social experience, one that expresses *and* shapes our bodily perceptual orientation in the world. To learn a different language is to learn of different bodily social habits, of different ways of perceiving and extending into the world. To be forced to give up a native language, or operate dominantly in a colonizing language, is to be forced to change one's being in the world, to be dominated by another group's tacit knowledges which may not resonate with my own. To demand a common language, then, is not only to demand a shared mode of communication: it is to enforce specific meanings, and because meaning emerges perceptually between body and world and is shaped by habit, it demands and enforces specific patterns of bodily movement aligned with the hegemonic perceptual grid; it demands unified, "normal" ways of being and perceiving in the world to keep the currents supporting social structures flowing strong.[65]

Liberation: A Theology of Sovereignty (Maryknoll, NY: Orbis Books, 2008), 25–28. I believe the same judgment may be applied (after thorough exploration and contextualization) to other colonial/colonizing dominations, such as the conquest and bodily removal and re-orientation of African bodies, the British conquest and usurpation of lands and peoples in India, or the Spanish conquest of South America, even the global reach of capitalism today.

65. See also Steven T. Newcomb, *Pagans in the Promised Land: Decoding the Doctrine of Christian Discovery* (Golden, CO: Fulcrum Books, 2008). Newcomb analyzes the imagination of the US Supreme court regarding federal Indian law, relating Christian narratives and their metaphors to the colonizing of indigenous peoples and lands. He demonstrates how Christian narratives, words, and images have an inherently political meaning (established through metaphors and their bodily dimensions) which provided colonization of Indian lands moral and legal legitimacy. Newcomb asserts that the employed metaphors and narratives present a cognitive schema which still operates today not only in the United States, but also other places of colonization, where language and human cognition (conceptualization and categorization) are the perfect instrument of empire because of their bodily embeddedness. The consequences thereof, such as starvation, denigration and loss of cultural identity and traditions, loss of land—in short, genocide—always come with a certainty of moral justification found in schemas (bodily-linguistic) such as domestic dependent nation, tribe, etc. Newcomb, *Pagans in the Promised Land*, 16–18, 30–32, 68–71.

CONCLUSION

"I am as body": I am in this world as body touching, feeling, seeing, thinking, remembering, desiring, speaking; I am always as body and I am in bodily reference to my world with deeply embedded, pre-reflexive tacit and visceral knowledge and situatedness in my world.

Our involvement with others, our mutual immersion in the currents of social bodily interrelation, *haunts* us, as Merleau-Ponty sometimes describes it:[1] My style of walking, how I hold myself or silverware even when nobody is watching, what my eyes are drawn to in an image, my reaction to unexpected touch, how I consciously and unconsciously respond to music; our most intimate bodily lives indicate this dimension of pre-reflective interrelation, this involvement in a current of incarnate otherness which precedes my consciousness though it is present "in the flesh" at every moment. My bodily movement, gestures, and postures do not enable communication between me and others, but depend on it. Our bodies and bodily lives inherit the memory of a pre-reflective contact with otherness, a contact which might be irretrievable to conscious reflection, but which nevertheless haunts our experience in the here-and-now. Put differently, as this pre-reflective dimension precedes my subjective coming-to-be, it precedes my individual experience while it always embeds me in a historical context that both is and is not mine.[2] This pre-reflective dimension provides an inexplicable

1. Merleau-Ponty, *The Primacy of Perception and Other Essays on Phenomenological Psychology*, 162.
2. Marratto, *The Intercorporeal Self*, 9.

familiarity of me as body with things and bodies of others and a same inexplicable sense of strangeness of "my own" body.[3] This is the bodily perceptual dimension from which individual and communal achievements emerge historically and culturally.

The pre-reflective currents in which I and the world are embedded imply an exposure, and even more, an inherent openness and ambiguity, in which my being-in-the-world is grounded and on which it depends. In other words, inherent to my existence is a relation *to* the other/world, which shapes our capacities and possibilities of relation *in* the world. This relation marks our bodies as open to and pervaded by a reality which is beyond our grasp insofar as it does not wait for us to set the terms of its appearance (as a Kantian a priori would have us do). But it is a reality that is not separate and mutually exclusive—it is not a realm transcendent of matter. Rather, it is the realm of transcendence, a transcendence that is made up of the matter of our bodies, a transcendence that only appears because of our bodily existence and our bodily outward reach. This appearance brings exposure and vulnerability (and with it fecundity) to my experience as sentient body:[4] I am always already in the world as body interrelated with this world, and as such I am already inheriting certain ways of moving in and relating to the world. This leaves my body open to and pervaded by currents which are beyond my grasp; in other words, as body I am immersed in a world already marked by gender, race, and normalcy; the world does not wait for me to enter it and dictate the terms of these concepts. I am already exposed and vulnerable to the bodily effects and alignments of these concepts, though in my bodily experience I also embody creativity and choice in how I employ these concepts as social and bodily habits, how I "interfere" bodily in our transcending movements.[5]

3. Ibid.
4. Ibid.
5. See, for example, a sociological discussion of three ethnographies (of bodybuilders, HIV/AIDS in heterosexual men, and obesity in men), discussing the social aspects of bodies, the fluid and mutable meanings and experiences depending on processes of symbolic interaction in Lee F. Monaghan, "Corporeal Indeterminacy: The

The significance of conceptualizing my being as always bodily per‐ceptually oriented and always embedded with pre-reflective, inter‐corporeal dimensions, is that it enables me to think of the meaning emerging from bodily perceptual experience as always traceable back to bodily experience, but neither experience nor meaning are properties of an individual self. Rather, being as body is the indispensable condi‐tion of one person's sharing of experience with another.[6]

Implied in the observations about bodily intentionality and pre‐reflective dimension of perception was a pushing of the subject's boundaries beyond the skin "out into the world":

> Whether we are concerned with my body, the natural world, the past, birth or death, the question is always how I can be open to phenomena which transcend me, and which nevertheless exist only to the extent that I take them up and live them, *how the presence to myself (Urpräsenz) which establishes my own limits and conditions every alien presence is at the same time depresentation (Engegenwärtigung) and throws me out‐side of myself.*[7]

What Merleau-Ponty problematizes is that the environment, or the world of the subject, has often only been of interest as object of percep‐tion, and also only insofar as its features correlated with perceptual structures and capacities. To assert with Merleau-Ponty that our bodily existence is organically interrelated with that of the world strongly implies that this interrelation of being is a dependency in becom‐ing. In other words, becoming and existing as embodied subject is to depend on other living bodies and the world I relate in and with. This

Value of Embodied, Interpretative Sociology," in *Body/Embodiment: Symbolic Interaction and the Sociology of the Body*, ed. Dennis Waskul and Phillip Vannini (Burlington, VT: Ashgate, 2006), 125–140. Monaghan carefully highlights how bodies have no intrinsic meaning, rather, meanings emerge *because* of this indeter‐minacy, meanings are forged bodily-creatively, and social meanings are transmitted and habituated in embodied ways.

6. Samuel Todes, *Body and World* (Cambridge, MA: MIT Press, 2001), 2.
7. Merleau-Ponty, *Phenomenology of Perception*, 363. Emphasis in original.

dependency or intertwining of embodied experience and world is not simply a product or manifestation of being.

The pre-reflective dimension, the current of sedimented habitual schemata, inhabits me as body and other bodies at the same time. We have seen that the parts of my body and my sensory capacities form an organic unity and my perceptions come together in things (such as my perception of a lump of dough rolling between my fingers). In the same way,

> as the parts of my body together comprise a system, so my body and the other's are one whole, two sides of one and the same phenomenon, and the anonymous existence of which my body is the ever-renewed trace henceforth inhabits both bodies simultaneously.[8]

My body schema, my tacit knowledge of bodily capacities in a given environment, is possible because of the mutual involvement of inter-related bodies. Only because I am already immersed in sedimented habits—and therefore in communion with other bodily movements and other bodies forming social relations that precede me—can I emerge with individual bodily movements. In other words, it is not "I" who enters the world and chooses my own style "from scratch." Rather, because I am already always bodily involved in a world in which bodies before me and around me are already relating to each other, already taking up a terrain full of habituated relations, I can emerge as a bodily being who "knows" how to be in her body.[9]

My subjectivity, my individual experiences, transcends me. My experience is that

> I do not feel that I am the constituting agent either of the natural or of the cultural world: into each perception and into each judgment I bring

---

8. Ibid., 354.
9. Marratto, *The Intercorporeal Self*, 145. It is not by accident that Merleau-Ponty invokes "communion," as he sometimes refers to this interrelation of bodies as transubstantiation, as mysterious intertwining in the process of perception: in perception, the perceived is inseparable from the perceiver. Merleau-Ponty, *Phenomenology of Perception*, 320.

either sensory functions or cultural settings which are not actually mine. Yet, although I am outrun on all sides by my own acts, and submerged in generality, the fact remains that I am the one by whom they are experiences . . .[10]

I and others are "outrun by [our] world, and [we] consequently may well be outrun by each other."[11] I am not completely ignorant about the other's existence as subject: Once I encounter the other as bodily perceptually oriented intentionality (i.e., a subject who perceptually transcends, as in movement or speech), then the other is not an object of my perception, or a subject-mind hidden in a body to me, but a perceivable subject-intention.

For example, as my grandmother moves her hand to cover herself with a blanket, or moves her eyes around the room in search of something, she is not a body-thing with questionable cognitive abilities, nor a consciousness hidden away in a body cut off from communication with me. Rather, in her bodily perceptual movements she has an intention toward and an orientation in the world. And while I have no absolute access to her or her experience (just as I have no complete access to mine), we are both inserted and participate in an interrelated bodily world in which our perceptual movements are as much our own as they are the other's. She cannot *not* be an experiencing subject, because she still inhabits a shared world on which she holds a bodily perceptual grasp. We are both present in a world, and our bodily perceptual intentionality opens us both to a world; we are both enmeshed with each other as we are enmeshed with the world.

As I join my mother at our German home in the outdoor kitchen, and she instructs me in the preparation of a Thai dish, our bodily perceptual orientations to each other and to our environment are full of alignments, orienting mechanisms, and pre-reflective currents which allow for indeterminate meaning to emerge as we get ready for a meal of gaeng neua. My underlying discomfort or embarrassment of cooking

10. Merleau-Ponty, *Phenomenology of Perception*, 358.
11. Ibid., 353.

outside is more than just mental knowledge that "something is not right"; it is also emerging out of bodily habituations of taking gendered home spaces outside the family home, of not having acquired bodily perceptual capacities of moving with my mother and within this space. Emerging are also "imported" (habituated during my living in the US) bodily perceptual orientations, such as a tacit awareness of two racialized brown women pushed to the margins of a German home, infusing the home space from the outside with ethnic fragrances. My apprehension, judgment, evaluation, thoughts, memories, and emotions in this situation are arising out of and within my bodily perceptual orientations, out of and within my bodily experiencing and perceiving the situation, and emerging out of and within social sedimentation of habits that encompass me as body.

It should not strike us as paradoxical or surprising anymore that the English term "sense" implies the ambiguity or duality of bodily perception and meaning as discussed in this chapter: *Sense* can connote "making sense," inferring sense as meaning found in order and through understanding. And *sense* or *the senses* refers to our perceptual experiences, our sensing and feeling of ourselves and/in the world through sensory capacities. The Latin *percipere* (from which the English *perception* derives) denotes "to take a hold of, to feel, to comprehend." Here too, the ambiguous connotations of the word *perception* in common usage describe reception of information through sensory capacities and as mental insight or activity of sense-making, meaning derived from sensory information. The dual use and implied aspects of *sense* and *perception* point to sensory perception as the reaching out, the extending into the world we have explored and to the understanding of the world gained in perceptual processes. Bodily perceptual experience is grounded in and dependent on my individual bodily capacities and history, and framed by socio-cultural orientations and habits.[12]

Sensing, perceiving, understanding, and knowing are inseparable dimensions of bodily experience; they are sides of the same coin (though

12. Paul Rodaway, *Sensuous Geographies: Body, Sense and Place* (New York, NY: Routledge, 1994), 5, 10.

I am stretching the coin metaphor here beyond the usual two sides). A complex understanding of bodily perceptual experience needs to recognize this ambiguity, which must not be resolved in favor of the bodily or mental aspect, lest we reinstate a body/mind dualism. Taking perceptual differences seriously raises the stakes when doing theology—not only when *not* beginning with bodily experience, but especially *when* doing so. Underestimating the bodily, visceral, deep-seated perceptual orientations which give rise to our experiences, and therefore reach into all our human endeavors, can too easily excuse potentially violent forces of speech, and even retain ideologies and though systems as "just thoughts" that may simply be exchanged in favor of others.

We must understand this interrelation and embeddedness of body-consciousness in its complexity, or we resort to naïve conceptions of perception without accounting for the way in which bodily perceptual experience is a relationship to the world, a mutual constitution with the world, a meaning-making process with respect to that world, and a habituated, culturally specific, style of being in the world. And we cannot underestimate differences in bodily perceptual orientations. When I do not take care to account for how my own individually and socio-culturally acquired perceptual "common sense" is a bodily experience shaped by concrete bodily, social, historical, and cultural forces, my own tacit knowledges may appear pre-cultural or a-historical to me. Contextual perceptual knowledge is then too easily presupposed as universal, natural, and therefore applicable to bodily experiences of others.

In my introductory remarks, I commented on relevant Christian theology demanding engagement in cultural analysis. Because of my own Western cultural location, and Western culture's interlocking structures with Christian theological imaginations, my own cultural imagination is informed by Christian theological orientations. The theoretical analysis thus far has provided me with a way to understand how what has come to be a matter of the mind and individual personal faith confession since the Protestant Reformation may be a deeply embedded bodily perceptual orientation. In other words, Christian theology is always more than "just" a matter of belief or a discipline devoted to connecting spiritual practices with ever more rational or thought-ful doctrinal formulations. Christian theologies and their continuing legacies need to be understood as embedded in our bodily perceptual orientations. They may be part of the sediment pre-reflective current, supporting perceptual emergences of nationalized or normalized bod-ies. They may be orienting devices, maintaining alignments of gender or race. Or Christian theologies may be orienting lines which support directionalities of perception, maintaining perceptual intentionalities, movements, and emergences so that we cannot but perceive, say, "one nation under God."

It is to theology, again, that I turn to in the final part of this book. More specifically, I will revisit and continue our explorations into bodily perceptual orientation—theologically. Attending to the ways in which our existence in bodily experiences situates and orients us in the world is the key feature of what I will present as "body theology."

PART THREE

PERCEIVING

BODY THEOLOGY

I began this project by stating that to think of our existence in the world as bodily perceptual orientation is to think beyond common tropes of nature/culture and essentialism/constructivism used in feminist and poststructuralist discussions to talk about embodiment. In such explorations, the body is often located at the intersection of nature/culture. In my investigation of our existence in the world as bodily perceptual orientation, I showed that our bodily experiences are located in interrelated dimensions of body-world-culture. Our perceptual experiences, our language, and other bodily movements shape this space and are shaped in this space. Our existence as lived body is neither solely natural or essentially biological nor exclusively cultural or discursively constructed. It is even more than both natural/biological and cultural/discursive. If we begin with bodily experience, our existence is bodily, naturally, and culturally, intertwined and interrelated: we learn and create meaning only in bodily experiencing. In bodily perceptual experience, we create, transmit, and express our bodily selves, cultural values, and the world we inhabit.

The body theologies we surveyed so far at times turn out to be inadequate in their conceptual and methodological approaches. Body/mind dualisms may be upheld by positing sensory perception in unreflective or naïve ways and/or by fixing bodily experiences statically to meaning when moving too quickly to establish theological metaphors. My contribution to body theology, rather than presenting a fully conceptualized theological work, is to present commitments which may help us to inquire into bodily experience more complexly. I am putting forward a framework within which to understand bodily experience in order to conceptually and methodologically strengthen those theological projects which seek to be grounded in embodiment. In this chapter, I will present what theological analysis can do when thinking through bodily perceptual orientation.

Body theology, as we will explore it throughout the remainder of this book, is a way of doing critical analysis that begins by inquiring into the many ways in which we are oriented in, toward, and by the world and others. To effectively understand how we come to be in this world, we need to understand what constitutes our being in this world, including how certain ways of valorizing the mind and devaluing bodies gain such bodily and socio-cultural force that some lives get violently pushed to the margins, such that some bodies are dismissed as holding no (more) value.

In the previous chapters, I showed how our bodily perceptual experiences *are* how we exist in this world, how our feeling, smelling, touching, seeing, thinking, speaking, remembering, and so forth are bodily perceptual experiences which orient us in the world and are oriented by the world. There are mechanisms at play—bodily movements, socio-cultural habituations—which may work in ways so that our bodily perceptual orientations position us within bounds of gendered, raced, normalized, nationalized, classed lines. These alignments are so powerful that we cannot escape their influence, reproduction, and naturalization.

To begin to counter the effects of sexism, racism, nationalism, ableism, classism, and so on is to begin understanding how these ideologies are not simply words or beliefs, and not even just perpetration of visual stereotypes (though these might be prevalent in Western cultural orientations). They take on a biopower, to use Foucault's term.[1]

---

1. "Biopower" is Foucault's descriptor for power over bodies, for the set of mechanisms through which bodies and groups of bodies become controlled by and aligned

And this requires conceiving of how the gendering, racing, and nor-matizing of bodies is made through the full range of the human senso-rium, as Paul Gilroy named it.[2] Or to follow Mark Smith, perceptual orientations are central to the way in which dividing lines in the world are created.[3] The lines of division which come to be fundamental, even natural, in our experiences come to be experienced in a bodily perceptual way and through instances of complication, nuance, and subtlety: What we call man/woman, black/white/brown, normal/disabled, citizen/alien are hierarchies which are aligned through our bodily perceptual experiences (through our seeing, tasting, feel-ing, smelling, thinking, remembering, hearing, etc.). Social concepts are not solely surface impressions (in both senses, as in impressions about surfaces and impressions on/of surfaces), but are cultural cat-egories of deep bodily impact and deep social significances. While social hierarchies and cultural orders may be belied by everyday con-tingencies, compromises, and complications in the context of our experiences, bodily perception is central to the mutual emergence of body-world-meaning.

To abandon these alignments and thereby to counter violent "isms," inquiries into bodily perceptual orientations will allow us to grasp more precisely and complexly the origins and sources of the creation and reproduction of divisive imagery. This inquiry will allow us to begin with framing how bodies and experiences are made and which mechanisms turn our bodily experiences and perceived meanings to socio-cultural images so damaging and powerful that they can wage war on our lives. This is true even or especially when we pride ourselves in being unprejudiced, non-discriminating, and reasoned thinkers and actors regarding social matters. By beginning our analysis so, we can

with and through socio-political strategies. See Michel Foucault, *The History of Sexuality: An Introduction.* trans. Robert Hurley (New York, NY: Vintage Books, 1978). In later works, as Foucault elaborates on this, his terms become more tech-nically framed.

2. Paul Gilroy, *Against Race: Imagining Political Culture Beyond the Color Line* (Cambridge, MA: Harvard University Press, 2000), 42.

3. Smith, *How Race Is Made*, 9.

begin to experience, imagine, taste, and appreciate bodily crossings and subversions of dividing lines which induce harm in our bodily experiences. By beginning to understand how the shaping of our world comes about in and through our bodily perception, we may not "just" experience our visceral reaction to others, but can begin perceiving and experiencing differently, perhaps.

In this final part, I return again to some of the questions I posed in my opening chapter and sketch a framework for body theology as a set of commitments which advances explorations into the what and how of bodily perceptual orientation. I will offer commitments of body theology as framework for analysis. Two select constructive theologies, concerned with bodily experience, and with references to the pitfalls of body/mind dualisms and/or sensory perception, will then serve as my test cases for utilizing body theology within the wider field of constructive theology. After showing via these test cases how body theology can expand and strengthen some critical claims and avoid potential manifestations and/or reiterations of Cartesian dualisms for any theologian concerned with the related issues, I will take up some of my personal questions/interests and take a body theology approach to construct a body theology beyond god-talk. I will conclude with offering possible trajectories for constructing body theologies in the future.

COMMITMENTS

Bodily perceptual orientations emerge from and are dependent on particularities, contingencies, and contextualities of embodiment. Our specific incarnation in space and time, our cultural context and individual bodily capacities, our being immersed in social givens and our personal development, significantly matter in the way we experience in the world. To insist on these contingencies and fluid ambiguous specifics of embodied life and then to move toward articulating a step-by-step methodology for body theology would be antithetical to the concerns and concepts presented here. Distilling body theology into a systematic method would imply that there is a method which might be free from culturally informed presuppositions and could be universally applicable. But this project has begun by cautioning of such presumptions, and to present a universalized method would be to pay no heed to my own convictions.

However, I believe that this caution does not deny my presenting certain commitments for a body theology approach. To weigh in on the significance of sensory perception is to take a specific stand when it comes to analyzing bodily experience: appreciate discursive analysis, and also pursue a kind of material investigation which might be fleeting and more difficult to grasp. Guiding commitments then can inform theological projects that seek to be grounded in experience without fixing experience in textual concepts. To formulate commitments rather than a method allows me to remain flexible (and hopefully humble) enough to travel cross-contextually.

The overarching commitment in body theology is the framework within which I have presented bodily experience in the previous chapters: The basic condition of my existence in the world and toward the world is my bodily perceptual orientation. My bodily experiencing is a perceptual experiencing; how I see, touch, feel, intuit, evaluate, remember, and so on *is* how I come to be and move in the world. Bodily perceptual experiences are also cultural acts, and perceptual differences are not only bodily differences but cultural differences, as culture inscribes how the senses are formed, utilized, and attributed.

Considering my exploration of bodily perceptual orientation in this project, there are some notions that I consider especially significant and constructive as commitments for body theology:[4]

> *Bodily experiences make sense.* To do body theology is to turn to bodily experience not first to make sense *of* it, but to turn to it understanding that bodily experiences make sense, make meaning, in the world. To do body theology is to acknowledge that we bodily deal with meaning in the world, and that we also actively create and make meaning as we bodily move with and within our embodied contexts. We acknowledge that bodily experiences always already make sense, in both meanings of the

---

4. I would also like to add that I do not consider this list as complete or exclusive, but I hold these commitments loosely enough to be adapted or added to as contexts and experiences may inform specific body theologies.

word; namely, there is already a logic to our bodily experiences and our bodily experiences create and manifest meaning for us.

Body theology explores bodily experience considering perceptual dimensions. When using bodily experience as resource for theology, we must consider perceptual dimensions. This means that the strength of the theological grounding in experience rests with the attention to sensory perception. Perception is embedded in various dimensions—pre-reflectively in social/cultural habits, in language, in individual bodily movements, in perceptual alignments, orientations, and perceptual devices—and is open to change, ambiguous and fluid meanings, and tensions and contradictions. Perception may shape how I know the world, but the world may also shape how I know to perceive.

Body theology conveys ambiguity and paradoxes. To turn to bodily experiences and perceptual dimensions is to acknowledge ambiguity and paradoxes in our experiences. If we are serious about overcoming body/mind dualisms, then we cannot maintain dualisms in body theology, not even traditionally cherished theological dualisms such as good/evil, oppression/redemption, sacred/profane, and so on. Since bodily experiences and perception are ambiguous and paradoxical (i.e., meaning is not statically fixed to certain experiences or perceptions, and perception is paradoxically both bodily and social, both passive and creative, both inherent and acquired, etc.), then body theology must remain open to ambiguity and paradoxes, to disorientations, changing currents, new movements. Because body theology conceives of bodily experience as ambiguous and open to change, it cannot derive theological concepts or formulations that are absolute or dualistic. This must not be a theological problem or weakness, but may be the strength of body theology in that it can attend to the gaps, cracks, fissures, and occlusions in our (theological) perceptual orientations.

Body theology is epistemologically unsettled. As a body theologian seeking to acknowledge and maintain the ambiguity, I must refrain from seeking absolute certainty without being afraid to make contingent pronouncements. I might gain skill and knowledge—for example, skill regarding analysis of bodily perceptual dimensions, knowledge regarding the processes of bodily perceptual experiences and interrelated dynamics—but this does not necessarily coincide with complete or final understanding. Our exploratory movements through different historical and cultural contexts might have helped in gaining a more complex understanding of bodily perceptual processes involved in different experiences, but I cannot claim to fully understand a different perceptual orientation, a different way of being in the world. To claim such full understanding and fix it within my own knowledge system would be counterproductive to the commitment of body theology which frames our own epistemological perspectives as bodily and socially determined. While I might deepen my understanding, or gain more complex understanding of a specific experience, my understanding is always contingent and momentary, and needs to be flexible enough to engage ambiguities and newly encountered difference. This also allows body theology a motile constructivity, attending to new meanings emerging via new bodily encounters, different perspectives leading to new interpretations, whilst remaining grounded in lived bodily experience and speaking clearly, even prophetically, within a situation.

Constructive body theology is grounded in our bodily experiences that *are* our theological imagination. The construction of body theology does not have to be god-talk, and perhaps should not be—in that it should be able to acknowledge and cross orient lines of Western theological symbols such as "God" that subsume non-theistic experiences and meaning-making. This does not imply that we are forfeiting the transcendent realm. If anything, as we have explored in this book, bodily perception *is* our experience of transcendence—bodies transcending toward a fluid, dynamic, yet ultimate reality that *is* the matter of our bodies as well as imagining and shaping our bodily existence. Body theology may, but does not need to engage in the kind of god-talk that employs God-the-symbol, but must construct particular (rather than generic or abstract) claims: what and how we imagine truth about ourselves and others, how we experience despair and what is aligned with our desire for freedom, what and where we imagine hope and agency for change, where and how we sense ultimate accountability in our relationships, how we experience the emergence of creative life crossing lines of injustice and violence. Bodily experiences that are our knowledge of the world are our theological imagination in the world. There is an ethical demand to our theological construction embedded here: account to the best of our

perceptual capacities for ways in which we tend toward our preferred theological imagery, to risk re-alignments of our theological
imagination, of a crossing of lines and a re-orientation of our bodies
and bodily experiences so that we may perceive and know bodies out
of line, and desiring to know those bodies emerging out of differently
aligned spaces and queer orientations.

CHAPTER SIX

REVISITING BODY THEOLOGY APPROACHES

Different theologians might have different goals in mind when employing body theology, be it systematic exploration of theological concepts or practical theological investigations into specific situational contexts. Deciding that I want to begin with bodily experience, I begin with the experience/situation I perceive to be relevant or which caught my theological attention. As body theologian, considering the commitments outlined, I am now charged to explore this experience for various bodily perceptual dimensions, understanding that my explorations are limited by my own capacities and orientations. I can examine my own understanding by maintaining a critically open posture and checking my own self-knowledge (am I aware of my own bodily perceptual orientations that I bring to the experience and to the analysis of this experience?) while seeking to explain how certain bodily perceptual orientations might come into play in our experiences.

In this section, I will turn to two theologians, Carter Heyward and Marcella Althaus-Reid, scholars who served as exemplars in my critique of phenomenological notions in feminist theologies. Both theologians explicitly reflect on bodily experience and seek to construct liberative theologies, make reference to the pitfalls of body/mind dualisms, and highlight, in one way or another, knowledge via perception.

Bringing body theology commitments to Carter Heyward's theological project, I will discuss ways in which body theology can go beyond naïve appeals to sensory perception as epistemological venue. I will strengthen Heyward's appeal to "be in touch with our bodies" by framing it in a complex understanding of bodily perceptual processes. Marcella Althaus-Reid's work will serve as an example of what I have termed body metaphor theology. Exploring and suspending/delaying Althaus-Reid's theological method, I will show how body theology can strengthen theological aims, namely by dwelling on and exploring experience more thoroughly, thus avoiding to move too quickly from experience to metaphor.

TOUCHING THE STRENGTH OF CARTER HEYWARD

Much of Carter Heyward's theological "coming out" work was published almost 35 years ago, though it has lost none of its critical creative challenge to the way theology should be done.[1] The Christian theologian and Episcopal priest may be best known for not only discussing openly her being a lesbian but also drawing on this dimension of her life as an integral source to her theologizing.[2] I very briefly

1. Carter Isabel Heyward, *The Redemption of God: A Theology of Mutual Relations* (Lanham, MD: Pilgrim Press, 1982). Carter Isabel Heyward, *Our Passion for Justice: Images of Power, Sexuality, and Liberation* (New York, NY: Pilgrim Press, 1984). Carter Isabel Heyward, *Speaking of Christ: A Lesbian Feminist Voice* (New York, NY: Pilgrim Press, 1989). Carter Isabel Heyward, *Touching Our Strength: The Erotics as Power and the Love of God* (San Francisco: Harper & Row, 1989).

2. Heyward's theological approach was/is compelling and groundbreaking not only in the way she insists that theology must be grounded in the here and now of embodied realities in order to pursue critically and imaginatively the truths of our own lives-in-relation, but also in the way her theological work seeks to be intersectional in regard to race, class, religion, gender, nationality, and sexual desires. She speaks clearly of the interrelated dynamics which bring about oppressive ideologies—that sexism and homophobia must be understood in relation to capitalism, nationalism, and racism, for example. Her epistemological method is to revalue feeling as source of "objective" knowledge, knowledge of real life experiences and embodied realities. The epistemological folly of Enlightenment rationality is that particularity coupled with power leads to presenting as universal, normative, and true what is grounded in specific social locations. Thus we need to be clear about the limits of our knowledge, which is constructed in a social context, not simply out of intellectual honesty

brought up a component of her theological framework in the second chapter, where I highlighted that her appeal to be in touch with our bodily senses inadvertently reinstates a body/mind dualism she seeks to overcome. This conception of perception and framing of the sensual as access to knowledge leads into a critical dead end, though one we might sense our way out of.

This project established body theology as an inquiry into meaning emerging in our bodily experiences. As such, body theology can join Heyward's conceptual and methodological commitments: She defines theology as "the capacity to discern God's presence here and now and to reflect on what this means"[3] and as "critical, creative reflection on the patterns, shape, and movement of the Sacred in our life together."[4] Body theology echoes her emphasis on human embodiment as inseparable body-mind existence intertwined through mutual relations with others and the world.

Heyward's conception and use of relationality and mutuality are where I locate a challenge and contribution I bring to Heyward via body theology. Heyward's answer to the pervasiveness of evil in human life is to frame "God" as human power in mutual relation. The harmful legacies of separating material from spiritual, body from mind, are found today in the concept of individual personhood as autonomous and independent. This denial of interrelatedness is at the heart of structural forces such as compulsory heterosexuality or white male patriarchy. The answer, Heyward argues, is in rediscovering and fostering our mutual relationality, to understand being a person *as* social relationship. Sin and evil are lack of mutuality; liberation and the sacred are found in mutual relations. Mutuality, to Heyward, transforms alienated power into right relations, sharing power in a relationship that

---

(and perhaps, humility), but also because the particularities which limit us are also the ground and source of our truth-claims. Heyward, *Touching Our Strength*, 3–13.

3. Heyward, *Our Passion for Justice*, 7.
4. Heyward, *Touching Our Strength*, 22.

each involved may become more fully who she is. Mutuality is a relational movement which shapes us.[5]

Mutuality, according to Heyward, is right relation, and this is the cornerstone of her theological project. Mutual relations are just and loving relations. She is careful not to conflate mutuality with sameness or oneness, and insists on the ambiguity and inherent tensions which come with relation across and within difference.[6] All relations are social and embedded with power, interests, and desires. Yet we are born alienated and into alienation as consequence of unjust power relations; economic oppression, racism, sexism, etc., are patterns of alienation.[7] Heyward then charges that we live as embodied creatures in the world, and mutual relation is a "radical connectedness" not just of humanity but all of reality.[8] Thus, our bodies are affected by the social structures within which we inescapably live, and this is why we know about the

5. Ibid., 56, 91, 191. Importantly, Heyward's theological convictions are deeply grounded in her life experiences and social justice activism. She has been an activist for racial justice, beginning as a teenager, and was part of the first group of women to be ordained in the Episcopal Church in 1974. This first ordination event was also an "extraordinary" event, invalidated in an emergency meeting of the House of Bishops. Two years later, women's ordination into priesthood of the Episcopal Church was approved. After retiring from teaching at Episcopal Divinity School in Cambridge, MA, Heyward now lives in an intentional community and has founded a therapeutic horseback riding center in North Carolina, geared toward children and adults with emotional, mental, and physical limitations and disabilities.

6. To be loving is not to engender a feeling, but to be open to action, a willingness to participate with others in the healing of a broken world and broken lives. Heyward, *Our Passion for Justice*, 82, 187. "God" is power in right relation as well as resource and power of relation, thus for Heyward, human activity *is* divine activity whenever and wherever it is just and loving. Heyward, *The Redemption of God*, 222. Heyward, *Touching Our Strength*, 22. Mutuality, though, goes beyond human relation, as the structures of alienation encompass the alienation of humans from other earthcreatures as well as rocks, plants, water, air, etc. Heyward, *Our Passion for Justice*, xiii–xv. Heyward, *Touching Our Strength*, 92–93.

7. Heyward, *Touching Our Strength*, 105. Carter Isabel Heyward, *Staying Power: Reflections on Gender, Justice, and Compassion* (Cleveland, OH: Pilgrim Press, 1995), 80.

8. Carter Isabel Heyward, *Saving Jesus from Those Who Are Right: Rethinking What It Means to Be Christian* (Minneapolis: Fortress Press, 1999), 62.

world and ourselves through our bodies, yet as bodies participating in complex, tension-filled, ambiguous relations with other bodies.[9]

Experiences of mutuality, which are bodily, sensual, erotic experiences, are the grounds for incarnate knowledge of right relations, knowledge that is a vision of what is possible beyond oppression and suffering.[10] She appeals (in an empiricist vein) to sensory perception as fundamental to conception of ideas, because all knowledge is rooted in the sensory capacities of the body.[11] Because structures of alienation have disconnected us from our power to feel, and thus, to know, returning to embodied relationality via sensory and sensual means and "trust[ing] our senses, our capacities to touch, taste, smell, hear, see, and thereby know" is learning via the senses "what is good and what is bad, what is real and what is false [. . .]. [S]ensuality is a foundation for our authority."[12] Yet Heyward is also careful not to posit this kind of "body knowledge" as an individually gained knowledge. Because bodies are always bound up in ambiguous, complex relations with

9. Lucy Tatman, *Knowledge That Matters: A Feminist Theological Paradigm and Epistemology* (Cleveland: Pilgrim Press, 2001), 199.

10. Heyward, *Touching Our Strength*, 187. It is also important to note that Heyward understands the "erotic" as "the yearning to be involved." She leans here on Audre Lorde's definition of the erotic.

11. Heyward, *Our Passion for Justice*, 172. Heyward is citing feminist ethicist Beverly Wildung Harrison, "The Power of Anger in the Work of Love," in *Weaving the Visions: New Patterns in Feminist Spirituality*, ed. Judith Plaskow and Carol P. Christ (San Francisco: HarperCollins, 1989), 214–225.

12. Heyward's own experiences and consciously self-reflexive reflections on them are central to her own theological reflections. Heyward, *Touching Our Strength*, 93. Heyward recounts some of her own bodily sensory experiences, e.g., experiencing the call to priesthood and its confirmations, in Carter Isabel Heyward, *A Priest Forever: One Woman's Controversial Ordination in the Episcopal Church* (Cleveland, OH: Pilgrim Press, 1999). Her engagement of her own feelings and personal issues via a women's consciousness-raising group and psychotherapy are significant grounding experiences for her theological aim at personal contextualization. See also Angela Pears, *Feminist Christian Encounters: The Methods and Strategies of Feminist Informed Christian Theologies* (Burlington, VT: Ashgate Publishing Company, 2004), 71–82.

other bodies and the world, situated bodily knowledge is necessarily communal.[13]

I cautioned earlier against a romanticizing or universalizing of "relationality" as intrinsic to human existence.[14] Relationality is not inherently innocent, thus women's experience of relationships can be marked by oppression as well as complicity, be it in deference to cultural customs or survival struggles.[15] Similarly, mutuality, commonly used as signifier for *having the same relationship toward each other*, or *being directed and received by each toward the other*, or as *reciprocal relationship*, is not inherently innocent or justice making. I do not take issue with Heyward constructing and using mutuality to describe her theological aim (I also appreciate that her interest is not in abstract notions of mutuality per se, but in "God" as the justice-creating power in mutual relationships).[16] But given my exploration of bodily perceptual

13. Tatman, *Knowledge That Matters*, 199.

14. See chapter 2, note 74. My caution is informed by Serene Jones, who argues that relationality can serve as the structure to appropriate or fit in that which is marginal, and she also wonders if valorizing traditional stereotypes of women being more relational can really be liberating. Serene Jones, *Feminist Theory and Christian Theology: Cartographies of Grace*, Guides to Theological Inquiry, ed. Kathryn Tanner and Paul Lakeland (Minneapolis: Fortress Press, 2000), 47.

15. I do not mean to imply that Heyward is ignorant to systemic structures of oppression and our implications in it, far from it. Her emphasis on relationality should not be mistaken for primarily being concerned with individual one-on-one interpersonal relationships (though her conception does include them in a significant way). Heyward is clear that we are always in relation to people and other living beings, as groups and to groups, via economical, political, and other larger systemic relations. Right relations include concern regarding right relations between communities, nations, etc., and Heyward's conception of injustice indicates she understands it as multilayered, complex, with sometimes competing dynamics/types of injustice coming to bear in people's lives. For example, she explores interlocking and interrelated injustices such as racism, sexism, imperialism, classism, militarism, anti-Semitism, heterosexism, ableism, ageism in Heyward, *Our Passion for Justice*, 145–147.

16. Theologically, bringing to bear her concern with relationality and mutuality on the concept of God, Heyward defines God as "our power in mutual relation." God is then a quality of existence, rather than a metaphysical presence outside of and separate from of the world. Heyward, *Touching Our Strength*, 3.

orientation in the world as condition for our existence, I believe there are some noteworthy critical challenges to bring to her work.

With body theology, I approach Heyward's theology presupposing our pre-reflective involvement in the world and with each other, our emergent existence with bodily and socio-culturally specific bodily perceptual orientations. Perception is not a tool, but in line with the commitments of body theology, perception *is* how we experience. The way we experience (feel, think, speak, imagine, talk, touch) in the world emerges from a social habitual base, from the way we emerge as existing in the world, already experiencing (feeling, thinking, speaking, imagining, talking, touching) a certain way, along pre-established lines of orientation which align our perceptions and bodily habits. In other words, sensory perception is not an unutilized or undervalued set of (epistemological or ontological) structures which may help us enter mutual relations, but perception is already grounding, already structuring our existence.[17]

Our bodily experience is grounded in a mutual constitution of our existence and emergence in the world. We are already bound up in a mutual, pre-reflective relationship with others and the world; our bodily perceptions, movements, and expressions are immersed and grounded in the bodily social sediment which we are born into. To then diagnose sin and/or evil in the world as alienation from each other and from our bodily feelings is to disregard that this very alienation Heyward is writing about *comes about through* our mutual embeddedness in the world and with each other.

Heeding another body theology commitment, namely acknowledging that our bodily experiences contain ambiguity and paradoxes, requires a conceptualization of relationality which holds mutuality and alienation not in a dualistic either/or fashion. Rather, mutuality and alienation are embedded with each other, intertwined in experiences of both/and: relations can encompass mutuality and alienation; mutuality and alienation both come about in relation.

---

17. Therefore, when referring to perception as a tool to be utilized, Heyward naturalizes what is perceived (as I have demonstrated in chapter 2).

Bringing body theology to bear on Heyward's work, I can assert that the patterns of alienation (racism, sexism, nationalism, etc.) we are born into are patterns of bodily perceptual alignments. I experience alienation under oppressive structures not only/simply because I have been alienated from my bodily feeling, but because my socio-cultural context aligns me with others in a mutual constitution in a grid of individual, autonomous, mind-over-matter ideologies. My emergence in the world, the emergence of the world, and the emergence of others with me in the world is already constituted by being directed and received by each toward each other. We are already immersed in a pre-reflective reciprocal relationship: that of being perceptually oriented toward each other and by each other.

Heyward asserts that we are alienated by structures of oppression which prevent a familiarity and trust in—and necessity to return to—our sensory/sensual capacities. Yet body theology reveals that/how it is precisely our bodily sensory, sensual capacities which may produce those alienations from each other. Structures of oppression, systemic injustices, are cultural sensory perceptual expressions, bodily movements and orientations which come to be habituated and maintain alignments of alienation. So rather than the answer to oppressive "isms," mutuality and relationality take part in the significant process of how we come to bodily experience alienation. We are already perceptually directed toward and received by each other in specific ways, for example, in gendered and racialized habituations, and this aligns us with (and maintains through us) experiences of alienation from each other.

This body theology perspective significantly bears on Heyward's theo-ethical aim. She charges that to be in touch with our feelings, to claim our bodily perceptions as access to truth, makes the world intelligible to us and can alert us to danger, injustice, or violation of bodily and emotional integrity. Bodily senses, for example, allow me to feel safe or threatened as I walk "alone at night through a neighborhood that is strange to me," so that my immediate sensory apprehension alerts me to possible danger in difference.[18] Yet these perceptual apprehensions,

18. Heyward, *Touching Our Strength*, 113.

our bodily feelings in certain situations, are already shaped in a pre-reflective current. The meaning of "danger" or "threat" emerges from a mutual constitution of myself and my environment along bodily perceptual orientation lines (of say, whiteness, class, heteronormativity), meanings which are not fixed or settled "body knowledges," but contingent and fluid significances emerging in motile engagements within bodily relations.

Heyward writes of erotic justice as creating boundaries *with* each other, learning *with* each other how to cross them, strengthen them, or loosen them,[19] yet when we take our existence as bodily perceptual orientation in the world into account, we can see how that is already happening pre-reflectively, bodily, socially. To aim for just relations through bodily expressions, feelings, sensual movements, requires us to be able to account for how our bodily feelings come about. Reframing mutuality as that in which we are already embedded (not alienated from) does not negate an ethical trajectory. Rather, it can highlight the ambiguity, indeterminacy, and tensions inherent in relations Heyward highlights. It allows us to account for the bodily feelings, the sensual apprehensions of the world, which demonstrate social relations embedded with power and desires, and even "truth" about what a situation, a context, or a relation "means."

Without accounting for our bodily perceptual orientations, for the ways in which my feelings, my desires to touch, my imaginations expressed in speech come about, we are tempted to equate our feeling/perception of "danger" or "evil" with the embodied presence of it. I certainly agree with Heyward that the bodily sense of feeling threatened in the presence of an abusive, violent person is a perception of evil and sin. Sharing feminist commitments, I am sure we have common perceptual orientations which allow us to perceive the orientation lines of patriarchal sexism and heteronormativity and the effects they have on aligning bodily movements. Yet the examples I provided in chapter three and four showed that "danger" or "evil" as perceptually

19. Ibid., 112.

emerging meaning is also too easily attached to difference in a way that reinforces oppressive structures. To be in touch with one's bodily feelings may just as easily lead to my apprehension of truth about a black body encountered on the street signaling "evil." Tapping into our feelings/sensory perceptions does not necessarily lead to a world perceived in line with a feminist consciousness. I may be bodily aligned in ways so that experiences of oppression or abuse are part of my habituation and bodily movement in the world. My bodily perceptual orientations then situate me in a way that trusting or valuing my sensory perceptions does not necessarily lead me to liberative truths about my experience. I might not even perceptually experience in ways which might bring about meaning regarding relationality in the ways Heyward envisions it, that is, my bodily experiences of violence *are* what makes sense in my life and what creates meaning in a situation.

We do not need to dismiss attention to our bodily experiences, but we need to be able to complexly grasp why certain apprehensions or knowledges about others and the world come to be natural truth, even when they reinforce stereotypes and oppressive behaviors. It is *because* we are indivisible body-mind-selves that, for example, heteronormativity has such a hold on our embodied lives, not because we lost touch with our bodies. To aim for justice, for just and right relations, for mutuality which does not lead to emergence of oppression, is to be in touch with how our bodily experiences *are* us, for better or worse.

Theology as enterprise in Heyward is always, critically and fundamentally, a "communal or collective struggle to comprehend ourselves in a world in which relation is broken violently."[20] Therefore, it grows out of lived experiences and the needs felt in different, particularly embodied communities.[21] To do body theology in a Heywardian frame can allow us to do relational, communally-grounded theology that begins with the pre-reflective dimensions emerging in our bodily

---

20. Heyward, *The Redemption of God*, 68.
21. Heyward not only draws on personal experiences as I footnoted earlier. Her writings always acknowledge and account for (and describe her accountability to) the communities in which she resides and engages.

movements together. Tapping into our experience is then more than being in touch with our feelings (even as we might strive to overcome ambiguous or conflicting feelings toward each other or others through embodied social justice actions). Grounding Heyward's theology in experience can be crucially expanded by understanding how our bodily perception is what supports certain kinds of community feelings over others (including those supporting alienation and separation); it is to understand how all bodily experience, all bodily sensing, is bound up in pre-reflective relationality.

Rather than something we have simply lost touch with, sensory perception is how we got be in our current embodied situation in the first place. Bodily experiences can be a valuable tool in thinking about ethical implications, because it is in our bodily experiences that the currents which "float the boat" of our lives can be traced. Tracing bodily perceptual orientations to the best of our abilities can be a tool in demonstrating the intersections Heyward is careful to highlight. As I have shown, it can allow for complex investigations into how, for example, nationalism is aligned through racial alignments, or how class alignments are supported by currents of gendered perceptual orientation.

Broadening my attention on Heyward from her concepts of relationality and mutuality to her larger theological project, there are ways in which body theology can significantly strengthen and support the task of a relational theologian. Heyward's theology is worked out within a systematic approach, formulating coherent theological concepts regarding God, Christ, the Holy Spirit, and the church community. Since God is defined by her as power in mutual relation, and the shape of God is justice, all human activity can be divine activity (the Spirit of God moving on earth). God, rather than being a personal figure, but the ground of being, is seen in human behavior such as compassionate action. All human acts of mutual relating are "godding," allowing God the sacred sensual power which infuses our bodies to reach out to others. The theologian's task is to discern God's presence in the here and now and reflect on the meaning of it.

The Heywardian theologian cannot rely on the senses to tell truth in the way in which Heyward suggests, but can still appeal to sensory perception as significantly embedded in our bodily experiences. Bodily experiences then may still be the realm in which "godding"/genuine justice-love relations across difference are possible, even crucial and necessary. However, sensory perception is not access to this realm, but is embedded in it. Rather than appealing to the senses to guide us toward mutuality, appealing to sensory perception needs to be done in a complex and nuanced way. Because sometimes, justice-love relations require that we deviate from the ways our sensory perceptions are aligned. It requires we change directions in our perceptual facing and bodily move into relations our senses might tell us to turn away from or close ourselves off from. Rather than relying on feelings to guide us, we might need to acquire new bodily movements so that our feelings can "catch up" with the truth about just relations which can emerge when we face that which "feels" different. This can only strengthen Heyward's claim that right relations can be hard and difficult, and her belief that we ought to aim to foster human acts of love and making justice in everyday situations. While her appeal to the senses might get in the way of supporting just relations in a nuanced way, a body theology approach can help Heyward's aim for visceral, bodily, sensual "godding" toward just relations; perhaps in new, different, even queer orientations toward each other.

ALIGNING WITH INDECENCY AND MARCELLA ALTHAUS-REID

Marcella Althaus-Reid approaches the doing of theology in radical ways by "contextually queering" Christian theology, particularly liberation theologies, through recontextualizing, "a permanent exercise of serious doubting in theology."[22] She charges Christianity with being complicit in the colonization and domination of Latin America, not the least through imposing a heterosexual rule of decency which underpins oppressive economic, social, and sexual systems of

22. Marcella M. Althaus-Reid, *Indecent Theology: Theological Perversions in Sex, Gender and Politics* (New York, NY: Routledge, 2000), 5.

exploitation.[23] She highlights how theological discourses have domesticated bodies, excluding challenges from different perspectives, particularly those perspectives which seek to hold together the intersections of sexual identity with racial and political constructions.[24] I already discussed, albeit briefly, how Althaus-Reid's approach to utilizing experience is close to an intellectualist position, which leads to theologizing as interpretive endeavor, as Althaus-Reid quickly moves from description of experience to mining it as metaphor for a theological construction.

"Indecency" and "queering" become significant concepts at work in Althaus-Reid's theological project. Emphasizing the immanence of God in all bodily experiences, she particularly focuses on uncovering that which has been denied as site of divine revelation by the disciplining discourse of heterosexual, patriarchal colonialism. Because her theological concerns began and were significantly shaped in the streets of Buenos Aires, Argentina, she offers theological analyses through experiences of Latin American women, from theologians like her to the lemon vendors on the street.[25] These experiences, she claims, have been "decented" to exclude the sexual experiences of the poor, thus presenting a decent image of the poor as the focal point of liberation theologies, effectively fetishizing and oppressing the poor, especially poor women, yet again.[26]

23. Ibid., 17–20.
24. Ibid., 4–5.
25. Althaus-Reid was born in Rosario, Argentina, knowing about life in poverty first hand. She earned her first degree at ISEDET, the center for the study of liberation theology in Latin America. She then worked in social and community projects in marginalized and deprived areas of Buenos Aires. Her work was inspired by Paolo Freire. She was invited to establish similar projects in Dundee and Perth (Scotland), earned a PhD at the University of St. Andrews, and was the first female lecturer appointed at the University of Edinburgh.
26. Althaus-Reid, *Indecent Theology*, 22–26, 34–35. Liberation theologies, Althaus-Reid charges, have idealized a model of the poor, ignorant but faithful Christian mother," but not a poor woman who also has sexual experiences, sexual

Althaus-Reid is committed to beginning with and speaking back particular experiences, but requires that bodily experiences need to be approached with "sexual honesty."[27] The queering hermeneutical circle of indecent theology begins with experience, but does not pre-define or censor what counts as experience. Because the sexual experiences and desires of the poor and marginalized have been systematically excluded, Althaus-Reid makes those her explicit starting and focal point.[28]

When she critically deconstructs complex layers of oppression, her conceptualization bears resemblances to the way in which I have framed perceptual orientations and the supportive pre-reflective currents of bodily experience. She describes the orders of (sexual) decency, of what can enter church settings, theological constructions, and theological patterns, as the underlying and supportive orders of oppression.[29] She charges that (and here I am applying the conceptual language of body theology to her work) the decenting of theology aligns perceptual orientations in such ways that the enterprise of theology emerges as theological engagements with a given directionality (say, concern for the poor, social justice), along certain orienting lines (the poor, the oppressed, the exploited). Yet the "sexual ideology performed in a socializing pattern" perceptually disappears behind certain naturalized Christian notions of decency.[30] Or, put differently through a body

desires, and preferences. While decency for men has been posited as honesty and trustworthiness, for women it involved gendered expectations and regulations regarding sexuality and sexual behavior. What is expected of women, and what is considered proper for them, masks a multitude of oppressions regarding gender, sex, race, and economical arrangements.

27. Ibid., 7.
28. Althaus-Reid's scholarship, activism, and personal involvement are testimony to the concern and personal commitment she held for marginalized communities and their suffering from structural injustices. For example, she was committed to justice for transgender persons, and was involved in this community personally but also advocated tirelessly for recognition and acceptance of transgender persons in the social realm, as well as for legal recognition and protection.
29. Althaus-Reid, *Indecent Theology*, 25–26.
30. Ibid., 87.

theology frame again, pre-reflective currents of sexual ideologies (sediment habits of heterosexist patriarchal Christianity) give rise to perceptual emergences of proper liberation theologies and alignments of proper theological subjects.

When Althaus-Reid then turns to bodily experiences, she seeks to queer theology by making it "indecent," that is, attend to what has been habitually excluded. For example, our bodily experiences of sexuality do include experiences of exploitation, but also lust; they might incorporate heterosexual tendencies, but also queerness. When making sense of human experiences, sexuality in all its various expressions needs to be available as a resource for theology. Althaus-Reid seeks to present experiences rendered too taboo for public theologizing as instances of experiencing the divine. The hermeneutical circle of indecent theology works well for a body theology approach because she understands her hermeneutics to be more an event than a method. The hermeneutical event that starts with experience and the naming of it uses sexuality as a way of thinking to unmask ideological constraints, and understands reflective analysis to demand action in regard to liberation from political, sexual, and religious oppressions.[31]

What makes Althaus-Reid's work compelling for my framing of body theology is that she is not simply charging us to be "in touch with our sexuality" (as in similar calls referring to our senses). Rather, she challenges us to go further in our attending to the sexual in our experiences,[32] and understand it more extensively as (what I have called) the pre-reflective current and tacit knowledge informing political and economic constructions, shaping discourses on divinely ordained ideologies and alienations of embodied lives/experiences via alignments of decency codes.[33] Furthermore, her refusal to apply her indecenting

31. Marcella M. Althaus-Reid, *The Queer God* (New York, NY: Routledge, 2003), 2. Althaus-Reid, *Indecent Theology*, 126.
32. For example, she challenges feminist theologies for focus on sex beyond connections to gender, but not on "sex as 'having sex,'" which includes "sex as lust." Althaus-Reid, *Indecent Theology*, 87.
33. Ibid., 2.

method to developing a closed narrative of liberative systematic theology, that is, a solid structure for a/one revised Christian story that is liberative in its indecency, makes her theological approach appealing to the body theology commitment I put forth; like me, she is less interested in systematically formulated content than in theology as critical reflection that is always contextual, localized, and embodied. Her theology aims to remain flexible and able to travel to various indecent experiences.[34]

To think sexually when doing theology in Althaus-Reid is to queer theology by grounding reflections in particular bodies, and more specifically, in their sexual practices. In the relationships of marginalized bodies, especially their sexual practices, we can find experiences to queer theological imagery, that is, which unveil God from and in those places typically excluded.[35] In her frequently invoked and cited example of the lemon vendors on the street of Argentina, Althaus-Reid directs our attention to the important economical, political, and theological structures and oppressions she seeks to deconstruct by invoking the underwear-free women selling goods on the streets.[36] When she

---

34. Ibid., 101–102. Pears, *Feminist Christian Encounters*, 150.

35. Althaus-Reid, *Indecent Theology*.

36. After leading with quotes describing women without underwear in public life and condemning them as immoral, indecent, or comically dismissing them, Althaus-Reid comments, "Should a woman keep her pants on in the streets or not? Shall she remove them, say, at the moment of going to church, for a more intimate reminder of her sexuality in relation to God? What difference does it make if that woman is a lemon vendor and sells you lemons in the streets without using underwear? Moreover, what difference would it make if she sits down to write theology without underwear? The Argentinian woman theologian and the lemon vendors may have some things in common and others not. In common, they have centuries of patriarchal oppression, in the Latin American mixture of clericalism, militarism and the authoritarianism of decency, that is, the sexual organization of the public and private spaces of society." Ibid., 1. She then describes a street scene of the lemon vendors, weaving together imagery of their presence in the street with histories of conquest and oppression. She continues, "The everyday lives of people always provide us with a starting point for a process of doing contextual theology without exclusions, in this case without the exclusion of sexuality struggling in the midst of misery. [...]

charges that the everyday lives of people provide us "with a starting point for a process of doing contextual theology without exclusions," she wants us to include "sexuality struggling in the midst of misery."[37]

Yet her move from experience to employment of it as metaphor or site of textual inquiry takes place rather quickly. When Althaus-Reid posits the sexual and political practices of the marginalized as point of departure for theology, she turns rather quickly to particular experiences as "living metaphor for God," employing the "*images* of lemon vendors,"[38] seeking to "sexually deconstruct Christ" in order to allow for re-significations. She positively appropriates words, such as "God, the Faggot; God, the Drag Queen; God, the Lesbian"; exploring and unpacking seemingly shocking juxtapositions of the sexual and the theological in "leather salvation," "Bi/Christ," "French-kissing God," investigating in cultural terms that "God is a Sodomite." She describes "God's voyeuristic vocation," and "God the Whore" who empties herself in a brothel.[39]

Althaus-Reid urges us to consider these bodily sites metaphorically and symbolically as the epistemological site for doing theology.[40] The indecent experiences of the poor become the experiences that Mariology or Christology are made of. So when she employs the sexual experiences of the marginalized, she explores, for example, the Bi/Christ as the hard-to-pin-down sexual body, misunderstood on both sides of dividing lines and providing openings to borders and categories. This Bi/Christ operates outside of heteronormative and heteropatriarchal binaries and liberates the poor *and* the rich, those on the sexual and economic margins *and* those in the center.[41] Althaus-Reid has been

A living metaphor for God, sexuality and the struggle in the streets of Buenos Aires comes from the images of lemon vendors. A materialist-based theology finds in them a starting point from which ideology, theology and sexuality can be rewritten from the margins of society, the church and systematic theologies." Ibid., 4.

37. Ibid., 4.
38. Ibid., Emphasis mine.
39. Ibid., 89, 95, 114, 125. Althaus-Reid, *The Queer God*, 39, 86, 95.
40. Althaus-Reid, *Indecent Theology*, 3–4.
41. Ibid., 114–118.

lauded for the radical, subversive, and liberatory theological potential in her indecent images of human and divine relationships. Yet she also has been challenged for the inherent limitations that her utilization of poststructuralist and queer methodologies brings to her doing of theology, for example, her failure to spell out what a Bi/Christ really means, or what substantial difference lies in using these bodily groundings.[42]

I diagnose this failure as resulting from the phenomenological position she falls into. As I pointed out in chapter 2, Althaus-Reid connects perception to recognition of meaning, recognition that is situated in particular embodiments. Perception is alternatively considered as bodily function which can be accessed to gather information; other times it is a socially-shaped recognition and interpretation of what is sensorially perceived. While she does not make any explicit appeals to perceptual capacities, her utilization of experience appears to be informed by a common phenomenological method in religious studies which understands perception as the capacity for objective observation and for "truthful" description of sensory information of a lived experience/phenomenon.[43]

42. Thomas Bohache, *Christology from the Margins* (London, UK: SCM Press, 2008), 223.
43. Phenomenological approaches in the study of religion view religion as experiences with different components to be studied. Religious phenomena can be studied as consistently as possible with the orientation of the practitioner. This approach owes its origin and conceptual development to a large extent to scholars like Pierre Daniel Chantepie de la Saussaye, William Brede Kristensen, and Gerardus Van der Leeuw. These phenomenologists of religion commonly build on and appropriate Husserl's influence on the phenomenological movement. Husserl recognized that prior beliefs and interpretations come to influence one's thinking. So his phenomenological method recognizes the role of the subjective observer in apprehending the world. It asserts that knowledge begins from within, with the subject moving outside itself into an objective description of the world. But to do so, one must bracket attitudes and presuppositions, suspend judgment. This allows us to describe phenomena as they appear, and to attain understanding of their structures and patterns. James Cox, *An Introduction to the Phenomenology of Religion* (New York, NY: Continuum International Publishing Group, 2010), 25–30. For a compilation of select essays on the phenomenology of religion by various religious or phenomenological scholars (such as Schleiermacher, Feuerbach, van der Leeuw, and

Body theology can begin in this space in which Althaus-Reid is limited by her phenomenological stance, slowing down the move to metaphorical use of radical indecent imagery found in bodily experiences. Maintaining the focus of exploration in bodily experiences themselves aids in articulating significant differences found in marginal bodily sexual experiences and is also useful in spelling out the meanings which might emerge from a bisexual body, or from selling wares without underwear.

When Althaus-Reid invites us to visit her city, Buenos Aires, and to take walks in the barrios, she invites us to take in the sights of humans, animals, houses, trees; to take in the smells of garbage and flowers, food and humans, coffee and sex; to tune into the sounds of political songs and theological discussions. She then invites us to think about what we thought when seeing her streets, because "[i]mpressions in foreign lands are so deceptive."[44] She then presents this image as metaphor for the fragmentation of subjectivity, the multiple consciousness effected by violently imposed Christian and European narratives. The lemon vendors provide Althaus-Reid with the imagery of bodily experience, and Althaus-Reid insists that "[t]hose lemon vendors can tell you a few things about postmodernism."[45] Though as Althaus-Reid continues, it appears that it is the *image* more than the actual lemon vendors speaking, it is what the lemon vendors may invoke in the interpreting theologian rather than their experiences themselves, that does the telling in Althaus-Reid's work. Thus, the intellectual agency of decoding and interpreting this imagery is clearly aligned with theologian Althaus-Reid, while the lemon vendors fade into the background as material, rather than as agents of theology.[46]

others) see Joseph Dabney Bettis, ed. *Phenomenology of Religion: Eight Modern Descriptions of the Essence of Religion* (New York, NY: Harper & Row, 1969).

44. Althaus-Reid, *Indecent Theology*, 3.

45. Ibid.

46. Ibid., 3–4. A similar reservations is expressed by Emilie Townes when she challenges Althaus-Reid's descriptions of the lemon vendors in a fashion which casts the reader in a voyeuristic position, deliberately perhaps, but voyeuristic nevertheless. Townes is troubled by the way in which Althaus-Reid's invocations maintain

Yet how might I follow this invitation to do theology from the sexual experiences of the marginalized, without falling for what Althaus-Reid called (and criticized) "theological voyeurism"?[47] Body theology intervenes at this junction, inviting me to feel and sense a bit longer, to pay attention to sensual cues and the sensory limits I am traveling with. Possibly, having been schooled by postcolonial feminists, I might already be aware that I am meeting her lemon vendors *not* in perceptual innocence. And I might be cued into my own visualist biases, paying attention to how I look and position myself in relation to the lemon vendors, and what my visual judgments of or in the encounter are. Thrown into perceptual unknowns, I might experience offense, surprise, disorientation. Body theology commitments challenge me to look for the sense in bodily experiences (e.g., the lemon vendors bodily movements already make sense and create meaning, before and without my acts of interpretation). And I am challenged to refrain from using body theology as framework of certainty in interpretation, but rather remain unsettled and attend to meaning emerging in bodily (and interpretative) encounters.

Sexuality and its embodied manifestations have often been posited as antagonist to theological enterprises. When Althaus-Reid seeks to establish the sexual as integral to critical theological analysis of economical, political, cultural, colonial structures, she might be invoking the emerging smell of lemons blending with genital scents. But she immediately connects smells to sex, invoking a metaphorical connection between sexuality and economics, locating theological messages

---

the object status of the lemon vendors throughout her work, as she falls short of engaging for them and with them their materiality, nakedness, sex, race, class, etc. "The too-flat descriptions of the indigenous lemon vendors does not help me understand the tie this region has to the United States, Great Britain, France or the Netherlands, or the horror of 1492 and the death it brought through violence and disease to three-quarters of the indigenous population within a hundred years." Emilie M. Townes, "Marcella Althaus-Reid's *Indecent Theology*: A Response," in *Dancing Theology in Fetish Boots: Essays in Honour of Marcella Althaus-Reid*, ed. Lisa Isherwood and Mark D. Jordan (London, UK: SCM Press, 2010), 64.

47. Althaus-Reid, *Indecent Theology*, 26.

at this intersection in the street of Buenos Aires. Yet this might be a rushed connection to make. Lacking bodily perceptual immersions in this context myself, bringing body theology commitments to Althaus-Reid can nevertheless provide a way to more fully ground her theology in the experiences she invokes.

For example, exploring bodily experiences in terms of perceptual dimension, what meanings could be detected emerging when paying attention to the smells on the street? Is it the smell of sex and/or the smell of poverty blending with the lemons? Is it a perceptual movement which claims space? How does smell align bodily movements, and what might be pre-reflective currents, and what might be perceptual emergences, or alignments of bodily orientations, supported by them? What emerging meanings might be perceived and expressed by the lemon vendors? While the lemon vendors might lack the jargon of cultural criticism (and even body theology), what *do* they speak and to whom, in other words, what are their linguistic expressions, their movements of sound, smell, touch, taste, intuition or knowledge and within which relationship does this sensory movement happen? What are the sensory relations within which religious, sexual, economic, and political practices are performed? What is the full sensorium through which these performances take place, and what emerges from it? What is the significance of sensory hierarchies and orders, how do the senses (e.g., the smell/ing of lemon vendors) interact with and engage in the political, the economical, and so forth?

Exploring more fully the sense in bodily experience, I am urged to consider the significances of different sensory perceptions and their interactions. How do particular women create their own sexual, economic, political, personal spaces through their bodily movements, how do they bodily-habitually engage in life? What are the aspects of culture and power that are difficult to unravel by simply gazing at the lemon vendor? What kinds of agency and resistances are perceptually embodied as a bodily subject selling lemons without underwear? To learn of this, and be implicated by my own immersions in sensory dominations, I need to be able to take up theology from the epistemological site that is Althaus-Reidian bodies filled/filling space with senses, rather than be immediately thrown into the theological imagery presented. Moving too quickly from observed experience to metaphor may reinstall a dualism when the intellectual activity of interpretation and metaphorical representation of experience as theological critique takes up almost immediate focus.

Ambiguity and paradoxes may emerge in the perceptual dimensions on the streets of Buenos Aires. Smells may evoke memory, place, and agency, as anyone who has experienced nostalgia at the smell of whatever you consider comfort food can attest to. Smells might signify inclusion and/or they can signify distance and cultural difference. As beauty lies in the eye of the beholder, so does the scent of home lay in the nose of the one smelling it. In the case of our hypothetical visit to the imagined lemon vendors in Buenos Aires, perceived olfactory differences often turn to oppression when class and cultural differences are turned into "filth" and "stench," which are associated with uncleanliness or immorality. So Althaus-Reid is right when she charges that the private and the public, the sexual and the economic are mixed. But there might be compelling ways in which this interrelation can be explored and articulated, ways in which I might be implicated beyond my positioning as theological voyeur.

The refusal to comply with the olfactory sensibilities of the decent theological tourist (me) or upper class sensory ideologies might be the sensory disruption of hegemonic spaces. Aromas, sights, and textures are not autonomous from their political and economic milieu. A bodily contestation of olfactory aesthetics can disrupt colonial spaces, and the lemon vendors may create a place in which their bodies, their olfactory emissions, rule; they may create a scented place in which they cope with their embodied reality and displacements, in which they make their bodies and their places a home.

Attention to bodily perceptual orientations and exploration of sensory dimensions might not significantly alter the theological output of Althaus-Reid's work, but it would support and strengthen her resourcing of experience, especially when she seeks to maintain the bodily/sexual aspects therein. Body theology in this case would be able to provide a methodological contribution to indecent theology by lingering with/in bodily experiences. Body theology not only provides indecent theology with questions to raise regarding experience, but also with ways to draw the material connections, and show the connections that (are) matter, between the experience drawn from and the historical, political, economical, etc., dimensions. Because sexual decency is enforced through experience, through bodily perceptual experience, indecent theology can only gain from in-depth inquiries into perceptual orientations. Even as outsider, I might be able to inquire into a bodily situation exactly by implicating myself by asking questions that might reveal my own bodily perceptual limits and limited orientations.

Attending to bodily experiences of others or of my own in search of metaphors, even with the explicit and passionate concerns held by Althaus-Reid, needs to delay the departure into the symbolic until the layered and multifaceted perceptual experiences and movements are felt rather than abstracted. To ground theology in lived experiences is seeking to be fully present to them and attending to the ways in which I might be drawn into experiences to which I do and do not belong. Put differently, I am bodily encountering the other, and my own bodily perceptual orientations and alignments habituate me to experience in certain ways and pay attention to certain components. Yet there are also ways in which some dimensions or components of this experience I want to draw from are perceptually hidden, or habitually not perceived, by me. This is the ambiguity and the paradox of bodily experience which requires that I remain epistemologically unsettled when exploring experience.

Althaus-Reid's indecent theology and Heyward's relational theology have been my test cases to show how body theology can expand and strengthen some of the theologies which seek to be grounded in bodily experience in different ways. I will now turn again to bodies and experiences familiar and personal to me. With the commitments of body theology framing my inquiries, I will go after the questions which initiated this project and bodily experiences of and in my family's home.

CHAPTER SEVEN

ORIENTING FAMILIAR BODY THEOLOGIES

I am re-entering my experiences in and with my family after having travelled through theoretical and theological spaces to explore how our bodies and experiences situate us in the world. To conclude this book, I will return to familiar experiences and explore them through body theology. With a commitment to experience, I will offer a few constructive performances within different existing theological models and put body theology to the test in a construction of "god-talk" grounded in bodily experiences.

By re-visiting shared experiences with my grandmother and mother, and setting out with body theology and attention to bodily perceptual orientation, I acknowledge our bodily movements, social habituations, and perceptual repertoires as loci for meaning to emerge. For example, my mother's cooking in the garage and her inhabiting the marginal spaces of our home is a place where every day experiences give rise to meanings shaped by bodily/cultural/religious differences running through and across our household.

The starting point for a critical inquiry into the shared experiences at my childhood home is an appreciation for these differences as bodily encounter, and an understanding that this inhabited space is one of the dimensions through which we can see how our bodily experiences "are us." What (feminist) analysis of the visual aspects and/or textual meanings embodied in the marginality of my mother's position in the home have enabled me to do thus far is to inquire into the inscription of "immigrant," "daughter-in-law," "foreigner," and/or "mother" on my mother's body. But taking bodily perception seriously, now that I conceive of the senses not as intrinsic, natural-biological properties of the body, I can inquire into the ways in which our perceptions and perceptual movements are not "innocent," but the situated practices and theological imaginations of our lives together with various meanings emerging.

MAKING HOME IN NEW SPACES

It was the middle of World War II. My pregnant grandmother fled the invading Russian army, leaving her home in West Prussia with three toddlers but without her husband (who was detained and later died in a Siberian camp). Displaced for three years in a refugee camp in Denmark, losing the newborn twins, Oma and her three children were resettled after the war ended. She was brought to a small rural Mennonite community in southern Germany, where residents were obligated to take in fellow Mennonite refugees. Dropped off in the middle of the village and lined up for residents to come and chose "their" Flüchtling, as single mother with three small children, Oma was the last one "picked, as if spoiled wares on the market." She was not the kind of help the farmers were hoping to acquire. For ten years, Oma tried to move out of the arranged accommodations and looked for a place of her own to rent for her small family, but was denied for various reasons (children too little, too big, no husband, etc.). When the state offered grants for families seeking to establish a new farmstead, she jumped on the chance and started a poultry farm with 20 chickens. After some years, the chicken house turned into a shed and the farm was no more, but Oma's family had a home. My uncle and my father designed and built the house, but it was Oma's dream and efforts that allowed a home to emerge.

Oma was determined to stay in this house, her home, for as long as she lived. In her will, she gave the house to my father, her favorite son and the last of her children to get married. The will legally established her right to stay in the house until her death. When Oma slowly came to need various kinds of care, my father Gernot was designated her power of attorney and her caretaker. His siblings who lived close by offered much advice, yet very little bodily care.

My mother was born in the poor outskirts of Bangkok. She was the foreign woman who married Oma's favorite son and moved into the house Oma fought to provide her children with after living as refugees in one room for years. My grandmother was the matriarch, and my mother tried her best to learn how to be a good German wife and daughter-in-law. But severe homesickness and the need for familiar cuisine led my mother to cooking Thai cuisine at home, an act that offended my grandmother's sense of proper nurture and her basic sense of proper smell. My mother was increasingly seen as the unruly, unthankful, renegade daughter-in-law who, much later after Alzheimer's moved into our family, rather than nursing Oma to "help out her poor husband," went off to work twelve hour shifts of physical labor tending to vineyards.

Today, if you pass our home during non-meal times, all you see is a house and a two-car garage with two adjoining garden huts. Yet during meal time, the garage opens and reveals a gas stove my father built, a fridge, and an array of tables with dishes and German and Thai kitchen tools. One of the garden huts is an outdoor dining room, with a table, more kitchen ware, and memorabilia from visits to Thailand. When we are home together, we gather around a table, food brought out from the garage. We hear my mother calling us to "Sit down and eat, eat, eat, before it gets cold!"

This narrative, a compilation of stories shared with me and recollections/depictions of my own experiences, is, of course, not "all that there is to it." To do body theology with these experiences, framing them through bodily perceptual orientation, I can explore the theological imagination in/of bodily experiences whilst also maintaining a constructive flexibility. By that I suggest: meaning emerges in experience, and as we have seen, experience is perceptual; and my telling and thinking about past experiences is an experience itself, thus always open to new meanings emerging. Constructive body theology then resists fixing a narrative, but rather "moves with" experience. Considering my family's bodily perceptual movements as extensions of their body-selves into the world in real, tangible ways, body theology takes as resource our experiences at home as motile engagements with the world that orient us towards ways of achieving objectives and meaning, as projections of meaning, and as patterns that shape our way of being in the world.

The physical house, our family home, came to be an extension of my grandmother's body. The house as home was the settling of her bodily habits and desires into her environment (the ways in which bodies extend through and construct culture); the house was incorporated into the way she moved and existed in her world. The presence of my mother, as non-Mennonite, non-Christian, non-German, and my mother's alien ways of moving (through language, cooking, bodily relating, etc.) were intrusions into my grandmother's physical space, into her home-body. Tension of sounds and smells were bodily perceptual tensions and invasions. My mother, aligned with her own socio-cultural habits of honoring elders, especially mothers and grandmothers, sought to make bodily sense of her new space, her new home, by becoming part of this bodily space in the bodily ways she tacitly knew.

My grandmother's prohibition against cooking certain Thai dishes for the whole family was then, in some ways, a way to maintain bodily sense at home, to maintain certain meanings emerging, certain bodily habits of nurture. But in other ways it was also a way of dominating family practices and asserting control over my mother's decision making. To my mother, it also emerged as bodily perceptual re-orientation of her experiences, as sensory re-education/re-habituation, as restriction of bodily perceptual movements which impinged on habituated and tacit knowledges about herself and meanings familiar to my mother. If my mother chose to align with the family of my father, she had to align (or fail to make sense trying)—among other things—with a certain food culture of tastes, smells, and presentations in order to be able to emerge as fit mother and nurturer.[1]

---

1. For a variety of investigations into taste and food cultures, inquiring into difference and meaning, see the volumes Carolyn Korsmeyer, ed. *The Taste Culture Reader: Experiencing Food and Drink*, ed. David Howes, Sensory Formations (New York, NY: Berg, 2005). Carole Counihan and Peny van Esterik, eds., *Food and Culture: A Reader*, 2nd ed. (New York, NY: Routledge, 2008). Noteworthy

The struggle over who and what dictated bodily movements, and with it, ways of being in the world that was our home, required that certain bodily and social habits needed to be changed, and certain sensory desires came to be out of reach. The two women inhabited a space in ways which in their bodily movements and habituated tacit knowledges called attention to the multicultural and multiperceptual tensions woven into their relationship: regarding what is meaningful, what conforms to family values, what emerges as meaningful and communicative bodily perceptual movements, what emerges as family body perceptually aligned with "home."

My mother's cooking within and despite certain rules and restrictions is not just a development *of* differential consciousness,[2] but *is* the recognition and identification of technologies of power which subscribed her place and subjectivity.[3] In my mother's culture, elders are

to the trajectory of this project are particularly the chapters on gender and consumption, and food and identity politics, for example, Lisa Heldke, "Let's Cook Thai: Recipes for Colonialism," in *Food and Culture: A Reader*, ed. Carole Counihan and Penny van Esterik (New York, NY: Routledge, 2008), 327–341. For a thorough study of food, taste, and their interrelations and connections with cultural performances such as kinship, mothering, and nurturance in the specific context of Greater Mexican culture, see Ramona Lee Pérez, "Tasting Culture: Food, Family and Flavor in Greater Mexico" (Ph.D.diss., New York University, 2009). Pérez traces complexly and insightfully the relationship between cognition and bodily habits and again their involvement in kinship relations.

2. Differential consciousness is Chela Sandoval's term for a key strategy employed by dominated peoples to survive demeaning and disempowering structures and ideologies. It is the skill to recognize and identify technologies of power as consensual illusions, and also to move differently through these technologies of domination, generating alternative beliefs and tactics of resistance. Chela Sandoval, "Dissident Globalizations, Emancipatory Methods, Social-Erotics," in *Queer Globalizations: Citizenship and the Afterlife of Colonialism* (New York, NY: New York University Press, 2002), 25–27. This is akin to the "hidden transcripts" articulated by James C. Scott, transcripts developed by oppressed groups to undermine public discourses of hegemonic power structures. James C. Scott, *Domination and the Arts of Resistance: Hidden Transcripts* (New Haven, CT: Yale University Press, 1990).

3. I appreciate Carole Counihan's description of the development of differential consciousness in Mexicana women of the San Luis Valley in southern Colorado

honored and family values are aligned with the mother who is every-thing: children are indebted morally and practically to the mother, a bodily perceptual alignment which informs Thai socio-cultural life, pri-vate and public.[4] When talking about her garage kitchen, mom often lets me know that she did move cooking outside not because she was angry or because she wanted to be separate. Her main reason, she con-tinues to tell me, are because she has respect for Oma and wanted peace in the family:

> "You can't change a situation by fighting or being greedy and wanting everything for your own. You bring about peace in the family by adjust-ing, not by forcing others to change for you. Changing what you do with your body is how you change the world around you. That's how you bring about peace. You start with yourself. You show respect."[5]

Yet my mother's desire for bodily perceptual familiarity—the feeling of being home and with family through the taste, smell, and touch of food and process of preparation and presentation—is also connected to a recognition and identification of oppressive power dynamics extended through my grandmother. Mom would never call it that, or even refer to it negatively. Her linguistic signifying of this situation still embodies respect: "She didn't like it very much;" "She said Gernot would like the Königsberger Klopse for dinner." So she spatially and temporally

---

to help me develop my analysis. Yet Counihan seems to make a distinction (or at least an inattentive separation) between food practices and consciousness, food work and liberating beliefs, a distinction I cannot uphold given my own framing of body-consciousness. Carole Counihan, "Mexicana's Food Voice and Differential Consciousness in the San Luis Valley of Colorado," in *Food and Culture: A Reader*, ed. Carole Counihan and Penny van Esterik (New York, NY: Routledge, 2008), 354–368.

4. From conversations with my mother. See also Niels Mulder, *Inside Thai Society: Religion, Everyday Life, Change* (Chiang Mai, Thailand: Silkworm Books, 2000), 58–73.

5. Telephone conversation with my mother. Denver, Colorado and Eichenhof, Germany. April 12, 2013. Translation mine.

moved her food habits to the margins of the kitchen first, keeping a hot plate in a kitchen corner. She often begged my father to set up a separate kitchen in a different room of the house, but when this request was not fulfilled, she moved her kitchen to the margins of the home, into the garage. From the margins, she extends olfactorily and inhabits space and bodies. She survives demeaning and disempowering structures and nationalistic-racist ideologies by moving resistantly in the home, saturating herself and her space with marvelous aromas.

The garage kitchen is a spectacle and a subversion[6] as well as displaced variation: It is a spectacle in that my family and our familial social relations are mediated by the visual imagery of the way in which the home and the kitchen(s) are arranged and presented, but visible only during certain times and to certain observers or partakers. It is subversion in that this marginal inhabitation critiques and resists my mother's position in the family. She navigates my grandmother's intrusive and abusive movements (treating her as the maid, questioning her ways of being a wife and mother) in bodily perceptual ways. She is unwilling to give up certain bodily habits (such as cooking and eating in ways she chooses), just because my father, even after she pleaded with him to move out of the home, or to make her a kitchen of her own, is unwilling/unable to accommodate her desire for meaningful bodily movements, for a way of being in the world and in her home that was meaningful to her. It is a variation of habits, though geographically and culturally displaced: travelling to Thailand this year, walking through streets in cities, towns, and villages, I saw variations of my mother's garage kitchen, similar in arrangement and look, appearing very much "normal" as part of Thai households and social customs. Spatially aligned in and with Thai social movements and recognizable as variation of social norms, emerging in a German setting it is

6. I borrow these terms from the analysis presented in Lisa Law, "Home Cooking: Filipino Women and Geographies of the Senses in Hong Kong," in *Empire of the Senses: The Sensual Culture Reader*, ed. David Howes (Oxford, UK: Berg, 2005), 224–241.

curiously and disruptively out of line, dis-placed from the home, and dis-placed from its home.

A discursive or visual analysis cannot relate the embodied dimensions involved in the emergence of multiple and indeterminate meanings here. An analysis through concepts of power, identity, and struggle for respect and dignity cannot grasp the full sensorium which makes up bodily experiences in my family: neither the pre-reflective terrain and habituated orientations and habits supporting this family, nor the ambiguity and tensions emerging.

The bodily perceptual orientations of the rural German Mennonite village still align my mother with otherness, her food practices now emerging even more as alien and associated with strange habits. My mother's olfactory and culinary extensions are not autonomous from the socio-cultural, familial, and moral mechanisms and currents. She is wrapped up in perceptual orientations, "This is not how normal people do it, but I don't care," and perceptual alignments, "You go and get your degree, so you can get a good job and you don't have to live like I live." Yet she also expresses that her difference is as much personal choice as it is tacit knowledge out of/about bodily difference. "I can do what I want out here. You wouldn't be able to do any of this; you are not used to these kinds of things. And I want you to have a different life," she says as she fluidly moves around her garage kitchen space and invites me to sit down and watch her. Because there is no body without consciousness, and no consciousness without body, and because the way we move, see, smell, eat, speak, cook, feel *is* our consciousness of our world, my mother's bodily experiences and perceptual movements are her differential consciousness, her differential bodily perceptual orientation resisting consensus with oppressing socio-cultural schemata.

In bodily perceptual movement—such as cooking and consuming certain foods prepared a certain way—the meanings of home, objects associated, and the bodies making up our family are mutually constituted. Only in the experience of bodily habits (even as they change) can our bodily movements be meaningfully grasped, and I as body moving into and within this space am implicated in the meanings and the tacit knowledges emerging perceptually. Even after my grandmother began requiring more intensive care than my father could provide and moved into a nursing home, my mother refused to use the inside kitchen again, or any other room previously occupied by my grandmother. She would often refer to not wanting to appear as the greedy daughter-in-law, but even more she would talk about the smells dominating certain rooms of the house, smells she did not want to dwell in.

My grandmother still extended in bodily perceptual (olfactory, visual, tactile, and more) ways in/through the house. Her way of being in the world, and perceptual manners meaningful to my mother, still extended and moved and made meaning in the home. Though my grandmother could not verbally abuse or control my mother anymore, and her body did not dwell in the house anymore, her bodily perceptual reach still extended into the home in powerful ways, aligning my mother in ways so that she could only perceptually emerge on the margins of the home. Today, over three years after my grandmother's passing, with rooms now renovated and smells expelled, my mother utilizes her garage kitchen, cooking Thai dishes outside, baking German cheesecakes inside. "It's too tight in there sometimes. I need air."

Body theology demands that I recognize bodily experiences as making sense: My mother inhabits certain spaces. She is still inhabiting marginal spaces and only slowly moving into others. She now cooks in two kitchens and has different habits of eating in three different rooms. This is not a coincidence, nor indecision. Her bodily movements and perceptual extensions infer and imply sense, make conceptual order in her world, and make her world meaningful. And her bodily experiences are her sense-making in the world, her sensing and feeling herself in the world and as part of her world through various sensory movements and extensions. Her body theology is a taking hold of her home through extensions of smell, through adjustment and acquisition of bodily habits such as eating in a way that feels meaningful to her. She bodily reaches out and extends her garage kitchen as the smell of fried garlic and fish sauce wafts across the patio and into the living spaces of our home. In the space of home, bodily (re)orientations and movements align the meanings emerging regarding home, body, world and emerging meaning through perceptual means.

Body theology allows me to gain a more complex understanding of these experiences. My mother's emergence was/is perceptually aligned in the community with her foreign religious habits, her lack of conforming to "Christian" or "German" values. The strong loyalties towards mothers in Thai culture led my mother to try and take care of Grandmother, but Grandmom made clear she did not want my mother to care for her in ways that left her feeling less than a matriarch. So my mother, failing and then refusing to conform to the role of primary caretaker of my grandmother, crosses perceptual lines of the community she lives in. Her bodily movements are not perceived as liberating herself from verbal and emotional abuse experienced by my grandmother, so she does not perceptually emerge as for example, victim-turned-survivor of emotional violence, but rather perceptually emerges aligned with national and religious foreignness and moral otherness.

There are different sediment cultural and social habits, pre-reflective currents supporting the emerging meanings of my family's bodily movements: Currents of nationalism and sediment habits of isolation of a non-mainstream religious community supported attitudes towards my grandmother and her children that ranged from hostile to indifferent, despite the theological commitments to hospitality and inclusion valued in Mennonite communities and preached in the village church. My mother emerges and moves into the family space as immigrant through marriage, which threatens the already hard-won perceptual alignment of my family as decent and belonging within the village community.

But the very bodily, emotional, social, and spiritual marginalization of my mother is supported by the similar pre-reflective currents which aligned my grandmother as refugee and then re-aligned her with national and religious sameness. Nationalism, religion, and rural community culture shape the ways in which our family bodies emerge, which bodily movements gain greater currency in shaping what our bodies "can." My grandmother's desire for home and a space of her own—induced by experiences of war, homelessness, poverty, and widowhood—brings about bodily perceptual movements through which she engages her world in a way meaningful to her. But these movements, these perceptual extensions in the world regarding home and family, supported by pre-reflective currents or nationalism and religion, also support and establish perceptual habits and devices which allow for tacit knowledge about my mother, her foreignness, her unruliness, her strange bodily habits which do not make sense in the home my grandmother inhabits. "Thai people cook outside," my mother says. Struggling to emerge bodily perceptually in ways that make home meaningful to her, my mother takes up and tries on different bodily movements, attempting to orient herself in this new space. Yet what might be meaningful to her might not allow her to perceptually emerge in ways in which home, or other desires, are available to her.

There are ambiguities emerging in the garage kitchen and the bodily movements within it. The bodily perceptual alignments arranging our family bodies and the ways we perceptually face each other and move toward each other give rise to my mother as a marginal body, a daughter-in-law who moves in many foreign ways and who refuses to comply with certain social habits. Yet my mother's bodily perceptual movements also give rise to habits which orient her in her space, which bring forth and project meanings for her invoking, for example, home and agency. The knowledges inherent in her perceptual acts are knowledges gained through specific perceptual orientations and movements. And from the margins of the family home, she knows how to raise/ habituate her daughters in ways to maximize their perceptual passing as Germans and Mennonites, and she knows how to bodily move in ways so that even given the pre-reflective social and familial currents, she can inhabit space and extend in space in a way that makes her way of being meaningfully "home" to her.

This body theology approach to my family home and our family bodies allows me to enter a more complex exploration on the meanings emerging in and through bodily experiences. This exploration is contingent on what I can perceive from within my own orientations to perception and on what I can perceive when crossing or being queered to my perceptual habits. I continue to experience space and time with my parents, and through the glimpses of and into difference I can deepen my understanding of my family's history or my mother's culture. The experiences I recalled and revisited here for this project are, of course, my own bodily perceptions, what I turn towards as meaningful and significant in, from, and through what I have seen, heard, smelled, touched, felt and thought with my family. And meanings emerging may shift and change, as I remember, analyze, and imagine the family situations I have described here. My own perceptions must remain open to new experiences (remembering, analyzing, imagining being bodily perceptual experiences as well), new reflections and interpretations, different orientations and re-alignments, they must remain as motile as our bodily existence.

My understanding is partial and must remain unsettled. My grasp on the habitual schemata, the tacit knowledges concerning bodily habits that are meaningful and communicative in my family space is tentative and continuously open. I continue to experience *with others*, thus I must remain open to the experiences, perceptions, challenges and complexification others might bring to me, and new meaning arising in our interrelation. This is a positional, yet motile, openness that is not without tension, gaps, or fissures. For example, as my mother listens to the descriptions of her kitchen I used in this book and we seek to find common, meaningful understanding in German, we both continue translating—me doing English/German, her doing Thai/German cultural-linguistic-perceptual movements—as we speak about our experiences and experience each other.

I might "miss" certain knowledges about what is meaningful, about which bodily movements may bring about the meanings and desired values to be perceived. I might not come to know or understand everything my mother knows or understands. Some meanings cannot emerge perceptually within my "other" perceptual hierarchy, in other words, there might be meaning extending for and perceived by mother, but not for me, Meanings lost in translation as my bodily perceptual orientations do not tune me into her habituated meaning-making processes; words we share in common may not represent experiences in their sensorial significance. Yet this openness and tentativeness can be a strength of body theology, granted we are willing to embrace this epistemological transitoriness.

Body Theologies at Home

To do body theology is to talk about our bodily perceptual orientations, our body-sense in and of the world, connected to specific contexts, locations, and experiences. Body theology can be done while pursuing other overarching theological goals, for example, within a systematic approach or a contextual/sexual theology. Or it can be done as constructive body theology "on its own," focusing on the specific ways in which bodily experiences make sense and create meaning, without connecting it to specific theistic concepts or commonly associated religious artifacts such as scripture or rituals. In other words, because body theology is more a set of commitments rather than a step-by-step method for theological application, it can accompany a theology to assist in more complex resourcing of experience, or it can provide commitments from which to construct a specific body theology grounded in particular experiences.

My family experiences as resource can "do" things theologically. Just like experience is not fixed to inherent meanings or significances, so is the connection between experience and theology. Next, I will offer glimpses and experiments of what body theology looks like constructively. I will provide body theological re-orientations to the aforementioned theological models of Heyward and Althaus-Reid, and conclude with my own constructive god-talk with/in bodily experiences.

Mutuality at Home

By putting body theology to work in Heyward's theology of mutual relation, I can attend to my own experiences by exploring my family's emergence in the world. The alienation or alignments with marginality emerging in my family relations are multiple and complex but can be grasped through a body theology approach. The mutual embeddedness of my family in various pre-reflective currents gives rise to perceptual emergences, so that my mother's emergence on the margins of the family home in the garage kitchen can be connected to interpersonal relations *and* national, religious, cultural, racial, gendered, and economical dynamics, pre-reflective and immediate.

To inquire into the perceptual dimensions of our existence allows us to understand complexly how bodily feelings or apprehension of meaning emerge from the ways in which we and our environment are aligned and shaped. The specific meanings of home emerging, the specific desires for home, and the specific ways in which we face, access, and can move towards this desire are constituted and made bodily and perceptually available through the ways in which we bodily perceptually exist in our specific context.

To live as a family through the erotic justice Heyward conceptualizes as "God," we must aim for just relations through bodily expressions, feelings, and movements by taking into take into account the complexity of how our family bodies emerged together. The mutuality in which my family is embedded is in the interrelated family dynamics, and in the interrelations of culture, history, and community context. Erotic justice then goes beyond bodily relations that might rearrange space in a way that visually places my mother at the center of the home again. To move toward right relations is to move toward justice with our full sensorium, our touch, smell, hearing, seeing, and thereby our knowing, not abstract truth about my mother's agency, full humanity and dignity, but tasting, and smelling and touching and seeing her way of being in the world.

Yet these movements toward right relations remain ambiguous movements, because the meaning emerging between our bodies (as we eat in the garage or turn a dining room into a bedroom for my grandmother to make easier her increased need for care) may shift, and may continue certain alienating perceptual alignments as they disrupt others. In other words, bodily moving to disrupt perceptual orientations of and within our relational space may align my mother more closely with desired meanings and experiences of mutuality; and currents of nationalism and Christian supremacy align her possibly more strongly as a foreign and alienated body as she now more freely and more regularly moves in her own different cultural and religious habits.

Body theology embraces the uncertainty and unknowing emerging in the bodily existence of my grandmother in her last years. Because she always exists as body-consciousness, even when she might not be consciously self-aware, her bodily movements still display habits and thus she still engages in meaning making, still has a way of being in the world.[7] Since bodily experience *is* how we exist, and bodily experience makes sense, Grandmother might show no "intellectual grasp" on her environment anymore after thirteen years with Alzheimer's disease, but as body-self she still holds agency. We still extend perceptually towards and with each other; she still holds power over our movements around the house. Her bodily presence still affects how mine obtains meaning. She is still making sense to me and with me because she participates in the world we inhabit together.

Body theology commitments allow me take a close look at the way bodies are aligned in space, how bodies follow certain lines of perception and movement, tracing how mutuality and relationality may be emerging. Now the ambiguities and paradoxes emerging might align my Grandmother as "just a body," aligning her with values in which her life doesn't make much sense to us anymore. The pre-reflective current, our mutual embeddedness in life orients us toward her already perceiving her and her dementia fearfully and doubtfully. Our social habituation idealizes the mind and all the control over life we *think* it affords us, so she cannot possibly be fully human if she "lost her mind." To live in just relations might entail living with the ambiguities emerging between our bodies, acknowledging that my bodily movements extend hopelessness, disdain, and patronizing attitudes. But always also right there, not breaking in from the outside, but as godding among us, as part of the terrain we navigate

---

7. I am grateful to David N. Scott for bringing to my attention the significance of differentiating between consciousness and self-consciousness. See also Raymond Gibbs' pointing toward a possibility of consciousness not necessitating self-consciousness, though his focus in the chapter referenced is on exploring emotion and consciousness as interrelated through embodiment. Raymond W. Gibbs, Jr., *Embodiment and Cognitive Science* (New York, NY: Cambridge University Press, 2006), 239–274.

in together, is also hope, love, care; laboring dances of mutuality because my being is still bound up with hers and so her body still makes sense with mine.

INDECENCY AT HOME

Putting my family's explored bodily experiences in conversation with Althaus-Reid's indecent theology, I am urged to attend to the full sensorium of sexual experiences. How do the bodily experiences I decently described connect to sexuality, and then again interrelate to the cultural, national, racial, political, economical; in other words, how do we think through sexual experiences within the complex matrices of social power? I can begin by wondering about the bodily perceptual orientations regarding sexual and marital decency my grandmother and my mother sought to teach me growing up. My grandmother could only perceptually emerge as a decent widowed refugee by being aligned with cultural habits which made only her own children and relations available for familial desires. Even though she was widowed at a young age, she never remarried, nor became emotionally or romantically involved with another man. Decent sexual relations were marital relations, which she not only aligned with heteronormative nuclear families, but also Mennonite and German alignments. Her children crossed those perceptual alignments, the first marrying a Protestant, the second a widowed Catholic, and the third, my father, a Thai Buddhist.

My mother, moving into a space of new and different pre-reflective currents, needed to emerge as sexually decent. German-Thai marriages are not uncommon in Germany, though these couples perceptually emerge as questionably decent at best, the meanings emerging often aligning the (commonly) younger Thai woman as sexual object of an economically superior and older German man. Perceived decency may be achieved through heteronormative alignments. My mother and father take care to emerge differently, to be perceptually aligned as a couple that emerges with a romantic love story, not a common or habituated social bodily perception of a German-Thai couple. These pre-reflective currents shaped their emergence as a couple, their bodily movements seeking re-alignments and seeking the shape of meaningful emergences between them and the world.

My parents movements and alignments with(in) decency then also shaped their perception of me as I crossed lines of decency and emerged as a lesbian body. My parents' concerns regarding my bodily movements, be it coming out or be it engaging in sexual relations, were/are significantly aligned with the perceived meaning emerging as I bodily move as lesbian. To them, these meanings are significantly shaped through economical alignments (will our daughter be able to have a career without fear of discrimination?), because of the way in which their own relationship and sexual alignments were supported by pre-reflective currents of racism, nationalism, and Christian supremacy affecting their family and home economically, for example, through my mother's career options or job discrimination based on her perceptual emergence as foreigner and sexually indecent woman.

An immigrant Thai-Christ might be found in the sexual body of a woman who dreams of freedom from poverty and finds romance in a German husband, yet who remains alien and queer in the many bodily perceptual orientations she finds herself in. There might be indecent redemption, found in maintaining peace in home spaces through physically distancing, yet intermingling and penetrating perceptually in space. There might be queer atonement, where experienced difference limits our actions, yet we act nevertheless and may even contribute to our own oppression, and yet we continue to live and struggle to protect and respect what is different. This kind of redemption and atonement of the immigrant Thai-Christ might be indecent, because it does not exclude tragedy. She crosses lines of decency, and her agency is found in subversive and persistent perceptual movements, ambiguous meanings emerging so that her daughter, too, can dream of a romance dis-orienting to social habituations. She does not redeem into decent liberation, but into ever new crisscrossing, queering, indecent indeterminate eschatologies.

When God Loses His Mind at Home

We are bodies, and we are bodies perceptually experiencing. Our bodily sensory experience *is* us. To do constructive body theology as intellectual work is to query our bodily theological imagination. By now, after our exploration into perception and our bodily existence, invoking theological imagination should not invoke god-talk as imaginative (i.e., creative, but not real, perhaps even false or illusory) for us. We have explored *that* and *how* our imagination of the world is intimately tied up with our bodily perceptual orientations in the world. Our theological imagination *is* our bodily experience: Our knowledge of the world, our knowledge of what it means to be human, how to account for ultimate reality, what we imagine as truth about ourselves and others, how we conceive of despair, what we know as aligned with our desires for life, where we imagine hope and creativity—that *is* our experience, this *is* our theological imagination. In other words, our bodily experiences are our imaginative activity, and already make up a god-talk we can work to constructively trace with the words available to us at the moment.

Oma bodily extended through and perceptually emerged within spatial movements and habits. I grew up watching and enjoying my grandmother's touch, the ways in which she held open her arms on Saturday mornings when I jumped into her bed for an hour of storytelling, how she tucked me in and sang me lullabies before I went to sleep at night. She would walk the perimeters of her property tracing the fence with her hands, inspecting the garden she was growing inside these boundaries. After having been pushed from her home land, been confined in a refugee camp, begrudgingly resettled, reluctantly granted a plot of barely fertile land many yards away from her temporary home, she finally found ways to build a house to call her own and that promised nourishing growth. She dreamed a home into being and moved in and within filling it with the meals of her own childhood, with songs sung and socks knitted and vegetables and fruit growing abundantly to rely on the work of your own hands and avoid perceptions of dependence on charity and government hand-outs.

In our shared terrain of existence, the ultimate transcendent emerges bodily and is experienced bodily. The condition of our existence is the reality that emerges from and between our movements and seeps back into and under our skin as perceptual orientation, habits, alignments, and is visceral intimate reality in our movements, language, and socio-cultural habits. We are immersed in, create, shaped by, and become the matter of this mystery. The condition that enables and makes up the possibilities of Oma and us and world interacting to outline "home" is a reality that is and is not mine. The terrain of life transcends me, there is a reality that holds "home" that does not wait for me to define it or structure its appearance. It is not content to remain within the concepts that are sense-able to me, and it is disruptive to my efforts to keep its meaning neatly arranged.

While only experienced because of our sensory perception, the transcendent is irreducible to the meanings I experience. The terrain that grounds experiences that are my home contains perceptual movements and meanings beyond my sensing, it contains historical and radical cultural differences and possibilities not perceivable to me, not meaningful to me, neither embodied by nor sense-able to me (ever or yet). It is the "there" for me to transcend towards and into. I-as-body-perceiving am not reducible to this terrain, yet I am part of making it—in my bodily perceptual orientations, my aligning or crossing of perceptual lines, my habituation by and participation in sensory formations.

This terrain of life is immanent in me; it is experienced in my taking up of its habits. "Home" would not be perceivable by me without my bodily experiences of it. The only way we know this ultimate reality is in our bodily perceptions, in embodied movements and places that carry unique histories and meanings through us and for us. The terrain that grounds my existence enacts itself on me as I become the site of our perceptions of it. I embody and "make real" this terrain of existence that makes me and that belongs to no singular body. Oma embodied and "made home real," yet she did not "create" it. Home is us and home is ours, though not merely. What holds my, her, our existence is that there is a condition to our lives which we embody with and for us, embodying and (re)creating a historical, cultural, personal specificity of its meanings.

We sense the terrain of our historical and cultural embeddedness within the lines of our home, we experience our oriented-ness in our world, we experience the power of something else on us that *is* the terrain within which I emerge, and that also *makes* a specific kind of landscape of experiences for and through me. I am already embedded in a reality more than myself, a reality that contains, enables, is pervaded by orientating lines and perceptual formations. I am embedded in a reality that holds out specific meanings to me to make sense of and embody, or possibly even subvert in bodily-ness: daughter, German, family, love, human, home.

This is the embodied life my mother was to make a new home in, a place so embedded in and crisscrossed with sensory grids and lines perceptually non-sensical to her, sensory lines related to and embodied in my grandmother's perceptual movements—her styles of caring, habits of nurturing and comforting (from how to make the marital bed to bodily expressions of love), her making familiar that which belongs. The cooking of food, the playing of music, the different caressing of children (maintaining the sanctity of the head), the aligning of spaces with "kitchen" became contested bodily movements. The tastes and fragrances meaningful to my mother were inhibited, even forbidden in the shared space in which my grandmother extended. From the margins, the scents of my mother's home penetrate the boundaries and walls of the house my grandmother built. Only after objects and home itself—the walls, the furniture, whole rooms—are realigned with new smells, more her own, my mother extends and moves within the walls of the house again as home space. My mother's simmering Thai curry, her singing to loudly played Thai folk music while she is ironing laundry is bodily extension, gendered and cultural perceptual movements claiming, inhabiting, embodying space, her making home through specific ways of facing and engaging the world.

The terrain of our existence, within and from which we make meaning of "home" holds irreducible differences. It is always in excess of my experiences and holds meanings, concepts, experiences which I do not, perhaps never will, really know embedded as I am in my bodily-socio-cultural conditioning. What is embodied in us and yet transcendent to me and my shared world with you, the excess of our experiences, is an intricate dynamic of interconnected irreducible ways of being. This is the condition of our bodily perceptual experiences—a paradoxical (deeply physical and deeply social) terrain in flux, transformation, (in)consistency, (dis)connectedness. Because it is so, it also makes possible overlaying, competing, re-affirming, demarcating, queering bodily movements that beckon and repel us, that claim and exclude us, that viscerally compete in our experiences and demand that we align home-base in this way or that.

In experiencing, I sense possibilities of difference that may be non-sensical to me, I get a taste of possibilities of queering and transformation and different-new-to-me experiences. There are ambiguous meanings emerging for me as I revisit "home"—the German-Thai daughter with Mennonite allegiances, married to another woman, turned feminist theologian in the space of the US academy—I return to an "old" home which now often appears strange to me, having made a new home and established new bodily perceptual movements in a space with different perceptual dimensions. My bodily experiences are paradoxical: I return to my family home as insider and outsider, *aligned with* my family's perceptual orientations *and queer* to them. My returning—physically, in conversation, in theological imagination, in recollecting—is present as well as presented to me, and queers me ambiguously. For example, I am queer to my mother's cultural and religious difference, out of line in my new "American" habits, disorienting as the lesbian in a straight family, but also aligned in my economic and familial habits, my taking up of familial alignments as daughter.

To be at home in our bodies, to create home meaningfully in our mundane every day bodily movements we extend ourselves, building home through perceptual lines of inclusion and exclusion, the ordinary lines within and behind which we find ourselves at home in our bodies. The mundane activities of cooking, preparing food together and/ or for each other, taking care of each other—our bodily movements at home—on closer look emerge as intricate transcendent movements in which we align what is to be our home. We include and exclude sensorialy that which is or should be familiar—tastes, sounds, smells, feelings recognizable as belonging to our family. Comfortable, cozy "homes" that are staked out by selecting and including that which belongs and excluding that which isn't, is constantly "under siege" by disruptions, fissures, and eruptions of differences. If we let it, if we can abide the traces of the disruptive transcendent in our embodiment and continuous creations of our home, we can experience being at home with and in difference, so that the emergence of difference in me or the familial other does not emerge as intrusion of the Outside, but as that difference which ultimately is real and at home in all of us.

My own habituation to the terrain of our existence compels me to perceive god in/as this terrain of our conditions and possibilities. God emerges meaningfully to me as that which makes my particularity possible, and which gives me a past and a future, that which is a transcendent ultimate reality that connects me to the world, to meaning. God is meaningful as our condition of existence, as/in this the terrain of our existence: In my bodily experiences of meaning I am aligned by German nationalism, Christian supremacy, chronological time, orientations to individual subjectivity, racialized gender alignments, Thai-Buddhist family habituations, Prussian sense of order and decency, heteronormative alignments of economical bodies. This is where my family moves, where we bodily perceptually theologize: We are embedded in a terrain that to us holds ambiguous meanings. God is not the alignment itself, god is not the orienting device, god is not the specific lay of the land in this terrain. God is that which enables drawing lines of belonging, that which enables our habituation as well as our re-aligning and following queer habits. God does not prevent or prompt our being swept up in racial hierarchies and violent exclusions, in perceptual habits of normalcy and pathologizing difference. God is the condition of our bodily perceptual orientations, that reality that transcends us and which we meaningfully know in our experiences.

What is gained by turning these accounts of transcendence in/through our bodily experiences into god-talk? In some respects, this view of our shared existence in the world can be maintained without bringing in the concept of god. Because of my theological commitments, this remains an intentional openness and frailty of my constructive work, since I am aware of the multicultural and multireligious context in which I am embedding this theological articulation. To speak of "god" is not how all of us in this shared world of my family experience meaning, and so it is possible to speak of our shared ultimate reality, its structures and excesses without a concept of god but with other religious concepts (e.g., those meaningfully emerging in my mother's experience), or even without religious concepts at all.

Yet there is vital work that "god" can do here for me as I am writing this. Bodies left out of or only spoken for/about in theology "proper" do the theologizing here, and my grandmother with advanced Alzheimer's and my skeptical of Christianity Buddhist mom with limited German tell me of god. And they ought to, as they can re-orient my perceptual habits and conceptions to sense that god that is emerging in our shared experiences. The god that emerges in our family movements is a messy, homely god, not neat and safe.

The terrain of god that embeds us, the ultimate reality that conditions our bodily experiencing, always already contains dimensions of experiencing differently. God messes with our efforts of out-lining safe homes and as our condition of existence embeds us in a terrain of possibilities, not a map of taxonomies. Working out god-talk from our experiences is a striving for articulating that which is strange and excessive to our concepts and embodied structures, that which remains incomplete in our embodiment of it. We experience knowing god always in deeply social and deeply physical ways. What we say and articulate about god is (ought to be?) always transforming (already changing as I write this), it always demarcates a ground of divine revelation and interrelation whilst simultaneously revealing inconsistencies and disconnectedness, a holy flux of visceral beckoning and repelling, claiming and excluding experiences.

Today, god lost his mind at home. God left the premises of a masculine, disembodied divine home, and emerged holding my grandmother's humanity out for me to meaningfully perceive. God does not speak about or make comfortable the bodily suffering at home. God is the condition that embeds our bodily knowing, reaching towards each other perceptually. God reminds me of human dignity in the visceral bodily mutual sensing, disrupting my attachments to cognition and consciousness, and inviting me to reach back towards and into the perceptual hold my grandmother has on my own being human.

The theologies emerging out of our bodily experiences might not be theologies I "like," they might not be reassuring me of that which I like to believe. Quite possibly, the theologies emerging from our bodily movements might indeed be of the kind that do not affirm difference, that value mind over matter, competence and capacities over embodied human limits. The theologies imagined in our bodily experiences, brought into focus because of my mother's misalignments, give rise to a God oriented around perceptions of a singular exclusive ultimate reality that reigns in and domesticates difference. And god beckons me to look at the unappealing, the ugly, the homely images and meanings created in the comforts of home, and beckons me towards it to understand its dynamics. God invites me to read the body theologies created about "Him" that violently render my mother foreign and abject. God disturbs "plain for everyone to see" theologies in our bodily movements, bodily hardened sedimentations of superior knowledge of a supreme Christian God.

The god that embeds our existence will not remain the static God emerging between us today. God embeds us in our perceptual orientations, and calls our movements towards each other into the space we share, and we make each other and are made in these movements. When we orient and dis-orient ourselves and each other in the spaces we share, we constructively theologize in our bodily experiences. In the terrain of our shared existence emerges also an ethical claim on me: the demand to not simply agree or disagree that ableism, Christian supremacy, heteronormative sexism, or colonizing racism are "real" experiences. Our bodies always already matter. The question that bodily experiences bring us, a question ever incompletely answered, is: As what to whom? How do we become the embodiment of our systems and relations? What makes us alien bodies perceived intrusive to someone's comfort? What kind of bodies embody sexual desires, who becomes the matter that is to be possessed and owned? Who is the matter kept "in check" by militarized policing of communities, who is the matter aligned in residential segregation and colonial reservation policies, who embodies the symbols of violence in our cultural imagination? Who is the body made pathological and how does it matter? Who is the matter of conquest, of abjection, of genocide? We are the matter of the theological homes we build.

God beckons in the ethical demand that have a claim on me in the terrain of my existence, the ultimate reality of my bodily perceptual orientations. I cannot simply *concede* that mom's experiences are valid expressions of pain and agency; that women's bodies should matter as more than they do; that Black lives should be different matter, human matter, in our social arrangements; that indigenous lives are of sovereign matter; that cognitive impairment is no pathological degrading matter; that embodied difference is always a matter of a common humanity. Because conceding the matter of humanity, conceding that other lives matter as human lives, is always already that: A concession that allows the Other to enter my line of vision, a concession that does not require me to change my perceptual alignments of what and how human live and dignity make sense, a concession that demands that other bodies get in line with my orientations of desire, get in line with bodily movements and knowledges that are mine.

The ethical demand is to the bodily sensorium of our morality: god does not concede, god conditions the "there" that is there for re-alignment, crossing, queering our theological imagination, god beckons to put our bodies on and across the lines of our habituated selves. Inclusions and exclusions into human concepts and systems depend on our flesh memories, and to re-align our theological imagination over against what we begin to perceive as unjust and violent exclusions in our bodily interactions is to bodily, perceptually cross orienting lines. Only in this visceral bodily movement may we perceive and know differently, out of line, and perhaps come to perceptually be oriented to different desires, different alignments, different imaginations emerging out of our shared terrain. And even our new-to-us perceptions of love, justice, truth, god will not be "more complete" or closer to the "absolute"—it will always be open-ended, incomplete, precarious and as such demands of us to continuously discern and investigate our theological habituations. I am accountable in this incompleteness of my experiences.

We may lose the God we are at home with—in our bodily experiences we may perceive traces of god beyond the exclusive premises of a rational mindful masculine dis-embodied being who is ours to know. In our bodily experiences we may even perceive traces of meaning-"less" god-talk—emergences that do not embody god, where god has no alignments (yet?). If we re-orient ourselves, peak behind the lines drawn in our movements, turn against the currents of our habituated perceptions, the terrain of our bodily existence is irreducible to that which we know. God transcends (us) towards contested and paradoxical terrain: Even abject bodily experiences are still bodily and experiences, they are already viscerally alive, with meaningful movements, alignments, trajectories of their own. What may make sense of god when we sense home there, in the abject bodily terrain of god?

My bodily experiences maintain an unsettled body theology: I gained a more complex understanding of what meanings emerge as we gather for lunch in a garage. Yet I am very aware that this more complex grasp, this deeper understanding, might shift and change—slightly or drastically—with each motile engagement that lies ahead: In my tracing of orienting lines and aligned desires, emerging meanings at home between the movements of grandmom, mom, and those that are mine declare what looks human, what tastes normal, what sounds good, what feels worthwhile. Resistance is not futile; it is built in, it makes sense: We already have bodily movements in which we cross perceptual habits, and the seemingly creative possibilities of our bodily perceptual crisscrossing of perceptual grids is already contained in our shared terrain. Because our bodily experiences *are* our theological imagination, we may begin to bodily theologize—not *instead* of intellectual articulation, but *so that* our intellectual theological work, our articulations in language can "catch up" with what our bodies already know, with what our bodies are beginning to make sense of, with what is already precariously becoming the matter of our lives. Rather than living into our intellectual imaginations, body theology propels us to imagine into and out of our other, queer, not-normal lived experiences. The discomforting, the breaking with habits, the moving into ambiguity, the crossing of lines into the meaning-"less" is our theo-ethical action that may become a sensible tune. For now.

CHAPTER EIGHT

SENSING FUTURIES

Body theology as I reframed it here contributes to and enhances the grounding of theology in experience by inviting complex investigations into the perceptual dimensions of bodily experience. It anchors theological construction in experience and fosters complex investigations that account for particularity and difference while also relating how commonalities and communally cohesive experiences may come about. Regarding experience, Merleau-Ponty's phenomenology of perception contributed concepts, such as intentionality, to explore the bodily processes orienting our existence in the world. To be bodily perceptually oriented in the world implies to experience others and the world habitually in specific ways, and these ways of experiencing (in) the world are fundamentally bodily as well as culturally specific, in other words, there are individual and cultural differences to account for in terms of accounting for experience.

But why the turn to theology? The personal, familial, social, political experiences I recount also occupy sacred, divine, spiritual, religious dimensions. The latter then are part of the full sensorium of human experience, be it as specific experiences of the divine, or as explanatory/analytical category for experiencing concepts such as race, ability or gender.[1] But ultimately, to frame this project and its outcomes

---

1. See, for example, J. Kameron Carter, *Race: A Theological Account* (New York, NY: Oxford University Press, 2008). Willie James Jennings, *The Christian Imagination: Theology and the Origins of Race* (New Haven, CT: Yale University Press, 2010). Deborah Beth Creamer, *Disability and Christian Theology: Embodied Limits and Constructive Possibilities* (New York, NY: Oxford University Press, 2009). Brian Brock and John Swinton, eds., *Disability in the Christian*

specifically as theology is not solely a scholarly self-situating, though I do engage this interdisciplinary work explicitly as a theologian. I am also seeking to establish a dialogical bridge where I perceive a methodological one way flux, thus I am insisting that theologians should not just be critical consumers of insights gained from other disciplines, but develop interdisciplinary projects decidedly theological in creative collaboration. Lastly, and importantly, theology allows me to inquire into human experiences and questions of meaning and value more creatively and holistically. Theological frameworks allow me to inquire into meanings experienced without having to take an objective or scientific stance regarding religious/metaphysical phenomena. Theology may go beyond conceiving of religious phenomena as inherent to our bodily existence in the world. As theologian, I can go beyond accounting for experiences of the supernatural as inherently connected to our meaning making. Even with acknowledging and accounting for potential gaps in understanding due to different perceptual orientations to religious experience, as a theologian I am able to go beyond descriptions and accounts toward constructions of and appeals to the supernatural.[2]

To do body theology is to tell of our bodily experiences in a way so we may see the world and meanings experienced in it in a different way, be it more complexly, or be it by taking on new perspectives. To do theology, in this case, to do body theology, is to think via bodily perceptual orientations of bodies and their intimate connections to manifestations

Tradition: A Reader (Grand Rapids, MI: Wm. B. Eerdmans Publishing, 2012). Amos Yong, *Theology and Down Syndrome: Reimagining Disability in Late Modernity* (Waco, TX: Baylor University Press, 2007). Paula M. Cooey, *Religious Imagination and the Body: A Feminist Analysis* (New York, NY: Oxford University Press, 1994). Jonneke Bekkenkamp, ed. *Begin with the Body: Corporeality Religion and Gender* (Leuven, The Netherlands: Peeters, 1998).

2. For example, my interests and concerns in this project are akin to Vásquez's materialist theory of religion. We do differ, however, not just in our situating ourselves as theologian or religious studies scholar, respectively, but significantly in what these disciplines allow us to do constructively. While Vásquez may be able to account for the supernatural in his reintroduction of embodiment to theories of religion, I may also be able to appeal to it. Manuel A. Vásquez, *More Than Belief: A Materialist Theory of Religion* (New York, NY: Oxford University Press, 2011).

of life in all its various shades, tastes, and tunes, be it the bitterness of oppression or the dance of abundance.

Resourcing the full sensorium of experience and engaging body theology, however, need not be limited to projects that are theological in nature. Because the commitments for body theology I presented urge us to attend to the particular ways of hearing, seeing, thinking, imagining, smelling, moving, etc., in short, the particular ways of experiencing bodily in the world, various areas for further application come to my mind, some immediate and directly connected to this project, some reaching further into deeper interdisciplinary conversations to be had.

For example, areas only hinted at in this project are connections between theological anthropological implications and ethical considerations, which may be made with body theology commitments in mind. Coming from my reflections on the last years in the life of my Grandmother, her mental and physical decline due to age and Alzheimer's disease, body theology will allow me to consider agency and ethical questions complexly. If, as I argue throughout, we need to forego notions of body/mind dualisms and understand our existence in the world as embodied consciousness, as conscious bodies, this understanding will have to bear on our consideration of bodily experiences such as dementia. Subjectivity and agency are theoretical terms to think through, but with concrete consequences for embodied life, medical and moral approaches and intersections of the two.[3]

---

3. For example, Marcia W. Mount Shoop engaged embodiment and ambiguities of lived experiences in her theological investigation of rape, pregnancy, and motherhood, presenting ecclesiology and Christology within a decidedly embodied framework. See Marcia W. Mount Shoop, *Let the Bones Dance: Embodiment and the Body of Christ* (Louisville, KY: Westminster John Know Press, 2010). This is a different theological project than those who take on embodiment and subjectivity within a more decidedly philosophical theological framework, as for example, David H. Nikkel has done. While we share certain philosophical convictions, his theological aim is toward re-rooting postmodern theologies in embodied life so that, e.g., concepts of God may be formulated within embodied pantheistic models. David H. Nikkel, *Radical Embodiment*, ed. K. C. Hanson, Charles M. Collier, and D. Christopher Spinks, Princeton Theological Monograph Series (Eugene, OR: Pickwick Publications, 2010). For an ethics of care building on Merleau-Ponty's

Another example of bringing body theology to theological concepts might be to construct a theological eschatology grounded through body theology, an eschatology which is based in the bodily experiences of change and endings, endings beyond end of life concepts but grounded in the endings and transformations experienced throughout life, reversible and final, sudden and gradual, expected and surprising. Theological constructions of atonement and redemption, grounded in experience via body theology, might yield imaginative theological work, considering atonement beyond metaphysical realities and queering justice through embodied acts.

Those interested in exploring other theoretical connections, such as theories of space, theories of architecture, or environmental studies, may find in body theology connections useful to their explorations. How we experience spaces—related to the social, political, cultural, and religious—is intrinsically connected to our bodily perceptual orientations, our individual bodily capacities as well as our socially trained and sensorially transmitted values regarding movement, and symbolic as well as embodied alignments of bodies in space.[4] To insist

notion of embodied habits, see Maurice Hamington, *Embodied Care: Jane Addams, Maurice Merleau-Ponty, and Feminist Ethics* (Chicago, IL: University of Illinois Press, 2004). A moral philosophy based in phenomenological inquiry is worked out by James R. Mensch, *Ethics and Selfhood: Alterity and the Phenomenology of Obligation* (Albany, NY: State University of New York Press, 2003). See also Bryan S. Turner, *Vulnerability and Human Rights*, ed. Thomas Cushman, Essays on Human Rights (University Park, PA: Pennsylvania State University Press, 2006).

4. For a philosophical exploration of body as place/space in relation with a larger place/space and bodily spatial experiences and conceptualizations thereof, see David Morris, *The Sense of Space*, SUNY Series in Contemporary Continental Philosophy, ed. Dennis J. Schmidt (Albany, NY: State University of New York Press, 2004). For a collection of provocative and insightful essays on conceptual and corporeal spaces, investigated from various angles and intersections (including Native American studies, architecture, women's studies, feminist theory, geography, postcolonial theory, moral theory, history, cultural studies, and more), see Susan Hardy Aiken and others, eds., *Making Worlds: Gender, Metaphor, Materiality* (Tucson, AZ: University of Arizona Press, 1998). For a Christian pastoral-theological engagement with human experience and the built environment, particularly urban spaces, see Eric O. Jacobsen, *The Space Between: A Christian Engagement with*

on inherent body-mind-world-culture interrelations is also to reorient ourselves to the human/animal/other divide and to investigate the ways in which anthropocentric conceptions of experience may be overcome.

This last trajectory is critical when continuing cross-cultural body theology inquiries. A comparative body theology would be able to embrace constructive comparisons of different religious theologies, but would significantly base such comparisons on experience connecting to theological themes.[5] Such religio-cultural comparisons need to be able to conceive of experience as not exclusively a human feature, rather, comparative work needs to be able to conceptualize orientations in which all that is in the world is sentient, and therefore, may experience in some way. Body theology can contribute to the framework of such comparative work, already presuming a body-world interrelation, while also remaining flexible enough to attend to specific shapes this interrelation is conceived of in other contexts.

In the end, however, I find myself significantly oriented in the world as a theologian, a feminist, postcolonial, queer, moral, Mennonite, body theologian, and therefore, a theologian through and on whose body different allegiances, alliances, transgressions, and desires crisscross, merge, and induce motile tensions and bodily-intellectual turnings. Theologically and personally, I want to see body theology contributing

---

the Built Environment, ed. William A. Dyrness and Robert K. Johnson, Cultural Exegesis (Grand Rapids, MI: Baker Academic, 2012). For an anthropological study regarding personhood and space and embodied tensions in light of Western individualism experienced in Melanesian communities, see Sabine C. Hess, Person and Place: Ideas, Ideals and the Practice of Sociality on Vanua Lava, Vanuta, ed. Jürg Wassmann and Katharina Stockhaus, Person, Space and Memory in the Contemporary Pacific (New York, NY: Berghahn Books, 2009).

5. See, for example, Michelle Voss-Roberts, whose comparative theology analyses metaphors grounded in bodily experience. Michelle Voss-Roberts, Dualities: A Theology of Difference (Louisville, KY: Westminster John Knox Press, 2010). And her comparison of affective dimensions in religious traditions in Michelle Voss-Roberts, Tastes of the Divine: Hindu and Christian Theologies of Emotion (New York, NY: Fordham University Press, 2014). For an example of comparative moral philosophy, see Erin McCarthy, Ethics Embodied (New York, NY: Lexington Books, 2010).

to the good life of all living beings, however goodness is sensed. To investigate into meaning of experiences and orientations of life towards each other may take theoretical-philosophical avenues, as I have done so in this project. But ultimately and significantly, the concerns that lead up to this project and which continue to stir in me as I move on from it, are connected to the sense of responsibility/response-ability to those other(ed) persons I am connected to, either by family, by choice, and/or by global implication. To investigate and to struggle, complexly and thoroughly, with the ways in which "I" came about—as product of cultures, privileges and absence thereof, personal choices, mentored growth, perceptual orientations, educational formation, etc.—to me is significant in order to construct body theologies for and on behalf of others who may find this specific project inaccessible, in word and/or space.

I am thinking of women like my mother, for whom education and sophisticated German and English language was/is out of reach, for whom books, computers, journals, and the internet are not part of her daily habits, a woman who worked hard to make all those things accessible to her daughter, yet who struggles to make her life meaningful and worth living without them, and who is proud of my academic successes but rightfully suspicious of academic projects (this one included). If body theology cannot matter in the embodied lives of especially those whose experiences have been excluded from decent theologies, then it would be indeed a futile exercise.

My hope for the future of constructive body theologies is that they can remain grounded in (and insistent on) the various and diverse kinds of good life desired to be lived. I wish for body theology to be diverse in its interdisciplinary investigations, sophisticatedly theoretical and poetically comprehensible, and always humble enough in its sophistication and poetics to acknowledge that inevitably, body theology will get it wrong, will fail to liberate, will contribute to alienation, will ignore what is significant to particular experiences. And body theology will be okay with it, will continue to investigate and imagine life and meaning as experienced. Because "isms" such as racism, ableism, sexism, nationalism, etc., are in fact embodied, visceral perceptual experiences, habituated in laws, regulations, behaviors, and beliefs, they may change and shift. Yet this does not deny us attempts to make the experiences of "isms" do theoretical work for us as analytic categories, granted that we allow for those categories to work for us in the ambiguity and fluidity that they do their work with in our embodied lives.

TO CONTINUE

I do not have to write *on* or *about* bodies but without doubt will always write *through* bodies, my own and those with whom I am mutually emerging and becoming. So then, what would "body" as adjective do, facing disembodied though divinized masculinities of the theological Word? Our bodily experiences are what immerse us in "the stuff" of who we are and what this life is made of, and we move as bodies in various perceptual dimensions. If bodily experience is difficult to express or narrate, it is because it is always on the edge of, never reducible to or arrested within, what is speakable.[1] But theologizing, if taken beyond thought and speech to perceptual movements, is not impossible.

Theologies that seek to be grounded in experience as a critical source for reflection—theologies that aim to robustly engage particularities of embodiment and construct complex arguments about the role of bodily particulars such as gender, race, sexual orientation, ability, or nationality—must attend to the way we exist in the world through our bodily perceptual orientations. To attend to experience as bodily perceptual existence, acknowledge the ways in which our experiences make sense, consider ambiguities and paradoxes of experience, and remain open to fluid and contingent knowledge is to do theology that has and makes "body-sense."

Understanding the extent of how our bodily perceptual orientations may also be intrinsically connected to experiences of violence,

1. I am paraphrasing here Catherine Keller's question regarding "feminist" theology. Catherine Keller, "The Apophasis of Gender: Fourfold Unsaying of Feminist Theology," *Journal of the American Academy of Religion* 76, no. (2008): 908.

be it socio-cultural conquest or individual victimization, we can now add body theology as critical mass when weighing in on how to move away/across from stereotypical imagery or sound bites. We may cross habituated alignments, but always must do so bodily, to change the domination of "lesser" beings, such as bodies with a sex other than male, races aligned differently than white, environments emerging other than industrial, and socio-cultural ways of experiencing other than linear-rationally.

We and the world emerge together through sense-making bodies. The significance of our place in the world emerges for us through sensing bodies. Our sensing is more than just structures of thought or embodied but biological or mechanical processes. Our sensing experiences are our perceptions, feelings, experiences, expressions, motivations, intentions, behaviors, styles, and rhythms.[2] We are existing in the world in/as/through sensing bodies; in and through our bodies and bodily senses we come to perceive the world and are perceived by it. Theology can and must gain body-sense if it seeks to be grounded in experience.

It is 2009, and I sit outside with my mother, enjoying some gaeng gai and German cheesecake. After talking about developing her own recipe for German cheesecake over six months of baking, she tells me about the first time I left Germany to go abroad for a year. "Your dad couldn't sleep well that first night. He was tossing and turning. I finally got up and got him your pillow that was still on your bed and put it next to him. It still smelled like you. He fell asleep then." She then tells me, "Go inside to your grandmother. Say goodbye. Who knows how long she will still be around? Maybe for a long time still." I go inside, already dreading the sight of my grandmother. She is lying in her bed. I think she might be looking at me, but I am not quite sure. I cannot bring myself to touch her hand, but I try to conjure up memories of her holding mine. I cannot quite remember. I try to say goodbye, but realize that I have grieved her passing some years ago already. There is a body in front of me that used

---

2. I am again returning to and adapting Long's definition of religion. Long, *Significations: Signs, Symbols and Images*, 7.

to hold me, whose warmth and comfort I sought when I was just a small child. I am crying a bit, but I think those are tears of guilt and confusion. I am trying to pray for her to die before too long, before bitterness consumes my mother more than it already has. I am not sure when this kind of God emerged for me, a God I can ask to deliver the death of a grandmother. But I get a sense that this kind of God emerged as meaningful in our experiences as family. I take this strange sense, this dis-orientation to my family, to my sense of self, to my theological conceptions, with me as I board the plane to leave home and return home to my spouse and my theological journey on foreign soil.

"The body is our general medium for having a world."[3] *Maurice Merleau-Ponty*

"In that sense we must remember that the starting point of our theologies are bodies, but the rebellious bodies: [...] the body 'as is' before theology starts to draw demonic and divine inscriptions in it."[4] *Marcella Althaus-Reid*

"That which does not bear directly upon human life and move toward the creation of justice in society is not worth our bother."[5] *Carter Heyward*

"Go tell them my story, tell them how I cook here."[6] *Unchalee Peckruhn*

3. Merleau-Ponty, *Phenomenology of Perception*, 146.
4. Marcella M. Althaus-Reid, "'Pussy, Queen of Pirates': Acker, Isherwood and the Debate on the Body in Feminist Theology," *Feminist Theology* 12, no. 2 (2004): 158.
5. Heyward, *Speaking of Christ: A Lesbian Feminist Voice*, 34.
6. Personal conversation, Eichenhof, Germany, July 1, 2010.

BIBLIOGRAPHY

Addams, Jane. *Twenty Years at Hull House: With Autobiographical Notes.* New York, NY: The Macmillan Company, 1911.

Ahmed, Sara. "Racialized Bodies." In *Real Bodies: A Sociological Introduction*, edited by Mary Evans and Ellie Lee, 46–63. New York, NY: Palgrave, 2002.

——. *The Cultural Politics of Emotion.* New York, NY: Routledge, 2004.

——. *Queer Phenomenology: Orientations, Objects, Others.* Durham, NC: Duke University Press, 2006.

Aiken, Susan Hardy, Ann Brigham, Sallie A. Marston, and Penny Waterstone, eds. *Making Worlds: Gender, Metaphor, Materiality.* Tucson, AZ: University of Arizona Press, 1998.

Alcoff, Linda Martín. *Visible Identities: Race, Gender, and the Self.* New York, NY: Oxford University Press, 2006.

Alcoff, Linda, and Elizabeth Potter, eds. *Feminist Epistemologies.* New York, NY: Routledge, 1992.

Alexander, Michelle. *The New Jim Crow.* New York, NY: The New Press, 2012.

Althaus-Reid, Marcella M. *Indecent Theology: Theological Perversions in Sex, Gender and Politics.* New York, NY: Routledge, 2000.

——. *The Queer God.* New York, NY: Routledge, 2003.

——. "'Pussy, Queen of Pirates': Acker, Isherwood and the Debate on the Body in Feminist Theology." *Feminist Theology* 12, no. 2 (2004): 157–167.

Althaus-Reid, Marcella M., and Lisa Isherwood, eds. *Controversies in Body Theology.* London: SCM Press, 2008.

Anderson, Benedict. *Imagined Communities: Reflections on the Spread and Origin of Nationalism.* London, England: Verso, 1983.

Avrahami, Yael. *The Senses of Scripture: Sensory Perception in the Hebrew Bible*. New York, NY: T&T Clark International, 2012.

Bal, Mieke. "Postmodern Theology as Cultural Analysis." In *The Blackwell Companion to Postmodern Theology*, edited by Graham Ward, 3–23. Malden, MA: Blackwell Publishers, 2001.

Banerjee, Mita. "The Hipness of Mediation: A Hyphenated German Existence." In *This Bridge We Call Home*, edited by Gloria E. Anzaldúa and Analouise Keating, 117–125. New York, NY: Routledge, 2002.

Barnes, Colin. "A Brief History of Discrimination and Disabled People." In *The Disability Studies Reader*, edited by Lennard J. Davis, 20–32. New York, NY: Routledge, 2010.

Baxter, Elizabeth. "Cutting Edge: Witnessing Rites of Passage in a Therapeutic Community." In *Controversies in Body Theology*, edited by Marcella M. Althaus-Reid and Lisa Isherwood, 48–69. London, England: SCM Press, 2008.

Baynton, Douglas. "'A Silent Exile on This Earth': The Metaphorical Construction of Deafness in the Nineteenth Century." In *The Disability Studies Reader*, edited by Lennard J. Davis, 33–51. New York, NY: Routledge, 2010.

Beauvoir, Simone de. *The Second Sex*. Translated by H. M. Parshley. Harmondsworth, England: Penguin, 1953.

Bekkenkamp, Jonneke, ed. *Begin with the Body: Corporeality Religion and Gender*. Leuven, The Netherlands: Peeters, 1998.

Betcher, Sharon V. *Spirit and the Politics of Disablement*. Minneapolis: Fortress Press, 2007.

Bettis, Joseph Dabney, ed. *Phenomenology of Religion: Eight Modern Descriptions of the Essence of Religion*. New York, NY: Harper & Row, 1969.

Birke, Lynda. "Bodies and Biology." In *Feminist Theory and the Body: A Reader*, edited by Janet Price and Margrit Shildrick, 42–49. New York, NY: Routledge, 1999.

Bloom, Paul. "Roots of Word Learning." In *Language Acquisition and Conceptual Development*, edited by Melissa Bowerman and Stephen C. Levinson, 159–181. Cambridge, England: Cambridge University Press, 2001.

Bohache, Thomas. *Christology from the Margins*. London, England: SCM Press, 2008.

Brock, Brian, and John Swinton, eds. *Disability in the Christian Tradition: A Reader*. Grand Rapids, MI: Wm. B. Eerdmans Publishing, 2012.

Brock, Rita Nakashima, Jung Ha Kim, Kwok Pui-Lan, and Seung Ai Yang. *Off the Menu: Asian and Asian North American Women's Religion and Theology*. Louisville, KY: Westminster John Knox Press, 2007.

Bryden, Inga. "'Cut'n'slash': Remodelling the 'Freakish' Female Form." In *Controversies in Body Theology*, edited by Marcella M. Althaus-Reid and Lisa Isherwood, 29–47. London, England: SCM Press, 2008.

Butler, Judith. "Sexual Ideology and Phenomenological Description: A Feminist Critique of Merleau-Ponty's Phenomenology of Perception." In *Thinking Muse: Feminism and Modern French Philosophy*, edited by Jeffner Allen and Iris Marion Young, 85–100. Bloomington, IN: Indiana University Press, 1989.

——. *Gender Trouble: Feminism and the Subversion of Identity*. New York, NY: Routledge, 1990.

——. *Bodies That Matter: On the Discursive Limits of "Sex."* New York, NY: Routledge, 1993.

——. *The Psychic Life of Power: Theories in Subjection*. Stanford, CA: Stanford University Press, 1997.

——. *Giving an Account of Oneself*. New York, NY: Fordham University Press, 2005.

Carman, Taylor. "Between Empiricism and Intellectualism." In *Merleau Ponty: Key Concepts*, edited by Rosalyn Diprose and Jack Reynolds, 44–56. Stocksfield, England: Acumen, 2008.

——. *Merleau-Ponty*, Routledge Philosophers, edited by Brian Leiter. New York, NY: Routledge, 2008.

Carman, Taylor, and Mark B. N. Hansen. "Introduction." In *The Cambridge Companion to Merleau-Ponty*, edited by Taylor Carman and Mark B. N. Hansen, 1–25. Cambridge, England: Cambridge University Press, 2005.

Carrington, Christopher. *No Place Like Home: Relationships and Family Life among Lesbians and Gay Men*. Chicago, IL: Chicago University Press, 1999.

Carter, J. Kameron. *Race: A Theological Account*. New York, NY: Oxford University Press, 2008.

Cerborne, David R. "Perception." In *Merleau-Ponty: Key Concepts*, edited by Rosalyn Diprose and Jack Reynolds, 121–131. Stocksfield, England: Acumen, 2008.

Churchill, Ward. *Fantasies of the Master Race: Literature, Cinema and the Colonization of American Indians*. San Francisco, CA: City Lights Publishers, 1998.

Classen, Constance. *Worlds of Sense: Exploring the Senses in History and across Cultures*. New York, NY: Routledge, 1993.

——. *The Color of Angels: Cosmology, Gender and the Aesthetic Imagination*. New York, NY: Routledge, 1998.

——, ed. *The Book of Touch*. Oxfod, NY: Berg, 2005.

Classen, Constance, David Howes, and Anthony Synott. *Aroma: The Cultural History of Smell*. New York, NY: Routledge, 1994.

Comaroff, Jean. "The Diseased Heart of Africa: Medicine, Colonialism, and the Black Body." In *Knowledge, Power, and Practice: The Anthropology of Medicine and Everyday Life*, edited by Shirley Lindenbaum and Margaret Lock, 305–329. Berkeley, CA: University of California Press, 1993.

Cooey, Paula M. "The Word Became Flesh: Woman's Body, Language, and Value." In *Embodied Love: Sensuality and Relationship as Feminist Values*, edited by Paula M. Cooey, Sharon A. Farmer, and Mary Ellen Ross, 17–33. San Francisco, CA: Harper & Row, 1987.

——. *Religious Imagination and the Body: A Feminist Analysis*. New York, NY: Oxford University Press, 1994.

——. "Bad Women: The Limits of Theory and Theology." In *Horizons in Feminist Theology: Identity, Tradition, and Norms*, edited by Rebecca S. Chopp and Sheila Greeve Davaney, 137–153. Minneapolis. MN: Fortress Press, 1997.

Corbin, Alain. *The Foul and the Fragrant: Odor and the French Social Imagination*. Cambridge, MA: Harvard University Press, 1986.

Counihan, Carole. "Mexicana's Food Voice and Differential Consciousness in the San Luis Valley of Colorado." In *Food and Culture: A Reader*, edited by Carole Counihan and Penny van Esterik, 354–368. New York, NY: Routledge, 2008.

Counihan, Carole, and Peny van Esterik, eds. *Food and Culture: A Reader*. New York, NY: Routledge, 2008.

Cox, James. *An Introduction to the Phenomenology of Religion*. New York, NY: Continuum International Publishing Group, 2010.

Creamer, Deborah Beth. *Disability and Christian Theology: Embodied Limits and Constructive Possibilities*. New York, NY: Oxford University Press, 2009.

Crossley, Nick. "Body-Subject/Body-Power: Agency, Inscription and Control in Foucault and Merleau-Ponty." *Body & Society* 2, no. 2 (1996): 99–116.

——. *The Social Body: Habit, Identity and Desire*. Thousand Oaks, CA: Sage Publications Inc., 2001.

Csordas, Thomas J. *Body/Meaning/Healing*. New York, NY: Palgrave Macmillan, 2002.

Daly, Mary. *Gyn/Ecology: The Metaethics of Radical Feminism*. Boston: Beacon Press, 1978.

——. *Pure Lust: Elemental Feminist Philosophy*. Boston: Beacon Press, 1984.

Davis, Lennard J. *Enforcing Normalcy: Disability, Deafness, and the Body*. New York, NY: Verso, 1995.

——. "Nude Venuses, Medusa's Body, and Phantom Limbs: Disability and Visuality." In *The Body and Phsyical Difference: Discourses of Disability*, edited by David T. Mitchell and Sharon L. Snyder, 51–70. Ann Arbor, MI: University of Michigan Press, 1997.

——. *Bending over Backwards: Disability, Dismodernism, and Other Difficult Positions*. New York, NY: New York University Press, 2002.

——. "Constructing Normalcy." In *The Disability Studies Reader*, edited by Lennard J. Davis, 3–19. New York, NY: Routledge, 2010.

de Saussure, Ferdinand, Albert Sechehaye, Charles Bally, and Albert Riedlinger. *Course in General Linguistics*. Translated by WadeBaskin. LaSalle, IL: Open Court, 1986.

Derrida, Jacques. *Of Grammatology*. Translated by Gayatri Chakravorty Spivak. Baltimore, MD: Johns Hopkins University Press, 1976.

Desjarlais, Robert. *Shelter Blues: Sanity and Selfhood among the Homeless*. Philadelphia, PA: University of Pennsylvania Press, 1997.

——. *Sensory Biographies: Lives and Deaths among Nepal's Yolmo Buddhists*. Berkeley, CA: University of California Press, 2003.

Dillingham, William Paul. *Reports of the Immigration Commission: Statements and Recommendations Submitted by Societies and Organizations Interested in the Subject of Immigration*. Washington, DC: Government Printing Office, 1911.

Eiesland, Nancy L. *The Disabled God: Toward a Liberatory Theology of Disability*. Nashville, TN: Abingdon Press, 1994.

Erlmann, Veit, ed. *Hearing Cultures: Essays on Sound, Listening, and Modernity*. Wenner-Gren International Symposium Series, edited by Richard G. Fox. New York, NY: Berg, 2004.

Fabella, Virginia, and Mercy Amba Oduyeye, eds. *With Passion and Compassion: Third World Women Doing Theology*. Maryknoll, NY: Orbis Books, 1988.

Fanon, Frantz. *Black Skin, White Masks*. New York, NY: Grove Press, 1962.

———. *The Wretched of the Earth*. New York, NY: Grove Press, 1968.

Foucault, Michel. *The Birth of the Clinic: An Archaeology of Medical Perception*. London, England: Tavistock Publications, 1973.

———. *The History of Sexuality: An Introduction*. Translated by Robert Hurley. New York, NY: Vintage Books, 1978.

———. *Discipline and Punish: The Birth of the Prison*. Translated by Alan Sheridan. 2, reprint, illustrated ed. New York, NY: Vintage Books, 1995.

Fulkerson, Mary McClintock. *Changing the Subject: Women's Discourses and Feminist Theology*. Minneapolis: Fortress Press, 1994.

Gannon, Jack. *Deaf Heritage: A Narrative History of Deaf America*. Silver Spring, MD: National Association of the Deaf, 1981.

Gardner, Martha Mabie. *The Qualities of a Citizen: Women, Immigration, and Citizenship, 1870–1965*. Princeton, NJ: Princeton University Press, 2005.

Garland Thomson, Rosemarie. *Extraordinary Bodies: Figuring Physical Disability in American Culture and Literature*. New York, NY: Columbia University Press, 1997.

Geertz, Clifford. *The Interpretation of Cultures*. New York, NY: Basic Books, 1973.

———. *Local Knowledge: Further Essays in Interpretive Anthropology*. New York, NY: Basic Books, 1983.

Geurts, Kathryn Linn. *Culture and the Senses: Bodily Ways of Knowing in an African Community*. Berkeley, CA: University of California Press, 2002.

Gibbs, Raymond W., Jr. *Embodiment and Cognitive Science*. New York, NY: Cambridge University Press, 2006.

Gilman, Sander L. "Touch, Sexuality and Disease." In *Medicine and the Five Senses*, edited by W. F. Bynum and Roy Porter, 198–224. Cambridge, England: Cambridge University Press, 1993.

———. "Jews and Smoking." In *Smoke: A Global History of Smoking*, edited by Sanders L. Gilman and Zhou Xun, 278–285. London, England: Reaktion Books, 2004.

Gilroy, Paul. *Against Race: Imagining Political Culture Beyond the Color Line*. Cambridge, MA: Harvard University Press, 2000.

Gossen, Gary H. *Telling Maya Tales: Tzotzil Identities in Modern Mexico*. New York, NY: Routledge, 1999.

Grant, Madison. *The Passing of the Great Race: Or, the Racial Basis of European History*. New York, NY: Charles Scribner's Sons, 1922.

Greenblatt, Stephen. *Marvelous Possessions: The Wonder of the New World*. Chicago: University of Chicago Press, 1991.

Grosz, Elizabeth. *Volatile Bodies: Toward a Corporeal Feminism*. Bloomington and Indianapolis: Indiana University Press, 1994.

Hamington, Maurice. *Embodied Care: Jane Addams, Maurice Merleau-Ponty, and Feminist Ethics*. Chicago, IL: University of Illinois Press, 2004.

Haney Lopez, Ian F. "White by Law." In *Critical Race Theory: The Cutting Edge* (2nd ed.), 626–634. Philadelphia: Temple University Press, 2000.

Harrison, Beverly Wildung. "The Power of Anger in the Work of Love." In *Weaving the Visions: New Patterns in Feminist Spirituality*, edited by Judith Plaskow and Carol P. Christ, 214–225. San Francisco, CA: HarperCollins, 1989.

Harvey, Elizabeth D., ed. *Sensible Flesh: On Touch in Early Modern Culture*. Philadelphia, PA: University of Pennsylvania Press, 2003.

Harvey, Jennifer. *Whiteness and Morality: Pursuing Racial Justice through Reparations and Sovereignity*. New York, NY: Palgrave Macmillan, 2007.

Heinämaa, Sara. *Toward a Phenomenology of Sexual Difference*. Lanham, MD: Rowman & Littlefield Publishers, Inc., 2003.

Heldke, Lisa. "Let's Cook Thai: Recipes for Colonialism." In *Food and Culture: A Reader*, edited by Carole Counihan and Penny van Esterik, 327–341. New York, NY: Routledge, 2008.

Hess, Sabine C. *Person and Place: Ideas, Ideals and the Practice of Sociality on Vanua Lava, Vanuta*. Person, Space and Memory in the Contemporary Pacific, edited by Jürg Wassmann and Katharina Stockhaus. New York, NY: Berghahn Books, 2009.

Heyward, Carter Isabel. *The Redemption of God: A Theology of Mutual Relations*. Lanham, MD: Pilgrim Press, 1982.

——. *Our Passion for Justice: Images of Power, Sexuality, and Liberation*. New York, NY: Pilgrim Press, 1984.

——. *Speaking of Christ: A Lesbian Feminist Voice.* New York, NY: Pilgrim Press, 1989.

——. *Touching Our Strength: The Erotics as Power and the Love of God.* San Francisco: Harper & Row, 1989.

——. *Staying Power: Reflections on Gender, Justice, and Compassion.* Cleveland, OH: Pilgrim Press, 1995.

——. *A Priest Forever: One Woman's Controversial Ordination in the Episcopal Church.* Cleveland, OH: Pilgrim Press, 1999.

——. *Saving Jesus from Those Who Are Right: Rethinking What It Means to Be Christian.* Minneapolis: Fortress Press, 1999.

Hogan, Linda. *From Women's Experience to Feminist Theology.* Sheffield, England: Sheffield Academic Press, 1995.

Howes, David. "Olfaction and Transition." In *The Varieties of Sensory Experience*, edited by David Howes, 128–147. Toronto, Canada: University of Toronto Press, 1991.

——. *Sensual Relations: Engaging the Senses in Culture and Social Theory.* Ann Arbor, MI: University of Michigan Press, 2003.

Hume, David, and L. A. Selby-Bigge. *Enquiries Concerning Human Understanding and Concerning the Principles of Morals.* 3rd ed. New York, NY: Oxford University Press, 1975.

Husserl, Edmund. *Cartesian Meditations: An Introduction to Phenomenology.* Translated by Dorion Cairns. The Hague: Martinus Nijhoff, 1964.

——. *Logical Investigations.* Translated by J. N. Finley. Vol. 2. 2 vols. New ed. New York, NY: Routledge, 2001. Reprint, 1921.

Irigaray, Luce. *An Ethics of Sexual Difference.* Ithaca, New York, NY: Cornell University Press, 1993.

Isasi-Díaz, Ada María. *Mujerista Theology: A Theology for the Twenty-First Century.* New York, NY: Orbis Books, 1996.

——. *En La Lucha = in the Struggle: Elaborating a Mujerista Theology.* 10th anniversary ed. Minneapolis: Fortress Press, 2004.

Isherwood, Lisa. "Will You Slim for Him or Bake Cakes for the Queen of Heaven?" In *Controversies in Body Theology*, edited by Marcella M. Althaus-Reid and Lisa Isherwood, 174–206. London, England: SCM Press, 2008.

Isherwood, Lisa, and Elizabeth Stuart. *Introducing Body Theology.* Sheffield, England: Sheffield Academic Press, 1998.

Iwakma, Miho. "The Body as Embodiment: An Investigation of the Body by Merleau-Ponty." In *Disability/Postmodernity*, edited by Mairian Corker and Tom Shakespeare, 76–87. New York, NY: Continuum, 2002.

Jacobsen, Eric O. *The Space Between: A Christian Engagement with the Built Environment*, Cultural Exegesis, edited by William A. Dyrness and Robert K. Johnson. Grand Rapids, MI: Baker Academic, 2012.

Jakobs, Monika. "Auf Der Suche Nach Dem Verlorenen Paradies? Zur Hermeneutik Von Ursprüngen in Der Feministischen Theologie." *Journal of the European Society of Women in Theological Research* 5 (1997): 126–139.

James, Jennifer C. "Gwendolyn Brooks, World War Ii, and the Politics of Rehabilitation." In *Feminist Disability Studies Reader*, edited by Kim Q. Hall, 136–158. Bloomington, IN: Indiana University Press, 2011.

Jay, Martin. *Downcast Eyes: The Denigration of Vision in Twentieth-Century French Thought*. Berkeley, CA: University of California Press, 1993.

Jennings, Willie James. *The Christian Imagination: Theology and the Origins of Race*. New Haven, CT: Yale University Press, 2010.

Joh, Wonhee Anne. *Heart of the Cross: A Postcolonial Christology*. Louisville, KY: Westminster John Knox Press, 2006.

——. "Violence and Asian American Experience: From Abjection to Jeong." In *Off the Menu: Asian and Asian North American Women's Religion and Theology*, edited by Rita Nakashima Brock, Jung Ha Kim, Kwok Pui-Lan, and Seung Ai Yang, 145–162. Louisville, KY: Westminster John Knox Press, 2007.

Johnson, Mark. *The Body in the Mind: The Bodily Basis of Meaning, Imagination, and Reason*. Chicago, IL: University of Chicago Press, 1987.

Jones, Serene. "Women's Experience between a Rock and a Hard Place: Feminist, Womanist, and Mujerista Theologies in North America." In *Horizons in Feminist Theology: Identity, Tradition, and Norms*, edited by Rebecca S. Chopp and Sheila Greeve Davaney, 137–153. Minneapolis: Fortress Press, 1997.

——. *Feminist Theory and Christian Theology: Cartographies of Grace*. Guides to Theological Inquiry, edited by Kathryn Tanner and Paul Lakeland. Minneapolis: Fortress Press, 2000.

Jones, Serene, and Paul Lakeland, eds. *Constructive Theology: A Contemporary Approach to Classical Themes*. Minneapolis, MN: Augsburg Fortress Press, 2005.

Joy, Melanie. *Why We Love Dogs, Eat Pigs, and Wear Cows: An Introduction to Carnism*. San Francisco, CA: Red Wheel/Weiser, 2010.

Kalekin-Fishman, Devorah. "Sounds That Unite, Sounds That Divide: Pervasive Rituals in Middle Eastern Society." In *Everyday Life in Asia: Social Perspectives on the Senses*, edited by Devorah Kalekin-Fishman and Kelvin E. Y. Low, 19–39. Burlington, VT: Ashgate, 2010.

Kant, Immanuel. *Critique of Pure Reason*. Translated by Marcus Weigelt. New York, NY: Penguin Group, 2008.

Kaufman, Gordon D. *An Essay on Theological Method*. Missoula, MT: Scholars Press, 1975.

Kaufman, Gordon D. *The Theological Imagination: Constructing the Concept of God*. Philadelphia, PA: Westminster Press, 1981.

Keller, Catherine. "The Apophasis of Gender: Fourfold Unsaying of Feminist Theology." *Journal of the American Academy of Religion* 76 (2008): 905–933.

Kerr, Anne, and Tom Shakespeare. *Genetic Politics: From Eugenics to Genome*. Cheltenham, England: New Clarion Press, 2002.

Kim, Taewoo. "Medicine without the Medical Gaze: Theory, Practice and Phenomenology in Korean Medicine." Ph.D.diss., University of New York at Buffalo, 2011.

King, Ursula. *Feminist Theology from the Third World: A Reader*. Maryknoll, NY: Orbis Books, 1994.

Korsmeyer, Carolyn. *Making Sense of Taste: Food and Philosophy*. Ithaca, NY: Cornell University Press, 1999.

——, ed. *The Taste Culture Reader: Experiencing Food and Drink*. Sensory Formations, edited by David Howes. New York, NY: Berg, 2005.

Kwok Pui-Lan. *Discovering the Bible in the Non-Biblical World*. The Bible and Liberation Series, edited by Norman K. Gottwald and Richard A. Horsley. Maryknoll, NY: Orbis Books, 1995.

——. *Introducing Asian Feminist Theology*. Sheffield, England: Sheffield Academic Press Ltd, 2000.

——. *Postcolonial Imagination and Feminist Theology*. Louisville, KY: Westminster John Knox, 2005.

Lakoff, George, and Mark Johnson. *Metaphors We Live By*. Chicago, IL: University of Chicago Press, 1980. Reprint, 2003.

——. *Philosophy in the Flesh: The Embodied Mind and Its Challenge to Western Thought*. New York, NY: Basic Books, 1999.

Lane, Harlan. "Construction of Deafness." In *The Disability Studies Reader*, 77–93. New York, NY: Routledge, 2010.

Langer, Monika M. *Merleau-Ponty's Phenomenology of Perception: A Guide and Commentary*. London, England: The Macmillan Press LTD., 1989.

Law, Lisa. "Home Cooking: Filipino Women and Geographies of the Senses in Hong Kong." In *Empire of the Senses: The Sensual Culture Reader*, edited by David Howes, 224–241. Oxford, England: Berg, 2005.

Locke, John. *An Essay Concerning Human Understanding*. New York, NY: Oxford University Press, 1975.

Long, Charles H. *Significations: Signs, Symbols and Images in the Interpretation of Religion*. Aurora, CO: The Davies Group Publishers, 1995.

——. *Significations: Signs, Symbols and Images in the Interpretation of Religion*. Aurora, CO: The Davies Group Publishers, 1996.

Mann, Barbara A. *The Gantowisas: Iroquoian Women*. New York, NY: Peter Lang Publishing, 2000.

Marratto, Scott L. *The Intercorporeal Self: Merleau-Ponty on Subjectivity*, Contemporary French Thought, edited by David Pettigrew and Francois Raffoul. Albany, NY: State University of New York, 2012.

Marshall, Helen. "Our Bodies, Our Selves: Why We Should Add Old Fashioned Empirical Phenomenology to the New Theories of the Body." In *Feminist Theory and the Body: A Reader*, edited by Janet Price and Margrit Shildrick, 64–75. New York, NY: Routledge, 1999.

Martin, Emily. "The Egg and the Sperm: How Science Has Constructed a Romance Based on Stereotypical Male-Female Roles." In *Feminist Theory and the Body: A Reader*, edited by Janet Price and Margirt Shildrick, 179–189. New York, NY: Routledge, 1999.

Marx, Karl. *Capital*. Translated by Samuel Moore. Vol. 1. New York, NY: International Publishers, 1970.

Masquelier, Adeline, ed. *Dirt, Undress, and Difference: Critical Perspectives on the Body's Surface*. Bloomington, IN: Indiana University Press, 2005.

McCarthy, Erin. *Ethics Embodied*. New York, NY: Lexington Books, 2010.

McClintock, Anne. *Imperial Leather: Race, Gender and Sexuality in the Colonial Contest*. New York, NY: Routledge, Inc., 1995.

McFague, Sallie. *Metaphorical Theology: Models of God in Religious Language*. Philadelphia, PA: Fortress Press, 1982.

——. *Models of God: Theology for an Ecological, Nuclear Age*. Philadelphia, PA: Fortress Press, 1987.

——. *The Body of God: An Ecological Theology*. Minneapolis. MN: Fortress Press, 1993.

McLuhan, Marshall. *The Gutenberg Galaxy*. Toronto, Canada: University of Toronto Press, 1962.

Mensch, James R. *Ethics and Selfhood: Alterity and the Phenomenology of Obligation*. Albany, NY: State University of New York Press, 2003.

Merleau-Ponty, Maurice. *Phenomenology of Perception*. Translated by Colin Smith. New York, NY: Routledge, 1962.

——. *The Structure of Behavior*. Boston, MA: Beacon Press, 1963.

——. *The Primacy of Perception and Other Essays on Phenomenological Psychology, the Philosophy of Art, History and Politics*. Evanston, IL: Northwestern University Press, 1964.

——. *The Visible and the Invisible*. Translated by Alphonso Lingis. Evanston, IL: Northwestern University Press, 1968.

——. *The Prose of the World*. Translated by John O'Neill. Evanston, IL: Northwestern University Press, 1973.

Mitchell, David T., and Sharon L. Snyder. *Narrative Prosthesis: Disability and the Dependencies of Discourse*. Ann Arbor, MI: University of Michigan Press, 2000.

Mitchell, Dolores. "Women and Nineteenth-Century Images of Smoking." In *Smoke: A Global History of Smoking*, edited by Sander L. Gilman and Zhou Xun, 294–303. London, England: Reaktion Books, 2004.

Moltmann-Wendel, Elisabeth. *I Am My Body: A Theology of Embodiment*. New York, NY: Continuum, 1995.

Monaghan, Lee F. "Corporeal Indeterminacy: The Value of Embodied, Interpretative Sociology." In *Body/Embodiment: Symbolic Interaction and the Sociology of the Body*, edited by Dennis Waskul and Phillip Vannini, 125–140. Burlington, VT: Ashgate, 2006.

Morris, David. *The Sense of Space*. Suny Series in Contemporary Continental Philosophy, edited by Dennis J. Schmidt. Albany, NY: State University of New York Press, 2004.

——. "Body." In *Merleau-Ponty: Key Concepts*, edited by Rosalyn Diprose and Jack Reynolds, 110–120. Stocksfield, England: Acumen, 2008.

Mu, Peng. "Imitating Masters: Apprenticeship and Embodied Knowledge in Rural China." In *Everyday Life in Asia: Social Perspectives on the Senses*, edited by Devorah Kalekin-Fishman and Kelvin E.Y. Low, 115–136. Burlington, VT: Ashgate Publishing Company, 2010.

Mulder, Niels. *Inside Thai Society: Religion, Everyday Life, Change.* Chiang Mai, Thailand: Silkworm Books, 2000.

Nelson, James B. *Embodiment: An Approach to Sexuality and Christian Theology.* Minneapolis, MN: Augsburg Publishing House, 1978.

——. *Body Theology.* Louisville, KY: Westminster/John Knox Press, 1992.

Newcomb, Steven T. *Pagans in the Promised Land: Decoding the Doctrine of Christian Discovery.* Golden, CO: Fulcrum Books, 2008.

Newell, Christopher. "On the Importance of Suffering: The Paradoxes of Disability." In *The Paradox of Disability: Responses to Jean Vanier and L'arche Communities from Theology and the Sciences.*, edited by Hans S. Reinders, 169–179. Grand Rapids, MI: Wm. B. Eerdmans Publishing Co., 2010.

Nikkel, David H. *Radical Embodiment.* Princeton Theological Monograph Series, edited by K.C. Hanson, Charles M. Collier and D. Christopher Spinks. Eugene, OR: Pickwick Publications, 2010.

Olkowski, Dorothea. "Introduction." In *Merleau-Ponty, Interiority and Exteriority, Psychic Life and the World*, edited by Dorothea Olkowski and James Morley, 1–23. Albany, NY: State University of New York Press, 1999.

Omi, Michael, and Howard Winant. *Racial Formations in the United States.* New York, NY: Routledge, 1994.

Padden, Carol, and Tom Humphries. *Deaf in America: Voices from a Culture.* Cambridge, MA: Harvard University Press, 1988.

——. "Deaf People: A Different Center." In *The Disability Studies Reader*, edited by Lennard J. Davis, 393–402. New York, NY: Routledge, 2010.

Panagia, Davide. *The Political Life of Sensation.* Durham, NC: Duke University Press, 2009.

Pandya, Vishvajit. *Above the Forest: A Study of Andamanese Ethno-anemology, Cosmology, and the Power of Ritual.* New York, NY: Oxford University Press, 1993.

——. *In the Forest: Visual and Material Worlds of Andamanese History (1858–2006)*. Lanham, MD: University Press of America, 2009.

Paoletti, Jo B. *Pink and Blue: Telling the Boys from the Girls in America*. Bloomington, IN: Indiana University Press, 2012.

Passenier, Anke. "Der Lustgarten Des Leibes Und Die Freiheit Der Seele: Wege Der Mittelalterlichen Frauenspiritualität." *Journal of the European Society of Women in Theological Research* 5 (1997): 192–216.

Pastoureau, Michel. *Blue: The History of a Color*. Translated by Markus I. Cruse. Princeton, NJ: Princeton University Press, 2001.

Patel, Tina G., and David Tyrer. *Race, Crime and Resistance*. Thousand Oaks, CA: Sage Publications, 2011.

Paul II, John. *Man and Woman He Created Them: A Theology of the Body*. Translated by Michael Waldstein. Boston, MA: Pauline Books & Media, 2006.

Pears, Angela. *Feminist Christian Encounters: The Methods and Strategies of Feminist Informed Christian Theologies*. Burlington, VT: Ashgate Publishing Company, 2004.

Pears, Angie. *Doing Contextual Theology*. New York, NY: Routledge, 2010.

Peckruhn, Heike. "Bodies as Orientation in/to the World—Bodies in Queer Phenomenology and Religious Studies." Presented at the *American Academy of Religion Annual Meeting*. Chicago, IL, 2012.

Pérez, Ramona Lee. "Tasting Culture: Food, Family and Flavor in Greater Mexico." Ph.D.diss., New York University, 2009.

Pink, Sarah. "The Future of Sensory Anthropology/the Anthropology of the Senses." *Social Anthropology* 18, no. 3 (2010): 331–333.

Pinn, Anthony B. *The End of God-Talk: An African American Humanist Theology*. New York, NY: Oxford University Press, 2012.

Polyani, Michael. *Personal Knowledge: Towards a Post-Critical Philosophy*. Chicago, IL: University of Chicago Press, 1964.

Priest, Stephen. *Merleau-Ponty*. The Arguments of the Philosophers, edited by Ted Honderich. New York, NY: Routledge, 1998.

Reinders, Hans S. "Human Vulnerability: A Conversation at L'arche." In *The Paradox of Disability: Responses to Jean Vanier and L'arche Communities from Theology and the Sciences*, edited by Hans S. Reinders, 3–15. Grand Rapids, MI: Wm. B. Eerdmans Publishing Co., 2010.

Rivera, Mayra Rivera. "Corporeal Visions and Apparations: The Narrative Strategies of an Indecent Theologian." In *Dancing Theology in Fetish Boots: Essays in Honour of Marcella Althaus-Reid*, edited by Lisa Isherwood and Mark D. Jordan, 79–94. London, England: SCM Press, 2010.

Rodaway, Paul. *Sensuous Geographies: Body, Sense and Place*. New York, NY: Routledge, 1994.

Ruether, Rosemary Radford. *Sexism and God-Talk: Toward a Feminist Theology*. Boston: Beacon Press, 1983.

Said, Edward W. *Orientalism*. New York, NY: Vintage Books, 1979.

Salamon, Gayle. *Assuming a Body: Transgender and Rhetorics of Materiality*. New York, NY: Columbia University Press, 2010.

Sanders, Todd. *Beyond Bodies: Rainmaking and Sense Making in Tanzania*. Toronto, Canada: University of Toronto Press, 2008.

Sandoval, Chela. "Dissident Globalizations, Emancipatory Methods, Social-Erotics." In *Queer Globalizations: Citizenship and the Afterlife of Colonialism*, 20–32. New York, NY: New York University Press, 2002.

Scarry, Elaine. *The Body in Pain: The Making and Unmaking of the World*. New York, NY: Oxford University Press, 1985.

Schulting, Dennis. *Kant's Deduction and Apperception: Explaining the Categories*. New York, NY: Palgrave Macmillan, 2012.

Schüssler Fiorenza, Elisabeth. *But She Said: Feminist Practices of Biblical Interpretation*. Boston: Becon Press, 1992.

——. *Jesus: Miriam's Child, Sophia's Prophet. Critical Issues in Feminist Theology*. New York, NY: Continuum Publishing Company, 1994.

——. *Sharing Her Word: Feminist Biblical Interpretation in Context*. Boston: Beacon Press, 1998.

Scott, James C. *Domination and the Arts of Resistance: Hidden Transcripts*. New Haven, CT: Yale University Press, 1990.

Sherry, Mark. "(Post)Colonizing Disability." In *The Disability Studies Reader*, edited by Lennard J. Davis, 94–106. New York, NY: Routledge, 2010.

Shildrick, Margrit, and Janet Price. "Vital Signs: Texts, Bodies and Biomedicine." In *Vital Signs: Feminist Reconfigurations of the Bio/Logical Body*, edited by Margrit Shildrick and Janet Price, 1–17. Edinburgh: Edinburgh University Press, 1998.

——. "Openings on the Body: A Critical Introduction." In *Feminist Theory and the Body: A Reader*, edited by Janet Price and Margrit Shildrick, 1–14. New York, NY: Routledge, 1999.

Shoop, Marcia W. Mount. *Let the Bones Dance: Embodiment and the Body of Christ*. Louisville, KY: Westminster John Know Press, 2010.

Silverman, Hugh J. "Merleau-Ponty and the Interrogation of Language." In *Merleau-Ponty: Perception, Structure, Language*, edited by John Sallis, 122–141. Atlantic Highlands, NJ: Humanities Press, 1981.

Singer, Linda. "Merleau-Ponty on the Concept of Style." In *The Merleau-Ponty Asthetics Reader: Philosophy and Painting*, edited by Galen Johnson and Michael Smith, 233–244. Evanston, IL: Northwestern University Press, 1993.

Smith, Mark M. *How Race Is Made: Slavery, Segregation, and the Senses*. Chapel Hill, NC: University of North Carolina Press, 2006.

——. *Sensing the Past: Seeing, Hearing, Smelling, Tasting, and Touching in History*. Berkeley, CA: University of California Press, 2007.

Spicker, Stuart F., ed. *The Philosophy of the Body: Rejections of Cartesian Dualism*. Chicago, IL: Quadrangle Books, 1970.

Spiegelberg, Herbert. *The Phenomenological Movement: A Historical Introduction.*, Vol. 5. 6 vols. 3rd ed. Boston, MA: Martinus Nijhhoff Publishers, 1982.

Spivak, Gayatri Chakravorty. "Can the Subaltern Speak?" In *Colonial Discourse and Postcolonial Theory*, edited by Patrick Williams and Laura Chrisman, 66–111. New York, NY: Columbia University Press, 1994.

Stafford, Barbara Maria. *Body Criticism: Imagining the Unseen in Enlightenment Art and Medicine*. Cambridge, MA: MIT Press, 1991.

Strong, Josiah. *Our Country: Its Possible Future and Its Present Crisis*. reprint ed. Bibliobazaar, 2010.

Stuart, Elizabeth. "Experience and Tradition: Just Good Friends." *Journal of the European Society of Women in Theological Research* 5 (1997): 49–71.

Synnott, Anthony. "Puzling over the Senses: From Plato to Marx." In *The Variety of Sensory Experience: A Sourcebook in the Anthropology of the Senses*, edited by David Howes, 61–76. Toronto, Canada: University of Toronto Press, 1991.

Tanesini, Alessandra. *An Introduction to Feminist Epistemologies*. Malden, MA: Blackwell Publishers Inc., 1999.

Tatman, Lucy. *Knowledge That Matters: A Feminist Theological Paradigm and Epistemology*. Cleveland: Pilgrim Press, 2001.

Tinker, George E. (Tink). "Missionary Conquest: The Gospel and Native American Cultural Genocide." (1993).

——. *Spirit and Resistance: Political Theology and American Indian Liberation*. Minneapolis: Augsburg Fortress, 2004.

——. *American Indian Liberation: A Theology of Sovereignty*. Maryknoll, N.Y.: Orbis Books, 2008.

Todes, Samuel. *Body and World*. Cambridge, MA: MIT Press, 2001.

Townes, Emilie M. "Marcella Althaus-Reid's *Indecent Theology*: A Response." In *Dancing Theology in Fetish Boots: Essays in Honour of Marcella Althaus-Reid*, edited by Lisa Isherwood and Mark D. Jordan, 61–67. London, England: SCM Press, 2010.

Townes, Emily M. *Womanist Ethics and the Cultural Production of Evil*. New York, NY: Palgrave MacMillan, 2006.

Turner, Bryan S. *Vulnerability and Human Rights*. Essays on Human Rights, edited by Thomas Cushman. University Park, PA: Pennsylvania State University Press, 2006.

Vásquez, Manuel A. *More Than Belief: A Materialist Theory of Religion*. New York, NY: Oxford University Press, 2011.

Vine Deloria, Jr. *God Is Red: A Native View of Religion*. 3rd ed. New York, NY: The Putnam Publishing Group, 2003.

——, ed. *Spirit and Reason: The Vine Deloria, Jr., Reader*. Boulder, CO: Fulcrum Publishing, 1999.

Vinge, Louise. *The Five Senses: Studies in a Literary Tradition*. Lund, Sweden: LiberLäromedel, 1975.

Vogel, Arthur A. *Body Theology: God's Presence in Man's World*. New York, NY: Harper & Row, 1973.

Voss-Roberts, Michelle. *Dualities: A Theology of Difference*. Louisville, KY: Westminster John Knox Press, 2010.

——. *Tastes of the Divine: Hindu and Christian Theologies of Emotion*. New York, NY: Fordham University Press, 2014.

Wade, Nicholas J. *A Natural History of Vision*. Cambridge, MA: MIT Press, 1998.

Wallner, Friedrich G, Fengli Lan, and Martin J. Jandl, eds. *The Way of Thinking in Chinese Medicine: Theory, Methodology and Structure of Chinese Medicine*. Frankfurt, Germany: Peter Lang, 2010.

Walvin, James. *An African's Life, 1745–1797: The Life and Times of Olaudah Equiano*. New York, NY: Continuum, 2000.

Wang, Robin. *Yinyang: The Way of Heaven and Earth in Chinese Thought and Culture*. Cambridge, England: Cambridge University Press, 2012.

Watkin, Christopher. *Phenomenology or Deconstruction? The Question of Ontology in Maurice Merlau-Ponty, Paul Ricoeur and Jean-Luc Nancy*. Edinburgh, Scotland: Edinburgh University Press, 2009.

Weiss, Gail. *Body Images: Embodiment as Intercorporality*. New York, NY: Routledge, 1999.

Welter, Barbara. *Dimity Convictions: The American Woman in the Nineteenth Century*. Athens, OH: Ohio University Press, 1976.

Wilhelm, Richard. *The I Ching*. London, England: Routledge and Kegan Paul, 1967.

Williams, Delores S. *Sisters in the Wilderness: The Challenge of Womanist God-Talk*. Maryknoll: Orbis Books, 1993.

Williams, Simon J., and Gillian Bendelow. *The Lived Body: Sociological Themes, Embodied Issues*. New York, NY: Routledge, 1998.

Wittgenstein, Ludwig. *Philosophical Investigations*. Translated by G. E. M. Anscombe. 3rd ed. New York, NY: Macmillan, 1958.

Yeğenoğlu, Meyda. *Colonial Fantasies: Towards a Feminist Reading of Orientalism*. New York, NY: Cambridge University Press, 1998.

Yong, Amos. *Theology and Down Syndrome: Reimagining Disability in Late Modernity*. Waco, TX: Baylor University Press, 2007.

Young, Iris Marion. *Intersecting Voices: Dilemmas of Gender, Political Philosophy, and Policy*. Princeton, NJ: Princeton University Press, 1997.

——. *On Female Body Experience: "Throwing Like a Girl" And Other Essays* Studies in Feminist Philosophy. New York, NY: Oxford University Press, 2005.

INDEX